10 MAY 2008

For: Anne and John
with warmest regards,

[signature]

Captain, U.S. Navy (Ret.), Ph.D.

Unknown Waters

A Firsthand Account of the Historic
Under-Ice Survey of the Siberian
Continental Shelf by USS *Queenfish (SSN-651)*

Alfred S. McLaren
Captain, U.S. Navy (Ret.)
With a foreword by Captain William R. Anderson, U.S. Navy (Ret.)

THE UNIVERSITY OF ALABAMA PRESS
Tuscaloosa

Typeface: AGaramond

∞

The paper on which this book is printed meets the minimum requirements of
American National Standard for Information Sciences-Permanence of Paper for
Printed Library Materials, ANSI Z39.48-1984.

Library of Congress Cataloging-in-Publication Data

McLaren, Alfred Scott.
Unknown waters : a firsthand account of the historic under-ice survey of the
Siberian continental shelf by USS Queenfish / Alfred S. McLaren, Captain, U.S.
Navy (Ret.) ; with a foreword by Captain William R. Anderson,
U.S. Navy (Ret.).
p.   cm.
Includes bibliographical references and index.
ISBN 978-0-8173-1602-0 (cloth : alk. paper) — ISBN 978-0-8173-8006-9
(electronic) 1. Queenfish (Submarine) 2. McLaren, Alfred Scott. 3. Arctic
regions—Discovery and exploration—American. 4. Continental shelf—Arctic
regions. 5. Continental shelf—Russia (Federation)—Siberia. 6. Underwater
exploration—Arctic Ocean. I. Title. II. Title: Firsthand account of the historic
under-ice survey of the Siberian continental shelf by USS Queenfish.
VA65.Q44M33 2008
359.9′330973—dc22

2007032113

To Vice Admiral Hyman G. Rickover, U.S. Navy,
and Waldo K. Lyon, Ph.D.—
Pioneers, Patriots, Visionaries

Contents

Illustrations

Chartlets

Foreword

Vice Admiral John Nicholson, U.S. Navy (Ret.), once observed that, whereas control of the seas generally required a combination of surface ships, submarines, and aircraft, control of the Arctic Ocean could come only through the nuclear-powered submarine. Nicholson, a true pioneer of Arctic submarining, knows by his own experience that true control can come only through exploration and mapping of uncharted waters under the ice spread across the Arctic. The most difficult and hazardous area of Arctic ice to explore is the shallow waters of the continental shelf north of Siberia, and that is exactly what this fascinating book is about. It is the true story of Captain Fred McLaren and his officers and crew of the nuclear submarine USS *Queenfish (SSN-651)*, who made, through every conceivable hazard of ice and seafloor, history's first survey of that remote and important region.

Although six times the size of the Mediterranean Sea, the Arctic Ocean is the world's smallest ocean and remains to this day the least understood and charted. Before hearing my own siren song of the Arctic, I visualized the region at the top of the world in terms of a lot of ice and snow. This is true, but the more important fact is that the ocean supports much of that ice and snow. Because ocean waters are on the move, the ice floating on top is also on the move—constantly shifting and heaving great pieces of ice one on another. This action creates pressure ridges: high ice projections on top of the ice and deep ice keels below the water surface. Even on tried-and-true routes, one must realize that the only thing predictable about sea ice is its unpredictability. A submarine exploring a new route can find itself in shallow water due to a rapidly shoaling seabed or face to face with an underwater mountain peak. Throw in the possibility of encountering an iceberg, and the underwater picture becomes quite crowded with hazards. For example, *Queenfish* encountered ice keels projecting more than one hundred feet below the ocean's surface. Such encounters were more likely to occur in missions such as mine and Fred McLaren's, where the main point of exploration was to gather information on these uncharted parts of the globe.

The year central to Captain McLaren's story, 1970, found Vietnam still difficult and the cold war at its height. It was thought the Soviets viewed the Arctic as a private backyard. Our own *Nautilus* had, in 1958, crossed that ocean and been to the pole, but we had not been to, and knew little about, the sea shelves immediately off the Siberian shore.

McLaren was among the first to recognize that this lack of information about a region of such great strategic importance could become a national embarrassment to the United States Navy. To gain the needed information, however, it would not be necessary to penetrate Russian territorial waters secretly; it would be adequate to survey along a path well north of the Soviet Union's territorial claim.

Selected and trained by Admiral Hyman Rickover, McLaren was chosen by Rickover in 1969 to command USS *Queenfish*. Possessing an outstanding ability as a submarine operator, and with considerable Arctic experience as a young officer on USS *Seadragon (SSN-584)*, McLaren set about planning and getting support for a two-phase exploration. The first phase was to retrace most of *Nautilus's* 1958 track, beginning in the Bering Strait. One aim was to compare ice conditions of 1958 versus those of 1970 and perhaps draw some conclusions. The second phase would start 240 nautical miles after passing the pole and divert south and east to the Laptev Sea and then commence a detailed survey of the Siberian shelf, working back to the Bering Strait through the Laptev, East Siberian, and Chukchi seas.

This was an extremely hazardous mission, and Captain McLaren, his officers, and crew deserve great credit for having accomplished it. Just to put the cards on the table, though in *Nautilus* we had some squeeze problems of our own, McLaren and *Queenfish* went some places that I doubt I would have gone.

In the three seas covered, the next squeeze problem was always just ahead, each with its own unpredictable characteristics and special challenges. The net result of this almost constant need to zig and zag around deep ice keels and to go up and down to clear sea-bottom obstacles demanded a special delegation of responsibility to three highly trained command watch sections. Otherwise the skipper would not have been able to get any rest at all. Captain McLaren and his officers and crew have my admiration and deserve congratulations for the success of this arrangement.

McLaren quite aptly characterizes the Siberian underwater environment as "extremely oppressive and relentlessly hazardous." The distance covered in the three seas approached thirty-one hundred miles over a period of some twenty days. This made for an average speed of a laborious 6.5 knots—a reflection of the difficulty of pressing forward.

Other than a hard-to-control fire while under heavy, compact ice, the thing we under-ice explorers fear the most is getting stuck while in shallow water and finding ourselves wedged in under deep-draft ice ridges with no way out. McLaren relates quite vividly how he found himself in just such a situation. Tellingly, he calls it an encounter with an "ice garage." Mind you, the vehicle parked in this case is 292 feet long, 54 feet high in the middle, with a weight of 4,640 tons. To add to the problem, his *Queenfish* had but a single propeller, which made it very hard to back in a straight line. When the one propeller was reversed, it tended to throw the stern down and to port.

As an example of his skillful delegation of authority, he called on the maneuvering watch to rotate the single propeller in precise, small, and quick revolutions so as to gain just a slight amount of sternway. This and the placement of the rudder at just the correct angle to compensate for the left drift tendency of the stern was the kid-glove maneuvering required to get out of the entrapment without damage to the ship.

McLaren told me that it took an hour to extricate his ship out of the "ice garage" but that the process was so intense it seemed like three. Having almost entered an under-ice garage on the north coast of Greenland in *Nautilus*'s first (1957) Arctic mission, I can attest that anything over five minutes would have seemed like an eternity.

Queenfish was the first of a new class of nuclear-powered attack submarines specially designed to include features that would optimize under-ice capabilities. This did not, by any means, result in a relaxation of their versatility to carry out a wide variety of missions, the primary one being the ability to sink other ships and other submarines. Other responsibilities included such duties as lifeguard for downed aircrews, transport of relief supplies, landing of specially trained raiding parties, monitoring of sea traffic along various routes, evacuation of American and Allied citizens caught behind combat lines, and the use of ship-to-shore tactical missiles.

When future submarines are called on to carry out one or a combination of these missions in the treacherous waters explored by Fred McLaren, they will benefit immensely from the knowledge gleaned from this unique voyage into unknown waters. But what about the Arctic scientists? Have they not already benefited? Of course the answer is a resounding "yes." Indeed, the author of this excellent book was inspired by his submarine Arctic experience to become himself one of the world's foremost Arctic scientists, focusing on polar and open-ocean oceanographic and bathymetric factors.

On his navy retirement as captain in 1981, Fred did postgraduate work at Cambridge University, England, followed by studies at the University of Colorado, Boulder, from 1983 to 1986, where he obtained his Ph.D. in the polar field. This work included a detailed analysis and comparison of sea ice recorded during the 1970 voyage versus the 1958 expedition along the joint *Nautilus-Queenfish* route. His conclusion was that the average ice thickness along that path had decreased 0.7 meters in the interim, although he is quick to point out that, subsequent to 1970, some years have continued to show a decrease whereas others show an increase in thickness. The total quantity or extent of sea ice, however, continues to decrease.

The exclusive, world-renowned Explorers Club elected Dr. McLaren its president in 1996, and he served a distinguished four years. As president emeritus, he continues a wide variety of exploration activities using manned underwater submersibles and contributing to research on global climate change. Readers will enjoy getting to know this outstanding man of science and exploration.

Captain William R. Anderson
U.S. Navy (Ret.)

Captain Anderson was skipper of USS *Nautilus (SSN-571)* during that vessel's 1958 ocean-to-ocean crossing of the Arctic Ocean, an 1,830 nautical-mile journey dealing with unexplored ice and ocean, becoming also, for the record books, the first ship to reach the North Pole. He was subsequently awarded the Legion of Merit by President Eisenhower and *Nautilus* the Presidential Unit Citation. Captain Anderson retired from the U.S. Navy in 1962, and in 1969 he was elected to the U.S. Congress, representing the Sixth District of Tennessee as a Democrat. He served in Congress for four terms. He passed away on 25 February 2007 and was buried with full military honors at Arlington National Cemetery.

Preface

Almost thirty-eight years ago the crew of the nuclear attack submarine USS *Queen-fish (SSN-651)* completed the first hydrographic survey ever undertaken in international waters of the entire continental pack-ice–covered shelf off the Soviet Union's Siberian coastline—a distance of some thirty-one hundred nautical miles. An arduous feat of seamanship and navigation under cold war conditions, it was accomplished under my command during the summer of 1970.

Our voyage of exploration began officially on 30 July 1970 in the Bering Strait with a retracing of USS *Nautilus*'s historic 1958 route across the Chukchi Sea and Arctic Ocean via the North Pole. A brief oceanographic survey of a section of the Nansen Cordillera (now called the Gakkel Ridge) was then conducted to determine whether it was tectonically active. From there *Queenfish* proceeded southward to the northwestern corner of the Laptev Sea, off the northernmost island of the Severnaya Zemlya Archipelago. Arriving on 10 August 1970, we began the main purpose of our voyage, a survey of the largely uncharted ice-covered shallow waters of the Laptev, East Siberian, and Chukchi seas. The survey was completed nineteen days later, on 29 August, in the southwestern Chukchi Sea just north of the Bering Strait. Altogether, from her departure from Pearl Harbor on 6 July 1970 to her return to Pearl Harbor two months later, on 11 September, *Queenfish* traveled more than fourteen thousand nautical miles, almost all of it submerged.

The Arctic-Siberian Continental Shelf Exploration, or SUBICEX 1-70 (Submarine Ice Exercise), as the expedition was officially termed, was one of many undertaken during the cold war by an extremely versatile and capable group of U.S.

Figure P.1 USS *Queenfish (SSN-651)* Arctic-Siberian Shelf Expedition voyage cachet/insignia. (Courtesy of the U.S. Navy)

Navy commanding officers and crewmen plying the Arctic waters in the *Sturgeon*-class nuclear attack submarine. *Queenfish* was the first of these to be launched, the first to go to sea, and the first to be commissioned. Her mission, the second major one under my command, into the unknown waters of the Arctic was recognized with a Navy Unit Commendation to both submarine and crew and the Legion of Merit to her captain.

The *Sturgeon*-class submarine was specially designed, constructed, and outfitted beginning in the early 1960s for year-around operation in the polar regions. As a frontline nuclear attack boat, ready for rapid deployment with a full load of anti-submarine and ship torpedoes and submarine rocket (SUBROC) antisubmarine missiles in war, her uses during the cold war were myriad. Primarily she was tasked with monitoring a rapidly expanding Soviet navy through the conduct of intelligence, surveillance, and reconnaissance missions, but her capabilities uniquely fitted her for exploring, charting, and collecting oceanographic data throughout the still largely unknown ice-covered Arctic Ocean and its peripheral seas.

Today this class has been consigned to the scrap heap of history as a direct re-

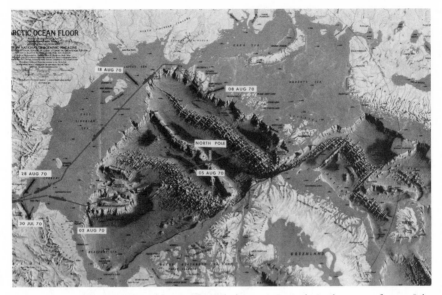

Figure P.2 Graphic of USS *Queenfish's* route through the Arctic Basin during her voyage from 30 July to 30 August 1970. (National Geographic, 1968 map)

sult of the abrupt end of the cold war with the Soviet Union and its bloc in the late 1980s. The first to be commissioned, *Queenfish* was also the first to be decommissioned, on 8 November 1991. She was subsequently stricken from the naval registry and entered the U.S. Navy's submarine and ship recycling program at Bremerton Naval Shipyard on the Puget Sound, Washington State, on 1 May 1992. By 7 April 1993, our tried, trusty, and much beloved "Queen of the Sea" had ceased to exist.

The last of the true Arctic submarines, USS *Parche (SSN-683),* was decommissioned in 2004, and now all but a few of the original thirty-seven have been completely scrapped and the materials of which they were made recycled. So ended one of the most extraordinary eras in U.S. submarine development, literally a golden age of nuclear submarine exploration, in which I was most fortunate to have played an active part.

In late 1971 I was authorized by Commander Submarine Forces Pacific's chief of staff, Captain Joe Russell, to tell the general public for the first time about *Queenfish's* voyage of exploration through the northern Siberian seas two years earlier. This occurred in late March 1972 at the famed Explorers Club's annual dinner, held at the Waldorf-Astoria Hotel in New York. Since then I have given numerous lectures and written many articles on the evolution and development of the Arctic submarine and on *Queenfish*'s operations in particular. It has not been possible before now, however, to relate more than just a few of the many significant achievements of her superb crew during my four-year command.

Early chapters of this book are devoted to the process of educating yours truly as a submarine officer in the late 1950s and 1960s and of preparing me for the command of *Queenfish*. The development of this submarine and the requisite training for her forthcoming cold war operations occurred in tandem. Both were new. The significance of *Queenfish*'s 1970 Arctic and Siberian shelf exploration cannot be appreciated without conveying to the reader all that was involved in learning how to safely operate and ultimately command an Arctic submarine of such complexity as *Queenfish*, particularly under so able and visionary a leader as Admiral Hyman G. Rickover, whose high achievement in developing a nuclear submarine force for the United States has never been exceeded. The same is true of Dr. Waldo K. Lyon, whose hope for the creation of a submarine capable of year-round operation in the polar regions was finally realized in 1958.

Although many aspects of this story will probably remain classified for years to come (for security reasons, ship movements included here are approximate), it is my intention in this book to provide as detailed a narrative as possible of the historic Siberian shelf expedition and to share the excitement of what it was like to be a submariner for our great country, the United States of America.

Acknowledgments

This book has been written in grateful recognition of the vision and valiant work of all the Arctic submarine pioneers preceding and during my era, in particular Admiral Hyman G. Rickover, Dr. Waldo K. Lyon, Mr. Walt Wittmann, Mr. Art Roshon, Mr. Art Molloy, Dr. M. Allan Beal, and, earlier in the last century, Sir Hubert Wilkins.

Three Arctic submarine pioneers gave me, and other Arctic submariners, invaluable advice and support over the years: Vice Admiral John H. Nicholson, commanding officer of USS *Sargo (SSN-583)*, without whose efforts the first true class of Arctic submarine, the *SSN-637 Sturgeon* class, would not have become a reality; and Captain Robert D. McWethy and Mr. Richard J. Boyle, both of whom in the very critical early years worked hard to get the Arctic submarines to sea.

Finally, I wish to acknowledge the extraordinary achievements of three other pioneering Arctic submarine commanding officers: Captain William R. Anderson of USS *Nautilus (SSN-571)*; Vice Admiral James F. Calvert of USS *Skate (SSN-578)*, and Vice Admiral George P. Steele of USS *Seadragon (SSN-584)*. All these men truly blazed the way and set the example and standards for the generations of Arctic submariners to follow.

Worthy of special recognition are the officers and men who served with me on USS *Queenfish (SSN-651)* and their families, who steadfastly supported them. Without them, this Arctic expedition would not have been so successful. In particular, they are Lieutenant Commander Toby G. Warson; Lieutenant Commander Ralph E. Beedle; Lieutenant Commander Walter A. Pezet; Lieutenant Stephen V. Gray; Lieutenant Robert J. Baumhardt; Lieutenant Karl T. Hoepfner; Lieutenant

Junior Grade Grant H. Youngman; Lieutenant Junior Grade Lars P. Hanson; Lieutenant Junior Grade Fred C. Moore; and Lieutenant Junior Grade William G. Blenkle.

In addition, I wish to mention Senior Chief Sonar Technician (SS) James C. Petersen; Sonar Technician First Class (SS) Frederick Miller III; Electronics Technician Second Class (Radar)(SS) Gordon W. Branin; Electronics Technician Second Class (Radar)(SS) Joseph R. Boston; Chief Quartermaster (SS) Jack B. Patterson; Quartermaster First Class (SS) Clarence F. Williams; Commissaryman First Class (SS) Michael L. Knaub; Master Chief Electricians Mate (SS) Mike Kotek; Senior Chief Torpedoman (SS) Kenneth E. Ickes; Chief Radioman (SS) Michael S. Hein; Senior Chief Electronics Technician (Nuclear) Richard L. Dietz; Chief Machinist Mate (SS) Harry Tample Jr.; and Chief Hospital Corpsman (SS) Andrew J. Gunn.

Others who played significant roles in my development as a U.S. Navy officer by their example and mentoring were my father, the late Captain William Fleming McLaren, USN; Commander Gerald F. Case, USN; Lieutenant George W. Dickey, USN; and Lieutenant Dale Kerfoot, USN, of USS *Gregory (DD-802)*.

Submarine commanding officers whose personal example influenced the development of my command philosophy and style of leadership were Commanders Jack Knutson and Al Davis (under whom I qualified for submarines), with whom I served on USS *Greenfish (SS-351);* Vice Admiral George P. Steele, with whom I served on USS *Seadragon;* Captain Les Kelly, under whom I qualified for both engineer and command and who, as submarine officer detailer, ensured that I was later assigned as prospective executive officer of *Queenfish;* and Captain Shep Jenks, with whom I served on USS *Skipjack (SSN-585)* as navigator and later engineer officer. Also playing a significant part were Rear Admiral Guy Shaffer, with whom I served on USS *Greenling (SSN-614),* and Captain Jack Richard, with whom I served, as executive officer, on USS *Queenfish.*

Noteworthy for their support and encouragement among my division and squadron commanders were Captain Mike Moore; Rear Admiral Shannon Cramer; Captain Jack Richard; Captain Hank Hanson; Rear Admiral Warren Kelley; Captain Roth Leddick; Rear Admiral Jim Wilson; and Rear Admiral Logan Malone. I am also particularly grateful to two submarine executive officers who were special mentors to me as a junior officer: Rear Admiral Bob Chewning of *Skipjack* and Captain Jim Strong of *Seadragon.*

Last, but by no means least, I wish to recognize the strong support of my family, especially my loving wife, Avery Battle Russell, without whose assistance this book might not have been brought to fruition.

UNKNOWN WATERS

I
Man Overboard!

Let him, who would see the genius of humanity in its most noble struggle against superstition and darkness, peruse the history of Arctic travels. There, in the north, are all secrets laid bare.

—Fridtjof Nansen, 1878

Only intermittent "cats paws" or slight breezes disturbed the vast, calm sea that lay ahead. USS *Queenfish* slowly approached, on the surface, the western end of the Strait of Juan de Fuca, due north of Cape Flattery, Washington State, shortly after midnight on a cool, clear, almost moonless night on 22 July 1970. The first truly polar regions–capable U.S. nuclear attack submarine, she was en route to the Arctic Ocean and the North Pole via the Bering Strait, heading toward her ultimate destination, the Siberian continental shelf. A final bow-to-stern inspection of our boat's topside superstructure, line lockers, and deck hatches had been in progress for almost an hour. The weapons and sonar officer, Lieutenant Robert Baumhardt, and James Petersen, chief sonar technician, were abaft the sail, carefully securing anything that might come loose or rattle or emit even the tiniest sound during the many weeks that we expected to remain submerged.

I had joined the watch on the bridge earlier in the evening for a last hour or so of fresh air before *Queenfish* proceeded beneath the surface, following our passage through the strait and into the northern Pacific Ocean. Preparations were in progress for sending Baumhardt and Petersen on deck for a final sound-quieting check.

Both men had already donned standard navy safety harnesses that, once they were on deck, would secure them with long straps and "U" rings to a recessed track, with several breaks or connection points that ran from bow to stern down the center of *Queenfish*'s deck. Standard safety equipment on the bridge generally consisted of a life ring, a coil of heaving line, a bullhorn, and a searchlight that could be used as a spotlight on the deck or water surface or for signaling other ships if necessary.

A peculiar sense of unease prompted me to order some extra precautions for the men's safety. A second life ring was thus sent to the bridge along with an extra heaving line, and the man-overboard party was placed on standby in the control room, with a wet-suited swimmer ready to enter the water if necessary.

Noting how dark the evening had already become shortly after arriving on the bridge, I further asked the officer of the deck, Lieutenant Tom Hoepfner, to have two battle lanterns sent up. One of the lookouts, an electrician, immediately volunteered, "No need, Captain, the searchlight is rigged and ready to turn on!" I insisted, nonetheless, and the two battle lanterns were tested.

Baumhardt and Petersen climbed down to the main deck to begin securing topside for sea. They started from the bow. By shortly after midnight, the two men had reached the afterdeck and were within minutes of completing their sound-quieting check when suddenly the lookout excitedly pointed to what appeared to be a dark gray wall, dead ahead, moving very fast from seaward into the mouth of the channel toward us. It was a startling and unbelievable sight. It was, in fact, a solid wall of water, at least ten to fifteen feet high, extending from port to starboard across the limited horizon ahead. A growing line of frothy white breakers could be seen along its top. The wall appeared to be completely solitary, with no apparent waves in its wake, such as one would see along a beach. It seemed to gain in height, speed, and menace as it closed on us. Considering the flat, calm seas we had been enjoying for hours, it was hard to grasp that we were not observing an apparition or an optical illusion.

Using both bullhorn and cupped hands, those of us on the bridge frantically shouted warnings to the two men on deck, "Look out!" and "Hold tight!" Within minutes the rogue wave slammed into *Queenfish's* bow with tremendous force and noisily engulfed the main deck and both men. Nightmarishly, the wave snatched Baumhardt and Petersen from the deck as it passed over us and literally hurled them toward the stern planes, rudder, and propeller as it continued rapidly down the channel. I instinctively ordered, "Right full rudder!" and "Stop the shaft!" to put both men to starboard and thus prevent them from colliding with the rudder or, even worse, being chopped up by the propeller as they were swept violently aft. Ordering "On searchlight!" I instructed the officer of the deck to locate and maintain contact with the men, whether they were still on deck or in the water, as soon as possible.

As bad luck would have it, the searchlight chose to burn out with a very bright flash at that exact moment. Quickly handing the battle lanterns to both Hoepfner and the lookout, I repeated, "Find them!"

Chief Petersen was immediately spotted by the lookout; he was sprawled on deck near the after hatch. Lieutenant Baumhardt, however, was nowhere to be seen.

Hoepfner was the first to spot Baumhardt's bright orange knit cap off our starboard quarter, bobbing just above the waves and drifting rapidly astern. I immediately ordered, "All back full!" followed by "Left full rudder!" and "Man overboard, starboard side!" Baumhardt's bright cap was already on the verge of disappearing into the black void astern of us. Although Baumhardt was dressed warmly and wearing a life jacket, the water temperature was less than 50° F.

Queenfish was a single-screw submarine, which meant that her single large seven-bladed propeller caused her to back to port during backing bells, or orders—even more rapidly so using left full rudder. The best method to use in our present situation was, therefore, to swing the bow around to starboard and pick Baumhardt up from there. Keeping Baumhardt in sight as the bow continued to swing around and toward him, I ordered, "All stop!" followed by "Ahead one-third!" Course and speed were then adjusted as necessary to permit us to retrieve him off the starboard bow.

In the meantime the man-overboard party, headed by Quartermaster First Class Clarence Williams, rushed to the bridge and with my permission rapidly proceeded down the side of the sail and onto the main deck. As we nervously continued to look for more monstrous waves, Chief Petersen was quickly helped to his feet and up the sail by Williams and sent below.

After what seemed an eternity, *Queenfish* came to a dead-in-the-water position, with her bow within a few yards of an extremely shaken and quite water-soaked Lieutenant Baumhardt. A life ring was thrown to him, and, as he hugged it for dear life, the swimmer assisted as he was rapidly hoisted back on deck. He was then rushed below to be thawed out and examined by our chief hospital corpsman, Andrew Gunn.

Amazingly, both men survived their harrowing experience with no more than a few scrapes and bruises. They soon became the envy of the crew when, having undergone extreme exposure to the elements, each was handed a generous shot of Hennessey's fine brandy to remove the last vestiges of whatever "chill" and fright they had suffered.

Assistant navigator Chief Quartermaster Jack Patterson later informed me, to my utter disbelief, that we had managed to get Lieutenant Baumhardt back on deck in less than six minutes from the time he was washed overboard. A near tragedy had been averted that could have ended the expedition before it had even begun. It was an important warning to us to expect the unexpected from that point on. On the other hand, the rapid and successful recovery of our two men seemed to portend well for the long and hazardous voyage ahead.

What had actually occurred? We would never know for certain. A sudden rogue wave like this one could have been a tsunami, but we were never able to determine its source. We were fortunate that it had not been any greater in size than it was and that we had come through the experience with no personnel casualties or damage to the boat.

Have tsunamis or such large rogue waves ever been experienced elsewhere along the West Coast by submariners? Absolutely! Three years later, on 1 December 1973, Commander Alvin Wilderman of the nuclear attack submarine USS *Plunger (SSN-595)* was abruptly swept off the bridge, never to be recovered, during extremely heavy seas just outside the Golden Gate.

The lesson was one that all experienced men of the sea have to learn, often the hard way: the sea will always have unpleasant surprises in store for the unwary, careless, and unprepared. This was certainly to be true in the northern Pacific and Arctic oceans.

2

Becoming a Submarine Officer

Looking back, I cannot help but wonder at the convoluted path that led me to become commanding officer of USS *Queenfish,* on 12 September 1969, after two years serving as her executive officer and twelve years of sea experience, most of them in submarines.

I had, in fact, never planned to become a submariner, much less a nuclear submarine commander. Long before entering the U.S. Naval Academy on 5 July 1951, my sights had been set on being a Marine Corps fighter pilot. Airplanes had been my passion since boyhood, so submarines were definitely the furthest thing from my mind when, approaching service selection and graduation from the academy, I learned from a final precommissioning physical that my right eye was 20/30, not good enough for flying. My fallback plan of becoming a marine infantry officer and going to a reconnaissance company following basic school at Quantico abruptly fell through as well when the U.S. Department of Defense mandated that 25 percent of our class was to be commissioned in the U.S. Air Force (its academy's first graduating class was still several years away).

To my utter dismay, following graduation I found myself headed for Navy line (instead of the U.S. Marine Corps) and a Pacific-based destroyer, USS *Gregory (DD-802)*. It was unbelievable, particularly for my family, which had heard me maintain for years that I would never be a naval officer. My attitude formed during my early teenage years when my father, Captain William F. McLaren, took me to sea on his destroyer, USS *Fraser (DM-24)*, for extended periods during the summers. Constant rough seas, not to mention all the unpleasant smells from a destroyer manned by several hundred men, kept me in a perpetual state of seasickness during those involuntary sojourns.

Two years as a young naval officer on *Gregory*, along with a lengthy deployment in the Far East with the Seventh Fleet, turned out to be an infinitely better experience than I could have imagined. The opportunity to qualify as an officer of the deck on a destroyer in U.S. fast-carrier task forces off the South China coast during a number of confrontations with the People's Republic of China, and to achieve early responsibility within the gunnery department as its department head, provided priceless background and preparation for the submarine career that was to come.

My subsequent decision to apply for submarine duty in early 1957 grew from my frequent contact with fellow members of the Naval Academy track team who had graduated before me. The many hours I spent with them on their boats and on liberty in San Diego, Subic Bay, Hong Kong, and Yokosuka convinced me that the U.S. submarine force's esprit de corps was as strong as that of the Marine Corps.

Following graduation from U.S. Naval Submarine School in Groton, Connecticut, in late 1957, I was assigned to the diesel-electric submarine USS *Greenfish (SS-351)* in Pearl Harbor, Hawaii. The chance to serve under two good skippers, Lieutenant Commander Jack Knudsen and Lieutenant Commander John ("Tiger Al") Davis, in operations off the Hawaiian Islands and during three special operations in the northern Pacific positioned me for formal qualification as a submarine officer and for selection for Advanced Nuclear Power School in the late spring of 1959.

My selection for the navy's new nuclear power program and my dreaded interview with Admiral Hyman G. Rickover were as memorable as they were unexpected. The admiral was at that time director of naval reactors within the U.S. Navy Bureau of Ships in Washington, D.C.

Not two weeks after one of Al Davis's more senior officers had been selected for nuclear power school and detached from *Greenfish*, I suddenly received dispatch orders to report to Admiral Rickover's headquarters. This was not taken well by my commanding officer, because I had not yet applied for nuclear power, much less been proposed for qualification in submarines. Nonetheless, I departed for Washington a week later, with time only to read a book on the atomic submarine and Admiral Rickover and to glean as much information as possible from a library book on nuclear physics.

One's interview with the "KOG," or "Kindly Old Gentleman," during those early years of the submarine nuclear power program was guaranteed to be traumatic, and mine was no exception. The day began with a series of rigorous preliminary oral examinations conducted by key members of his staff, who included

Figure 2.1 Admiral Hyman G. Rickover, U.S. Navy. (Courtesy of the U.S. Navy)

Bob Panoff, Jack Gregg, Commander Jack Crawford, and Captain Jim Dunford. I was anything but optimistic. The interview with Panoff was the most difficult; I was never sure he and I even spoke the same language. Commander Crawford questioned me about what preparations I had made for my meeting with Admiral Rickover. When I mentioned the physics book, he opened a huge desk drawer that contained a great number of such books and asked me to point out the one I had studied. He then removed the book, and we spent the next several hours going through it chapter by chapter while he asked me questions to confirm that I had actually studied it.

The following morning, as I entered the admiral's office, the intense, almost blazing blue eyes of a surprisingly diminutive man bored into me from behind a large, paper-cluttered desk some thirty feet away. His eyes literally riveted me to the chair that I was ordered to take, and his first words set the tone. Fortunately for me, they ignited my fighting spirit. "What are you, a wrestler?" the admiral snarled. My puzzled "Sir?" was followed by his declarative and mocking, "Well, you have cauliflower ears!"

Now, I had always been fairly thin as I grew up, and my ears were sufficiently large and noticeable as to excite occasional unwelcome comment. This was apt to lead to fistfights in school and later to caustic exchanges with my classmates at the academy over our respective anatomical features. It was the perfect thing for the admiral to say to me. Suffice it to say, my adrenaline was up. "No, I do not!" I shot back.

Rickover's next remark was, in retrospect, my moment of truth. "Well," he growled, "we have determined that you are stupid and lazy and will be of little use to the nuclear power program!" I rose from my chair. He started to dismiss me from his office with a wave, but I stood my ground and protested vehemently that I was neither stupid nor lazy. I was specific about the one but not the other, and to this day I cannot remember which! A senior member of his staff immediately entered the office and attempted to usher me out. I shrugged off her light touch on my sleeve and, refusing to go, spoke my mind for a few moments more. As I hastily exited Admiral Rickover's office, Captain Dunford intercepted me.

"Well, Mac," he said to me behind closed doors, "that was quite a performance!"

"What does that mean?" I demanded to know.

"All I can tell you," he replied, "is that you stand either at the top or at the bottom of the seven interviewed from Pearl Harbor today."

His demeanor indicating that the discussion was at an end, I left the Main Navy Building and slowly made my way back to the old Ambassador Hotel, where I was staying. As I entered the lobby, my fellow officers from Pearl Harbor, all of whom had preceded me into Rickover's office that day, were at the bar and uttering loud whoops of laughter as they swapped their experiences with the "KOG." Joining them, I soon learned to my amazement that I was the only one who had sat in "the candidate's chair" that morning and not noticed that one leg was shorter than the other three, causing it to wobble and giving the admiral the opening to yell, "Sit still!" or "Why can't you sit still?" to the hapless interviewee.

Returning to my room several hours and many beers later, I was surprised and happy to find a message from Captain Dunford informing me that I had been selected to attend the Advanced Nuclear Power School at the submarine base, New London, Connecticut, and would soon be receiving orders. I learned later that what got me through the interview and accepted for the program was how I handled myself under pressure.

My return to *Greenfish* expecting orders to the nuclear power school infuriated Captain Davis, who was facing a forthcoming cold war deployment to the northern Pacific and was already short experienced officers. Added to his indignation was the fact that I had been selected before being formally qualified in submarines. The

pressure on him from senior submarine force staff officers to "get McLaren qualified as soon as possible" did not help. Completing the in-port and at-sea phases of
final submarine qualification under a not only tough but also very angry skipper
was no picnic. In the weeks that followed, he would frequently jibe, "There goes
nuclear power!" whenever I made a mistake during workup preparations for my
final qualification exams.

During the tense months that followed, I tried to remain calm and cool. As
approach officer on *Greenfish* during my final underway (at-sea) examination for
submarine qualification, I managed to make a completely undetected approach
and attack, with two practice torpedo hits, on an auxiliary vessel escorted by two
echo-ranging destroyers and further demonstrated that I could conduct a successful evasion and escape if detected. Captain Davis grudgingly presented me with
the "gold dolphins" of a qualified submariner before the entire crew one Saturday
morning in early July 1959. There was no qualification or farewell party. I was detached from *Greenfish* and within days was on my way to New London to undergo
a year of intense academic and operational training prior to reporting to my first
nuclear submarine.

The next six months of Advanced Nuclear Power School were the most intel-
lectually grueling of my life. All the mathematics and physics studied at the U.S.
Naval Academy over four years were covered in the first two weeks. From there we
proceeded to the even more difficult mathematics and physics associated with nuclear energy, followed by a basic, but quite challenging, reactor design problem that
required us to draw on all we had learned during the course.

The last six months were devoted to a formal watch qualification program at the
prototype S3G submarine nuclear power plant run by General Electric for the U.S.
Navy at West Milton, New York. Identical to the two installed on the world's largest submarine, the recently commissioned USS *Triton (SSN-586),* this land-based
prototype enabled both officer and enlisted nuclear submariners to train twenty-
four hours a day on an actual operational nuclear power plant under all power levels
and operational conditions and every conceivable practice casualty imaginable.
Successful completion of this rigorous watch qualification program, based on expected duties aboard ship, was required of all prior to graduation and assignment
to their first nuclear submarine. We officers had to qualify on all stations, culmi-
nating as a chief operator (equivalent to engineering officer of the watch on a nuclear submarine) certified to supervise the operation of the entire nuclear power
plant under all operational and casualty conditions.

Particularly noteworthy was that, in the course of our training, most of us
learned to push back considerably, if not completely eliminate, any internal limits

to learning that we had acquired up until then or imposed on ourselves. We really discovered what was possible to achieve with the right focus and motivation. None of us doubted that maximum effort would be needed in our future submarine careers, when the stakes would be high. Failing to pass any part of the nuclear power course curriculum was not an option, therefore, because it would not only destroy our hopes of ever becoming captains of nuclear submarines but probably also mean the end of our submarine careers.

Fresh out of nuclear power training in early June 1960, I reported to my first nuclear attack submarine, USS *Seadragon (SSN-584),* just commissioned at the Portsmouth Naval Shipyard in Kittery, Maine. This assignment was providential in that I would be serving with an outstanding commanding officer, Commander George P. Steele, and, with my first voyage to the North Pole, I would be launched on a path of Arctic exploration and scientific research that would consume a significant portion of my life during the years to come.

As the most junior officer on board, I was kept plenty busy standing diving officer watches and, at the same time, formally qualifying as officer of the deck and engineering officer of the watch. Other duties were any that my seniors chose to assign me, always unexpectedly and frequently at the very last moment. My favorite was photographic officer because I had the privilege to work with and learn a great deal from Lieutenant Glenn Brewer, who was assigned to us for the trip by the U.S. Navy Photographic Center. Glenn, who was a trained navy scuba diver as well, was to record our expedition photographically both above and beneath the Arctic seas.

Absolutely my worst job was taking over *Seadragon's* commissary department and with it overall responsibility for all meals served to the crew during the remainder of the voyage. Considering the truth of the old axiom that "the quality of the food served is responsible for 95 percent of the morale aboard ship," the assignment was disheartening. *Seadragon* had been specially loaded out with largely dried or "ration-dense" foods for the voyage to determine how much additional food storage space, and with it extra days at sea, could be gained. The boat's stores included such delicacies as dried apples, apricots, and prunes; cabbage; potatoes; carrots; eggs; milk; bacon; and, worst of all, canned hamburgers. The so-called hamburgers were vile and would soon be termed "weirdburgers" by the crew and thoroughly detested no matter how they were prepared.

During the remainder of my two-year tour on *Seadragon,* I performed all the usual divisional and department head duties of a submarine junior officer, from weapons and operations to reactor officer and from main propulsion assistant to

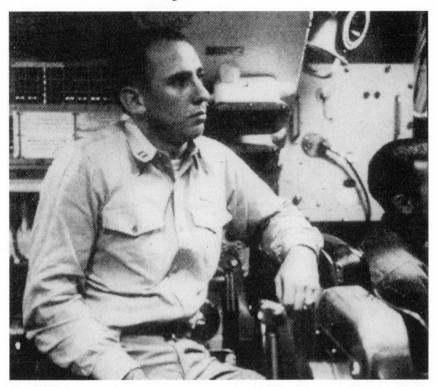

Figure 2.2 Lieutenant Alfred S. McLaren, U.S. Navy, diving officer of the watch, USS *Seadragon*, August 1960. (Courtesy of the U.S. Navy)

acting chief engineer. During this time I also took part in my third lengthy deployment to the western Pacific, which included several cold war operations.

Subsequent tours of duty up to 1965 included serving as both navigator and engineer officer on what was then the world's fastest submarine, USS *Skipjack (SSN-585)*, from 1962 to 1965 and officer-in-charge of *Whale (SSN-638)* in 1965.

In 1963, while on board *Skipjack* (Kelly),[1] I was formally qualified for command of submarines by our submarine division commander, Captain Shannon Cramer. I could now eagerly look forward to the day when I would have command of my own nuclear attack submarine.

3
The Advent of the True Arctic Submarine

Queenfish was the first of thirty-seven nuclear-powered attack submarines specially built by the United States for operating within the perennial ice-covered regions of the Arctic and Antarctic on a year-round basis. The design and subsequent construction and outfitting of this unique *Sturgeon* class was the direct result of the culmination and marriage of two major undersea technological advances in the 1950s, both of whose origins can be traced as far back as the fifteenth and sixteenth centuries.[1]

The first advance was that of the nuclear power plant, developed under the close supervision of Hyman Rickover, then captain (and later rear admiral), beginning in 1951. Nuclear power rendered the submarine capable of operating indefinitely beneath the sea without need to replenish its life-sustaining atmosphere, recharge its batteries, or refuel.[2]

The second and less well-known advance was the advent of the acoustic suite (consisting of all passive and active sonar equipment used for the detection and classification of potential targets, threats, or navigational hazards) and necessary submarine hull modifications that would enable a submarine to operate safely under the perennial sea ice of the polar regions. This innovation stemmed primarily from the vision and initiative of Dr. Waldo K. Lyon, a physicist then with the U.S. Navy Electronic Laboratory, Point Loma, California. Beginning in 1946, he directed an intensive period of research, development, and testing of submarine under-ice operating techniques and equipment on conventionally powered submarines, involving oceanographic expeditions across the Beaufort Sea by USS *Redfish (SS-395)* in 1952 and 1953. Successful testing led to the first formal proposal to the U.S. Navy for the creation of a United States polar submarine.[3]

The historic launch of USS *Nautilus (SSN-571)* on 21 January 1954 at the Electric Boat Company yard in Groton, Connecticut, and her subsequent famous "Underway on Nuclear Power" from there on 17 January a year later, signaled the birth of the world's first true submarine.[4] Commanded by one of the first submarine officers to be selected by Admiral Rickover for the U.S. Navy's new nuclear power program, Commander Eugene P. Wilkinson, USN, *Nautilus* was equipped with a nuclear-powered propulsion and electrical plant that enabled her to operate completely submerged and divorced from the outside atmosphere indefinitely.

By the time *Nautilus* returned to the Electric Boat Company yard in February 1957 for the refueling of her reactor core with just a few pounds of uranium, she had steamed 62,562 miles, more than half of that time completely submerged. A conventionally powered submarine would have required in excess of two million gallons of diesel fuel to duplicate *Nautilus*'s performance.[5]

On completion of *Nautilus*'s refueling two months later, and largely as a result of Captain Wilkinson's strong efforts, preparations were made to test her capabilities for under-ice operations and warfare in the Arctic Ocean during the forthcoming summer.[6]

Lyon, later to become director of the Arctic Submarine Laboratory, U.S. Naval Ocean Systems Center, San Diego, learning what was afoot in early March 1957, developed a proposal for a more comprehensive Arctic submarine program. With the invaluable assistance of Commander Robert D. McWethy of the Office of the Assistant Chief of Naval Operations for Undersea Warfare, Lyon prepared the proposal for presentation to the chief of naval operations (CNO), Admiral Arleigh Burke. The hope and expectation that the CNO would back the program and that the Commander in Chief Atlantic Fleet and the Commander Submarine Forces Atlantic would fully support an attendant nuclear submarine Arctic cruise was realized by early summer. The boat's new skipper, Commander William R. Anderson, who relieved Wilkinson in June of 1957, was equally enthusiastic about the proposed first-ever nuclear submarine Arctic operation.[7]

Commander Clay Blair, from the U.S. Navy Bureau of Ships, and Lyon set to work to ensure that *Nautilus* departed with all the equipment deemed necessary for safely operating under Arctic Ocean ice. The submarine was outfitted with five upward-beamed fathometers for detecting and measuring ice thickness overhead and a navigation system modified for high latitude. Her standard active-search sonar, the BQS-4, and mine-detection sonar, the UQS-1B, were considered sufficient for the detection of deep-draft ice in the submarine's path and small blocks of ice close aboard when coming to periscope depth.[8]

Between 1 and 6 September 1957, *Nautilus* steamed 1,383 nautical miles under Arctic Ocean ice during three probes, with the farthest taking her to latitude 87° N, only 180 nautical miles from the North Pole. Continuation to the pole was precluded, however, by a blown fuse that interrupted electrical power to both of *Nautilus*'s compasses at 86° N.[9] This quite serious casualty, coupled with the seven hours required to restore the operation of her special high-latitude MK-19 gyro compass, made it clear that installation of a more reliable navigational system capable of accurately determining position for sustained periods of time under ice was imperative for all future voyages into the Arctic Ocean. Damage to periscopes and masts during attempts to surface in leads or polynyas (openings within the ice) further revealed that the superstructure and hull of *Nautilus* and all follow-on nuclear submarines would have to be specially strengthened for sustained under-ice operations.

Despite these material setbacks, the overall success of *Nautilus*'s first under-ice voyage ensured that the vision of an operational under-ice submarine—a vision held by Lyon and by others in England, Germany, and Australia in earlier eras (Bishop John Wilkins, Professor Anschutz-Kampfe, and Sir Hubert Wilkins)—would soon become a reality.[10]

The high priority given by the CNO and the strong interest on the part of President Dwight Eisenhower left no doubt that *Nautilus,* still commanded by Anderson, would return to the Arctic Ocean in early June of 1958. Her top-secret mission this time was to make a historic first crossing of the Arctic Ocean from the Pacific to the Atlantic Ocean via the North Pole. *Nautilus* was to depart for sea equipped with a North American N6A inertial navigator, the first such navigation system to be carried by Arctic submarines.[11] It was, in essence, a very sophisticated dead-reckoning system that automatically measured, calculated, and recorded the submarine's relative motion from a known starting position or navigational fix.[12] Such a feature would enable the submarine to navigate accurately for long periods of time while fully submerged.[13] *Nautilus* would also depart for sea with an additional gyro compass and her standard MK-19 and MK-23 compasses modified for high-latitude operations.

Finally, Lyon, who would make this trip as science advisor to the captain, as he was on the 1957 voyage, came on board with a five-unit topside echo-sounder array and a high-resolution, variable-frequency, upward-beamed fathometer to be installed for more accurately measuring and analyzing the sea ice that *Nautilus* would be passing beneath. A precision depth recorder (PDR) was installed, in addition, for the specific purpose of collecting much-needed bathymetric data so that accurate Arctic Ocean bottom charts could finally be developed for this strategically important, yet virtually unknown, vast ocean area.[14]

Nautilus's first attempt at a transpolar crossing had to be aborted on 18 June 1958, to Anderson's and Lyon's acute disappointment. She had unexpectedly encountered deep-draft Arctic pack ice in the shallow Chukchi Sea at approximately 68° N, west of Point Hope, Alaska. The series of near collisions with massive ice floes that occurred while she attempted to proceed north while submerged beneath the pack made it inadvisable to continue without a forward-scanning sonar. Only equipment with the same capabilities as the no-longer-stocked QLA frequency-modulated, scanning mine-detection sonar (a short-range obstacle-avoidance sonar) used on the earlier *Redfish* under-ice operations would have enabled her to detect and safely pilot around such deep-draft ice in her path, and *Nautilus* did not have it.[15]

Nautilus returned to Pearl Harbor to await more favorable ice conditions. Still under top-secret security restraints, she departed once again for the Arctic on 22 July. She passed through the Bering Strait seven days later and reentered the uncharted Chukchi Sea on what would now be her third attempt to make a successful transpolar crossing of the Arctic Ocean. After a fruitless search for a deep-water route while operating on the surface in the northern Chukchi Sea, she closed on the Alaskan coast and slowly threaded her way through fingers of deep-draft sea ice en route to the Barrow Sea Valley to the east. The hope was that this valley would provide sufficiently deep water for the submarine to submerge safely beneath the ice pack and head north.[16]

Nautilus finally rounded a corner of the pack ice north of Point Franklin, Alaska, and, early on 1 August, headed directly for the sea valley's mouth. She encountered deeper water within hours and was at last able to submerge and gradually increase depth and speed as she left the North American continental shelf and entered the Canada Basin.

Well beneath the ice pack, *Nautilus* reached longitude 155° W later on the same day. Captain Anderson then ordered a course change to north for the run to the pole some 1,094 miles distant. Transiting at speeds of up to twenty knots and at a depth of six hundred feet, the submarine reached and passed beneath the North Pole just before midnight on 3 August 1958. Ninety-six hours from when she first submerged beneath the sea ice off Alaska, she emerged from beneath the ice pack northeast of Greenland. The first transpolar crossing of the Arctic Ocean had been achieved to worldwide acclaim.[17]

Figure 3.1 Artist's concept of USS *Nautilus (SSN-571)* under ice during 1958 transpolar voyage from the Pacific Ocean to the Atlantic via the North Pole. (Courtesy of the General Dynamics Corporation)

Coming from the Atlantic and close on *Nautilus's* heels, USS *Skate (SSN-578)*, under Commander James F. Calvert, reached the North Pole on 12 August. The first of a new class of nuclear submarines, *Skate* was equipped with a second North American N6A inertial navigator, a four-transducer topside echo-sounder array, a topside fathometer mounted on the sail, and, not least, a UQS-1 forward-looking mine-detecting sonar for detecting and piloting around deep-draft ice.[18]

Returning to the Arctic Ocean during the winter of 1959 with an improved model of the NK variable-frequency topside echo sounder carried by *Nautilus,* and with the top of the sail hardened with HY-80 steel, *Skate,* on St. Patrick's Day 1959, became the first submarine to surface through ice at the North Pole. In the course of twenty-five surfacings within the ice pack during both cruises, *Skate* developed

Figure 3.2 (*Left to right*) Dr. Waldo K. Lyon and Captain
William R. Anderson, U.S. Navy, on board USS *Nautilus*
(SSN-571). (Courtesy of the U.S. Navy)

the basic techniques for successfully surfacing without damage within open, and
through, ice-covered leads and polynyas.[19]

Two additional members of the *Skate*-class nuclear attack submarine, USS *Sargo*
(SSN-583) and USS *Seadragon (SSN-584),* skippered by Lieutenant Commander
John H. Nicholson and Commander George P. Steele, respectively, joined *Nautilus* and *Skate* as pioneer Arctic submarines in 1960. *Sargo's* Nicholson had served
on *Nautilus* and was executive officer and navigator during *Skate's* 1958 Arctic voyage. Under Nicholson's experienced leadership, *Sargo,* equipped with both an iceberg detector (IBD) designed by Art Roshon of the U.S. Navy Electronic Laboratory and a North American N6A inertial guidance system, completed a first-ever
all-winter expedition of more than 6,521 miles throughout the Arctic Ocean. Approximately 2,298 miles of the exhausting thirty-one-day mission were spent sur-

Figure 3.3 USS *Skate (SSN-578)* commanded by Commander James F. Calvert, U.S. Navy, surfaced at North Pole, 17 March 1959. (Courtesy of the U.S. Navy)

veying previously uncharted shallow waters of the Bering, Chukchi, and Beaufort seas. *Sargo* also carried the NK variable-frequency topside echo sounder and a prototype EDO Corporation BQN-4 five-unit upward-beamed fathometer. With this equipment and its HY-80 steel–reinforced sail, *Sargo* further perfected *Skate*'s techniques for surfacing through the ice.[20]

On 9 February 1960 *Sargo* broke through 39 inches of ice at the North Pole; she later surfaced through as much as 48.5 inches.[21] Altogether she achieved twenty successful surfacings through thick ice before ending her cruise. Nicholson improved the watch standing and operational procedures for piloting Arctic submarines in ice-covered shallow water—measures that were to prove invaluable to *Queenfish* during her 1970 Arctic expedition.

The transfer of a newly commissioned *Seadragon,* the fourth and last of the *Skate* class, from the Atlantic to the Pacific Ocean via the North Pole during August of 1960 was to conclude a historic two-year period of Arctic Ocean exploration of which I was privileged to take part.[22] The last of the Arctic submarine pioneers, *Seadragon* completed a final stage in the evolution and testing of what was to become the standard Arctic submarine suite.

Seadragon departed for the Arctic Ocean on 1 August 1960 equipped with all

Figure 3.4 USS *Sargo (SSN-583)* commanded by Lieutenant Commander John H. Nicholson, U.S. Navy, surfaced through three feet of ice at the North Pole in dead of winter 1960. (Courtesy of the U.S. Navy)

the components of what was to be the first integrated ice suite. She carried the NK variable-frequency fathometer for accurate measurement of ice thickness overhead, a rate-of-rise meter, a precision depth recorder (PDR), and an ambient light meter. She was provided, moreover, with a BQN-4 topside upward-beamed echo sounder (five transducers topside and one bottomside), a UQN-1 fathometer, and a mast-mounted, prototype EDO Corporation BQS-7 polynya delineator.[23] Completing the package of equipment considered necessary for the expedition was the installation of the first Sperry Corporation ship's inertial navigation system (SINS) for its initial test in Arctic regions. As science advisor to the captain, Dr. Lyon accompanied this voyage as he did those of *Nautilus, Skate,* and *Sargo.*[24]

Seadragon became the first and only submarine to examine the underside of twenty-two icebergs in Baffin Bay and Lancaster Sound. Many of these icebergs were unbelievably massive, exceeding several million tons and reaching hundreds of feet beneath the sea. *Seadragon* also discovered and surveyed a deep passage through the only partially charted Northwest Passage from Lancaster Sound through the Parry Channel to the McClure Strait via the Barrow Strait and Viscount Melville Sound in the Canadian Archipelago.[25]

On 25 August *Seadragon* reached the North Pole, where we crew members disembarked to play a wild game of baseball. The pitcher's mound was located as close to the North Pole as possible so that if you hit a home run you circumnavigated the globe. If you hit the ball into right field, it was across the international date line into tomorrow, and if the right fielder caught it, he threw it back into yesterday. Needless to say, sliding into base took on new meaning.[26]

An earlier task of *Seadragon* to survey the continental shelf of the Kara and Laptev seas before exiting the Arctic Ocean via the Bering Strait had been cancelled by the CNO, to the extreme disappointment of Steele and Lyon.[27] Little did I know that ten years later I would command the first in a new class of Arctic submarine that would finally accomplish the first survey of the Laptev Sea.

This earlier era of exploration drew to a dramatic close during the summer of 1962 when *Skate,* commanded by Joe Skoog, coming from the Atlantic by way of the Nares Strait and the Lincoln Sea (the first submarine transit of these waters), rendezvoused at the North Pole with *Seadragon,* commanded by Dan Summitt, which had come from the Pacific. On her return, *Skate* made the first transit of the Northwest Passage, from west to east, by way of the Parry Channel. Both submarines were outfitted with the standard Arctic suite carried by *Seadragon* in 1960.[28]

Plans for other submarine Arctic operations in the early 1960s were brought to an abrupt halt by the catastrophic flooding of USS *Thresher (SSN-593)* (Harvey) and the loss of her entire crew and more than thirty shipyard personnel in the spring of 1963. This horrendous and unforeseen tragedy triggered an immediate Navy-wide examination of all aspects of submarine safety. A committed navy assigned high priority to the development of a program that would prevent any further loss of deep-diving nuclear submarines and personnel due to seawater leaks while submerged. The Submarine Safety Program (SUBSAFE) would aggressively implement the many changes deemed necessary in shipyard construction and repair practices as well as at-sea operational procedures and training.

Full-scale submarine Arctic expeditions finally resumed in 1969, following implementation of the SUBSAFE program on all nuclear submarines. In the meantime the keel was laid for the first of the nuclear attack submarines of a new *Sturgeon* class, capable of operating within the polar regions year-round. Although she was ninth in the series of submarines whose construction was authorized by the U.S. Congress in 1963, *Queenfish* was the first of this superb class to go to sea and to test her ice suite and ability to operate under ice in Arctic waters, following her commissioning in 1966.

Completing the task of evaluating the class's under-ice operational capabilities were USS *Whale* (Wolff) and USS *Pargo (SSN-650)* (White), which departed for the Arctic in 1969. *Whale*'s and *Pargo*'s demonstrated ability to surface routinely through thick ice anywhere in the Arctic Ocean laid to rest most doubts about a single-screw submarine's ability to operate safely in ice-covered waters.[29] Both submarines also resumed the task of charting still-unexplored areas begun a decade earlier.

By the end of 1969, U.S. nuclear attack submarines had surveyed a considerable portion of the central Arctic Ocean, its two recently discovered deep basins, and the steep-sided, almost sill-like Lomonosov Ridge that separated them. Virtually no effort had been made, however, to penetrate and survey the more remote, uncharted areas along the Siberian continental shelf, the Kara Sea, or the myriad passages through the Canadian Arctic islands. Minor exceptions were *Nautilus*'s and *Seadragon*'s brief transits through the shallow Beaufort and Chukchi seas; *Sargo*'s more extensive search for and survey, under heavy winter sea ice, of deeper and more accessible portions of the Beaufort, Chukchi, and Bering seas; and *Seadragon*'s and *Skate*'s surveys, in 1960 and 1962, respectively, of the most direct route through the Canadian Archipelago (the Northwest Passage).

At this time, Lyon played a key role in setting CNO priorities for the testing of Arctic submarines and the exploration of uncharted areas within the perennially ice-covered Arctic Ocean and its contiguous seas. Suitable nuclear attack submarines had been made available for these missions by either the Commander Submarine Forces Atlantic or Pacific, as current cold war operational priorities permitted. But many large blank areas throughout the Siberian side of the Arctic Ocean remained to be filled in.

By 1970, therefore, exploration of the Siberian continental shelf, covered by the three sizable sea-ice–covered shallow shelf seas—the Laptev, East Siberian, and Chukchi—approached the top of the navy's operational priority list for both scientific and strategic reasons. *Queenfish* was tasked with this responsibility.

4
Construction and Commissioning
of USS *Queenfish (SSN-651)*

General Dynamics in Groton, Connecticut, was the lead shipyard and builder of the new *Sturgeon*-class submarine and began construction on the first boat on 10 August 1963. Follow-on submarines of the class were either under construction or scheduled to be built between 1963 and 1975 at General Dynamics' shipyards in Groton, Connecticut, and Quincy, Massachusetts, and at other independent shipyards at Newport News, Virginia; Pascagoula, Mississippi; Portsmouth in Kittery, Maine; and Mare Island, California.

I had been assigned as officer-in-charge of the second of these new boats, *Whale (SSN-638),* since early summer of 1965, until it became increasingly obvious that her construction at General Dynamics' Quincy Division was falling behind schedule. I was therefore shifted as precommissioning executive officer of *Whale* to that of *Queenfish,* which was under construction at the Newport News Shipbuilding and Drydock Company in Virginia. Dispatch orders came to me to report there in early November.

Queenfish's keel was laid on 11 May 1964, a full year and a half after that of the lead ship. She was the second submarine to be named after a small but beautiful metallic blue and silver fish of the Croaker family that lives along the California coast. The first was her illustrious World War II predecessor, USS *Queenfish (SS-393).* The first time I saw the new boat at the construction site during the fall of 1964, she was a huge dark shape behind a building-size tarp hanging in front, which prevented unwanted eyes from examining her more closely. Emblazoned on the tarp was a cross section of a submarine hull reading "*Queenfish (SSN-651)*." I felt a strong stirring.

The prospective engineer officer, Lieutenant Ron Burdge, and a number of engineering department senior petty officers arrived in Newport News a few weeks before I did. Commander Jack Richard, the prospective commanding officer (PCO) of *Queenfish,* and all remaining engineering department petty officers and firemen who had been assigned joined us before the end of the year. They were followed by a steady stream of officers, senior and junior petty officers, and seamen, rounding out our crew in early January of 1966. We would ultimately number eleven officers, nine chief petty officers, and some eighty-five men, making up all required technology support areas, plus cooks, stewards, storekeepers, yeomen, quartermasters, firemen, seamen, and hospital corpsmen required to operate the submarine at sea, by the early fall of 1966.[1]

The *Sturgeon*-class submarines combined the best of all design features needed for their missions: sound quieting, easy maneuvering, atmosphere control, and the latest in acoustic and electronic detection and war-fighting capabilities derived from the operational lessons of the earlier *Skate, Skipjack,* and *Thresher* (later *Permit*) classes of nuclear attack submarine. They were specially constructed and equipped to operate within the world's sea-ice–covered polar regions year-round.

The new boats slightly exceeded 292 feet and had a beam of almost 32 feet and a displacement of roughly 4,640 tons submerged. All seawater piping and main ballast tank blow systems met SUBSAFE standards.[2] Powered by a Westinghouse S5W nuclear reactor, two steam turbines, and a large seven-bladed, sound-quieted propeller capable of delivering 15,000-shaft horsepower, these boats could make speeds in excess of twenty knots submerged and reach ocean depths in excess of one thousand feet.

By the fall of 1965, construction of *Queenfish* was already several months ahead of schedule when the U.S. Navy offered Newport News a bonus of several million dollars if the submarine were completed and fully outfitted for sea in advance of the lead ship. Newport News accepted the challenge and immediately initiated maximum effort on a three-shift basis to deliver *Queenfish* on deadline.

Our new construction crew established a round-the-clock, seven-day-a-week watch team under the strong leadership of Commander Jack Richard. The three-section teams enabled us to monitor closely the shipyard's accelerated efforts and to keep a close eye on safety conditions and watertight integrity throughout the boat as its construction proceeded. The teams enabled us as well to follow closely the installation of all its components, systems, and equipments and to assist shipyard personnel in the subsequent inspection and testing of each system and equipment on their completions.

Queenfish's crew, moreover, had the responsibility for preparing the requisite valve and/or switch lineups and the operating instructions for all modes of operation and emergencies of each fluid and electrical system installed, in time to be used during initial operation and testing. It was an altogether monumental challenge that required extreme care and attention to detail.

As each system was completed, tested, and deemed operationally satisfactory in all respects, *Queenfish's* crew assumed full responsibility for her subsequent maintenance and operation. The net demand on both officers' and crew's time and skills in ensuring that all was accomplished satisfactorily and safely during the accelerated construction schedule proved to be incredibly taxing. Among the most demanding were those duties and tasks associated with such major events as submarine launch, initial fill of the nuclear reactor vessel, taking the nuclear reactor critical for the first time, and the testing and operation of the nuclear power plant and its myriad supporting primary and secondary engineering systems and equipments.

Queenfish was launched on 25 February 1966, a full day ahead of the lead ship, *Sturgeon*. We stood elated and proud as her sponsor, the Honorable Julia Butler Hansen of the state of Washington, smashed a champagne bottle across her bow and *Queenfish* slid rapidly and gracefully down the ways into the James River.

As a crew we now shifted our focus to assisting the shipyard in readying our boat for the extremely demanding series of first-in-the-class sea trials that would begin in early fall. An intense and well-coordinated effort by shipyard personnel and crew consumed the weeks and months that rapidly followed. Our collective efforts were not without a price: everyone, both officer and enlisted man, not to mention our families, felt the pinch. We had not only to stand watch for many hours throughout the ship but also to train for and perform all other duties normally expected for our rating or rank, including routine and preventive maintenance of a rapidly increasing number of systems and equipments accepted by *Queenfish's* crew on behalf of the U.S. Navy. *Queenfish's* accelerated schedule during 1966, moreover, demanded the scheduling of most crew members for special schooling and training on the many new equipments installed.

Queenfish gained her full crew complement by early summer and, with a few exceptions, was ready for the forthcoming sea trials. Almost 70 percent of the men were qualified submariners and seasoned veterans of cold war operations in both the Atlantic and Pacific. They were the cream of the submarine force, with both officers and petty officers carefully selected to assist in the completion and preparation of *Queenfish* for sea. The majority were well-educated, post–Korean War vet-

Figure 4.1 Launch of USS *Queenfish,* first of new class of Arctic nuclear attack submarine, at Newport News Shipbuilding and Drydock Company, Newport News, Virginia, 25 February 1966. (Courtesy of the U.S. Navy)

erans who possessed considerable technical ability and skills. As the months went by, these individuals quickly coalesced into an aggressive, proud, and well-qualified team—one heavily endowed with the submariner's typically rough sense of humor. *Queenfish's* commissioning crew, indeed, was to set the standard and become the prototype and example for all the superb crews that were to man her during an illustrious twenty-five-year life.

As executive officer, training officer, and de facto personnel officer, my routine on a typical day was similar to everyone else's, divided into three distinct parts or phases. First, and in many ways foremost, was standing a command/senior engineer watch in the maneuvering room (reactor and engineering plant control space). Each day from midnight to eight o'clock in the morning, my job was to monitor closely, and at times supervise, all that was taking place within the engineering spaces during that period, particularly the brand-new nuclear power plant and all its components and support systems.

The second portion of my day began shortly after I was relieved in the engineering spaces at eight o'clock by *Queenfish*'s engineer officer. After a "working breakfast" grabbed on the run at a local greasy spoon or vending machine, I spent the morning and afternoon until three o'clock performing normal executive officer duties. These duties encompassed preparing and supervising the daily training schedule, handling all personnel matters and problems and all ship's correspondence, and acting as a principal assistant to the commanding officer.

Other personal responsibilities of importance included the final preparation, verification, and promulgation of valve and switch lineups and operating instructions for all of *Queenfish*'s fluid and electrical systems and of the rig-for-dive and surface check-off lists and instructions for each of her seven watertight compartments. The most complex and challenging of these compartments were the newly designed control, torpedo, machinery, and engine rooms and the upper and lower level of the reactor compartment. Finally, I was frequently called on to assist in the final acceptance for the U.S. Navy "hand-over-hand" inspections and operational checkouts of a great number of the boat's fluid and electrical systems.

What was left of the day was devoted to my family, consisting of an all-too-brief visit and early dinner with my wife and three young children and a light sleep. Home life ended shortly after eleven o'clock at night, when I arose in a somewhat zombie state, quickly dressed, and drove to the shipyard in time to debrief and relieve Jack Richard, who had been on the command/senior engineer watch since four o'clock that afternoon.

Everyone on board was on a similar schedule, so if anyone needed a day off, those affected would often have to go on a port-and-starboard watch routine. Jack Richard, Ron Burdge, and I each tried to take at least one weekend off each month to be with our families. Unfortunately, this forced the other two to go on a twelve-hour-on, twelve-hour-off command/senior engineer watch routine until the third man had returned. There was little time for sickness, injury, or family emergency, much less recreational or personal leave.

The total effect of all these demands on the personal and family life of officers and crewmen throughout 1966 was horrendous, leading, not surprisingly, to a number of nervous breakdowns and divorces and ultimately the loss and replacement on an urgent basis of a significant number of our original and highly valued crew members.

Our sustained efforts as a team paid off handsomely, however. All aspects of construction, testing, and overall outfitting of *Queenfish* at Newport News proceeded unusually well and without incident or major problems. By early October 1966, her proud crew was fully prepared to take the first of the new *Sturgeon*-class nuclear attack submarines to sea.

How did we do it? I think, in retrospect, that our success stemmed not only from our great pride in being a handpicked crew for a very new, first-in-the-class submarine but also in large part from our dogged determination to do all that could be done to ensure that *Queenfish* was put to sea before the lead ship.

It was Admiral Rickover's custom to ride each newly constructed nuclear submarine during the initial sea trials. Both wardroom and crew pulled out all the stops to ensure that the admiral had a comfortable and successful ride. A special "Rickover Check-off List" had been developed, expanded, and steadily refined since *Nautilus* first departed for sea some twelve years earlier. The list included such essential items for the admiral as seedless grapes, SS Pierce lemon drops, comfortable pillows, sizable quantities of stationery and writing materials, and a number of navy foul-weather jackets (for later presentation to key members of Congress) that sported the new submarine's distinctive insignia patch.

The exhaustive preparations for the admiral's ride also required that the executive officer give up his tiny stateroom and bunk and find another place within an already crowded submarine to accomplish his many duties during sea trials and somehow sandwich in a few winks of sleep.

Near the top of the list of duties was drafting approximately one thousand letters for the admiral. These letters informed members of Congress and other senior U.S. government officials of the successful completion of the new nuclear submarine's initial sea trial. Heaven help the hapless executive officer and commanding officer if any typos, mistakes, or smudges were ever found on these letters or their envelopes. Hence both commanding and executive officer and, on occasion, senior shipyard officials spent every spare moment during this already stressful period carefully proofing each of these letters before it was presented to the admiral for signature.

Adding to the overall difficulties of getting through all phases of *Queenfish*'s initial sea trials was having to make the seven-hour surface transit from the Newport News shipyard through areas heavily trafficked by merchant and military ships before reaching water deep enough to conduct submerged operations. Our able navigator, Lieutenant Commander Bob Loewenthal, then had to return us safely by the same route, factoring in the proximity of shoal water and the times of high and low tide with the strengths of their attendant currents. If the winds were strong and the seas high, as they generally were off the Virginia Capes during the fall, the constant rolling and pitching of the submarine's rounded hull could trigger heavy bouts of seasickness. In sum, successful accomplishment of the complete series of sea trials was going to be a feat for captain, officers, and crew alike, none of whom had been to sea for well over a year.

Queenfish's initial sea trial was unique in the annals of new-construction submarine sea trials. On finally reaching the assigned diving area, we found to our utter consternation that we could not get our wonderful new boat to submerge no matter how hard we tried. Admiral Rickover stood by silently and, to our surprise, patiently in the control room as he observed our special sea-trials ship control team flood every conceivable tank, including both sanitary tanks, in our increasingly frustrated efforts to get below the surface. *Queenfish* remained so positively buoyant that we could not even drive her beneath the surface when Captain Richard ordered, "Make turns for ten knots," followed by "Fifteen knots!"

At length the admiral decided that "enough is enough" and directed Captain Richard to return to the shipyard. We arrived and moored quite late in the evening, whereupon shipyard workers swarmed all over *Queenfish*'s topside and began cutting holes in the top of each main ballast tank. They then proceeded to bring the boat in ballast by adding lead "pigs," or weights, in the upper part of each tank. It turned out that we had gone to sea that day almost 120,000 pounds lighter than neutral buoyancy. We all had nightmarish thoughts about what might have happened had we been 120,000 pounds heavier than neutral buoyancy.

Major reballasting was finished by early morning, and Admiral Rickover returned on board. Once again we departed for sea. To everyone's great relief and delight, *Queenfish* slipped smoothly beneath the surface, and the diving officer, Lieutenant Herb Mensch, soon brought her to neutral buoyancy or hovering position, all stop, at a depth of 120 feet and perfectly in ballast. The remainder of the initial sea trials, such as maneuvering the boat at various rudder and up- and down-angles and speeds, were completed without problem or incident. *Queenfish* ended the day proving she was fully watertight and seaworthy at test depth. We were now ready for more advanced testing during the weeks to follow.

Admiral Rickover left the boat shortly after our return to the shipyard with nary a cross word to either captain or crew. We noted with interest, though, that each of the senior shipyard officials who followed him out seemed to have gotten their ears sunburned during the voyage.

I was very happy to regain my small stateroom and, utterly exhausted, asked Senior Steward's Mate Emery Crite if he would please have the sheets on my bunk changed so that I could, at long last, retire for a full night's sleep.

Later, with my adrenaline still surging, I crawled between the fresh crisp sheets and lay on my back, trying without success to drift off to sleep. As I tossed and turned for what seemed hours, I began to notice little spots or deposits all over the overhead of my stateroom and the upper reaches of its bulkheads. There were hundreds! Was I having eye problems, or was there really something there? Might they be, God forbid, little seeps of heaven-knows-what vile substance through the overhead and bulkheads?

I asked Crite to come to my stateroom immediately with a flashlight. He arrived quite puzzled at being called with such urgency. Taking the flashlight from him, I began to point out the innumerable tiny blots and deposits. The minute Crite saw them he began to laugh hysterically. After he had calmed down, he told me that whenever Admiral Rickover found a seed in one of the grapes left for him in a bowl, he immediately tilted his head back and spit it into the air, whereupon it adhered to the overhead or on one of the bulkheads. I climbed back in my bunk, pointed out that the stewards had their work cut out for them the next day, and promptly fell asleep.

During the second sea trial, our ability to range at all speeds within our safe depth envelope was satisfactorily tested. We were now ready to proceed with the first of three special trials designed to check out operationally our underwater acoustic detection and analysis, or sonar, system and the fire-control systems used to compute the necessary lead or deflection angles and overall hitting solutions for our torpedo battery of four tubes. These trials would have to be completed before the submarine could be commissioned. It was during the first of these special trials that the crew's collective sense of humor and fun reared its head.

The sizable torpedo room contained four angled torpedo tubes, two to port and two to starboard. Our torpedomen had to be capable of actually manhandling a very heavy load of various warfish or torpedoes on a daily basis. Almost all torpedomen were big and burly old-time sailors: hairy-chested and well-tattooed, looking like wild men.

The morning of our third and what would be a weeklong sea trial arrived. Ready to embark early that morning were at least a dozen civilian engineers from the shipyard and the contractors who had produced and supported our fire-control systems. Immediately noticed by the crew was a young man with beautiful long blond hair that fell below his shoulders. Had he been of the opposite sex he would have been considered stunningly good-looking. He was definitely a novel sight to a hard-bitten and already tired submarine crew preparing for sea. Beyond a few brief comments by the chief of the boat and some of the crew, however, no mention was made of the man's appearance or presence on board. He was completely ignored. This struck me as strange, if not completely out of character, for "meat-and-potato sailors," especially because long hair in a man was still an uncommon sight.

We proceeded out to sea and, after a number of rough hours rolling about on the surface, eventually submerged and headed for our assigned operations area. Several days passed as each of the various tests of our fire-control equipment was completed. *Queenfish* was rapidly becoming a frontline attack boat capable of engaging and destroying any undersea or surface opponent with a variety of weapons, a serious threat to any potential enemy's military and merchant fleet. A growing sense of pride and confidence in the boat was becoming increasingly evident throughout the submarine crew.

By the fifth morning of the sea trial, I had long since forgotten about our rider with the long golden hair. I was eating a hurried breakfast in the wardroom when one of the cooks poked his head in and said, "Commander McLaren, it's not an emergency, but the chief of the boat thought you should take a peek into the crew's mess as soon as possible. Something very interesting is about to happen."

I crammed one last spoonful of cereal into my mouth and eased over to the door between the wardroom pantry and the crew's mess. Everything seemed normal as I observed some thirty crew members quietly eating breakfast. Standing at the far end, however, was our golden-haired rider peacefully pouring himself a glass of juice from the juice machine. Suddenly the door at the opposite end of the mess hall burst open with a loud bang. Everyone looked up, startled to see our biggest and burliest torpedoman literally filling the doorway as he lunged into the room. Naked to the waist, he stood about six foot five and weighed well over 250 pounds. His huge hairy chest and long, well-muscled arms were covered with strategically placed tattoos of every description. The general reaction from those eating was a quiet "what the hell?"

This fierce-looking apparition stopped abruptly and began to scan the mess hall with bulging, predatory, bloodshot eyes. When he spied the rider with the beautiful blond hair, he crouched forward as if about to spring. Fixing a hot, piercing glance on the luckless gentleman about to drink his glass of juice, the torpedoman rapidly charged him and with an enormous right arm pulled him to his side in a viselike embrace. Absolute silence prevailed. Our torpedoman turned toward the assembled crew members and with a deep growl that reverberated throughout the compartment announced, "We're engaged!" Loud laughter, cheers, whistles, and general pandemonium ensued as the "gorgeous critter," as he came to be known, slumped down and almost fainted. Reviving, he struggled valiantly against his seemingly love-struck attacker and managed to break free and escape through the nearest door.

The story concluded on the morning of our next and final sea trial just days later. It was early morning. We were once again joined by the same group of civilian shipyard representatives and contractors who had gone to sea with us the week before. I noticed that more members of the crew were topside than usual and that even our huge torpedoman of recent fame could be seen peering out of the torpedo room hatch forward. But, to the visible disappointment of all, the "gorgeous critter" had apparently not returned.

I silently counted the civilian scientists and engineers as they came on board and checked them against the cleared passengers' list by the topside watch. A final count revealed that we had exactly the same number on board as at our previous trial. I scrutinized the assembled group even more closely as one by one they headed below decks through the weapons-loading hatch amidships. One of their number appeared to be an entirely new rider. He was tall and thin with close-cropped blond hair. Here was the "gorgeous critter," shorn of his golden locks and trying to act as unobtrusive as possible. He had no intention of being subjected again to our brand of submarine humor.

With all sea trials successfully completed, *Queenfish* unfurled her commissioning pennant for the first time on 6 December 1966 following the traditional commissioning ceremony at which the featured speaker was Rear Admiral Elliott Loughlin. He had been the first commanding officer of our boat's World War II forebear, under whose leadership her crew had earned a Presidential Unit Citation for two war patrols in 1944 that sank seven Japanese ships totaling 29,160 tons. Also present was another famous World War II submariner, Vice Admiral Arnold F. Schade, Commander Submarine Forces Atlantic.

It was a proud day for shipyard workers and crew. *Queenfish* had not only succeeded in being the first of the new *Sturgeon*-class nuclear attack submarines to be launched and go to sea but also was commissioned several months ahead of the lead ship. We all believed, at the end of that memorable day, that we and our boat would sail into the future, whether for peace or war, with the combined good fortune of these two heroes of the Second World War.

5
The First Arctic Test of *Queenfish*
The Davis Strait Marginal Sea-Ice Operation

As the first of the *Sturgeon*-class submarines to be commissioned and made ready for unrestricted operations at sea, *Queenfish* was immediately subjected to a series of tests of her capability to operate under polar sea ice. A special add-on was a test of the under-ice capability of the nose cone of the new MK-48 antisubmarine warfare torpedo and all associated acoustic components.

The area chosen for conducting the tests, beginning in early February of 1967, was a marginal ice zone (MIZ) way up north within the Davis Strait, between Baffin Island and Greenland, approximately sixty miles south of the Baffin Bay pack ice. Even though this choice meant revising Christmas and holiday leave plans for most of the crew, we all turned to with enthusiasm to prepare and load out our new boat for an operational assignment considered by all to be a great honor.

The full list of major new hull and structural modifications and new equipments incorporated into *Queenfish* for operation under ice were as follows:

(1) The top of the sail and the rudder were reinforced with HY-80 steel to enable all submarines in the class to break through as much as six feet of sea ice in the polar regions.
(2) The forward diving-control surfaces (formerly "bow planes") were relocated from the bow to the middle of the sail and could be rotated to a 90° or vertical position to minimize impact and risk of damage to the sail planes and their operating mechanism during the process of surfacing through sea ice.
(3) All masts and periscopes housed within the sail, with the exception of the elec-

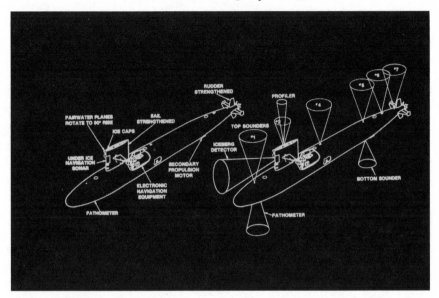

Figure 5.1 Schematic of Arctic submarine structural modifications, special equipments, and under-ice sonar of USS *Queenfish*. (Courtesy of the U.S. Navy)

tronics countermeasures mast (ECM), could be lowered within the sail suffi-ciently to prevent impact with sea ice during surfacing.

(4) A protective steel ice cap capable of withstanding impact with heavy sea ice was provided for the ECM during polar operations.

Each *Sturgeon*-class submarine was equipped, moreover, with the latest ver-sion of the AN/BQS-8 Arctic under-ice sonar suite. This consisted basically of a forward-looking frequency-modulated (FM) iceberg detector, or ice-obstacle-detecting sonar, to detect deep-draft ice in the path of the submarine and delin-eate the edges of open lakes of water during surfacing, together with a narrow-beamed acoustic ice profiler and accompanying recorder to measure and record sea-ice draft and underwater morphology above the submarine's sail. The acous-tic suite, furthermore, included a hull-mounted acoustic array of seven transduc-ers, numbered one through seven from bow to stern, which enabled the boat to de-termine ice draft, or thickness beneath the surface, above that hull location prior to surfacing.

There were, in addition, two hull-mounted fathometers (depth sounders)—one of which used a secure high frequency—to measure water depth beneath the keel. Also of considerable use under ice in Arctic regions was a secondary propulsion motor (SPM), which was housed along the keel aft. The SPM could be lowered, rotated up to 180° to port or starboard, and used like a thruster when operating at slow speed either on the surface or when submerged. It would prove particularly useful for dodging ice within polynyas in the pack ice.

Completing the basic equipment required for operating under ice was a navigation suite centered on the latest version of the shipboard inertial navigation system (SINS MK-3 Mod 4). This equipment consisted of the high-latitude-capable MK-19 and MK-23 gyro compasses; a state-of-the art satellite navigation system; and Omega, Loran C, and radio direction finder (RDF) worldwide electronic navigation systems.

Queenfish headed north from Virginia in late January of 1967 with Dr. Lyon, by then director of the Arctic Submarine Laboratory in San Diego; Richard J. Boyle, his principal assistant; and several MK-48 torpedo program personnel on board to assist us in accomplishing the rigorous series of tests planned.

The seas became steadily rougher and the weather more unpleasant as we continued to race north at deep depth. We continually thanked our lucky stars that we could remain well below the surface indefinitely if need be. An unplanned medical evacuation of Ron Burdge in St. John's, Newfoundland, gave us a taste of just how rocky conditions could get on or near the sea surface in northern latitudes during the winter. On first coming to periscope depth off Cape Farewell, Greenland, to communicate with the Canadian navy in St. John's, we were astonished to find ourselves wallowing around in trough-to-wave differences in excess of fifty feet. Wave heights approached twenty feet as we surfaced, dashed through the very narrow entrance to St. John's Harbour, and then came back out.

Reaching Davis Strait, we confronted an iceberg-studded, largely first-year sea-ice–covered MIZ. In spite of the loss of time and a key man, the various submarine and MK-48 torpedo tests were so well organized and refined en route that we managed to complete all successfully during the first two weeks of February. The operation culminated on 11 February when *Queenfish* completed the first surfacing by a single-screw submarine through a thin-ice-covered polynya near latitude 63° N, longitude 60°-30′ W. A large polar bear was spotted creeping up on us as we began a stationary dive to return beneath the ice and head for home. This short but intense operational excursion under sea ice confirmed to our satisfaction that the superb under-ice piloting and navigation capabilities of the *Sturgeon*-class submarine would enable it to operate safely within sea-ice–covered regions year-round.

It was during the preparations for the Davis Strait Marginal Sea Ice operation that I was to acquire the dubious nickname "Arctic Fox." In early January, *Queenfish*'s weapons officer, Lieutenant "Buzz" Galbraith, and I flew to St. John's, traveling via taxi through a heavy snowstorm to the naval air station at Argentia. A U.S. Navy "Birdseye" P-3-A antisubmarine warfare patrol aircraft was scheduled to take us over the exact route we planned to follow toward a suitable test area well within the Davis Strait MIZ.

The quite lengthy flight was a sobering one as Buzz and I sat on ledges behind and outboard of the pilot and copilot. We were dressed in full Arctic gear, including special long underwear that was not only heavy but also itchy; boots; huge gloves; polar trousers; and hooded parkas. Both of us looked as if we belonged behind dogsleds. No seat belts were available, much less required, at our perches, for as our pilot noted, "If this baby were to crash, you would not last more than two minutes in the water anyway." We flew north at altitudes within one hundred feet of the ice pack. The unusually close-hand view of the extent and severity of the ice cover throughout the flight, and particularly the great number of huge icebergs, gave us plenty to think about.

We finally landed on what seemed sheer ice at the Danish base at Thule in northwestern Greenland during the late afternoon. After clearing security we were escorted to lodgings for the night that looked like old-time iceboxes turned inside out. The rooms were clean and the beds comfortable, but the air was extremely dry. The degree of heat within was comparable to an Eskimo igloo full of people—in other words, hot. We later visited a quite exotic base exchange that sold everything from chewing tobacco to narwhal tusks and innumerable items of considerable interest and curiosity made by the local Thule Inuit or Polar Eskimos, who lived to the north of the base.

A former U.S. Air Force Officers Club served as the station restaurant, and although our fellow diners appeared perfectly normal, the dinner menu of seal, whale, guillemot, and eels was anything but. Curiosity led me to try a small plate of marinated seal as an appetizer. I immediately regretted it, as its smell and slimy consistency caused me to gag repeatedly. The experience left a vivid memory, as did my dinner of roasted dark guillemot flesh, convincing anyone wanting to return in a future life as an Inuit to reconsider. Fortunately, copious amounts of inexpensive wine and liquor were available to wash down the unsavory contents.

I arose early the next morning. Against all warnings about the dangers of encountering rabid Arctic foxes or a stray polar bear, I commenced to walk toward a nearby chapel to attend Catholic Mass several hundred yards away. No more than fifty yards from the chapel entrance I spotted a small, humped white shape moving rapidly toward me. It was, to my horror, an Arctic fox, hell-bent on attacking. There ensued a frantic battery of jumps, kicks, yells, and arm wavings as I tried to keep from being bitten. One well-placed kick among innumerable near-miss bites persuaded the fox to break off and run away. I stumbled toward the chapel where Mass was just beginning and gave fervent thanks for my escape. Seven people had been bitten by rabid foxes during the past several months at Thule, and the prescribed treatment was notoriously lengthy and unpleasant.

We took off from Thule later that day. Retracing our route and making further observations of the sea ice below, we safely returned to Argentia sometime after midnight. The entire Bird's-Eye flight was well worth the time and risk, considering what we had learned about the ice-littered sea surface along the prospective route and area under which we would be operating, but the experience of landing in a howling blizzard on full instruments that evening made us really appreciate the relatively safe operations life of a submariner.

On our return to *Queenfish*, I made the great mistake of sharing my exciting Arctic fox episode with my fellow officers. Our communications officer, Owen Brown, arranged a special wardroom Valentine's Day dinner during the transit home from the Davis Strait. The colorful and festive event included the posting of special Valentine's Day greetings for each of us on the wardroom bulkheads. My own special greeting happened to be a large photo of a well-endowed *Playboy* bunny with a personally inscribed message saying, "Happy Valentine's Day, Fred!" followed by "Try these on for size, you old Arctic Fox you!"

Queenfish's remaining months in the Atlantic were spent readying the boat for deployment on a cold war mission prior to our joining the Pacific Fleet. Having achieved every certification possible, we loaded for ninety days and, with a full complement of war shots, such as MK-16 steam and MK-37 acoustic torpedoes, departed in the late spring for our new homeport of Pearl Harbor. The long transit via Guantanamo Bay, Cuba, the Panama Canal, and the Pacific Northwest for advanced acoustic trials and weapons testing gave us further opportunities to train, test, and shake down our boat and crew for whatever might lie ahead following our arrival in Pearl Harbor.

We arrived at the submarine base at Pearl during the late spring of 1967, knowing that our boat and crew were fully ready for immediate deployment to the western Pacific or whatever cold war mission might be assigned us. The entire voyage from Atlantic to Pacific under Jack Richard's command, in my opinion, set the basic tone for, and firmly established, the high standards of professionalism and excellence that remained with *Queenfish* for the rest of her operational life.

6
Prospective Commanding Officer
Training for Submarine Command

Orders detaching me from *Queenfish* came in late August 1967. I was only the second nuclear submariner to be released by Admiral Rickover to attend the U.S. Naval War College in Newport, Rhode Island. Although it was not a prerequisite for taking command of a submarine, the Command and Staff course stood to broaden my knowledge of naval operations and history and help me appreciate more fully the requisite duties of the staff officers who would be involved in planning and scheduling the operations for whatever submarine I might one day command.

At the U.S. Naval War College I had the rare opportunity to meet and work with colleagues and more senior officers from other communities within the U.S. Navy and with those from the U.S. Army, Air Force, Marine Corps, and Coast Guard. The frosting on the cake, though, was obtaining a master's degree in international affairs from George Washington University, which had a branch at the Naval War College. My proposed joint thesis was the importance to our national security of the seasonal marginal ice zones that border polar ice packs worldwide during the winter months.[1]

Dr. Lyon, Dick Boyle, and I had remained in close contact during the months following the Davis Strait operation. When they heard about my thesis research, they expressed considerable interest and flew to Newport from California to discuss it with me in the early fall of 1967. During the course of several meetings, they offered many valuable ideas and insights as well as important references on the subject. As we examined where marginal sea-ice zones could be expected to occur during the winter months worldwide, they brought to my attention for the first time the need to explore the vast Siberian continental shelf.

In the decade that followed *Nautilus's* pioneering transpolar voyage in 1958, I learned that essentially no efforts had been made to penetrate, much less survey, the remote expanses of the Siberian continental shelf seas and the Kara Sea or the myriad passages through the Canadian Arctic islands. But this was about to change. Lyon was playing an increasingly key role in the establishment of U.S. Navy priorities for exploring the still largely uncharted Arctic Ocean and its contiguous seas. Approaching the top of his list for both scientific and strategic reasons by the time I entered the Naval War College was the accomplishment of an oceanographic and hydrographic survey of the three, virtually unknown, Siberian shelf seas: the Laptev, East Siberian, and Chukchi.

Needless to say, my interest was piqued, if not set on fire, and I dedicated myself to the goal of becoming the submarine captain who would actually accomplish this goal one day.

On graduation in June 1968 I received orders to remain an additional year at the Naval War College as an instructor in the war gaming department. Though I was disappointed at first, the assignment turned out to be a blessing in disguise, for I had use of the college's world-class library to research all that was known about the Siberian shelf at the time. Over the months I gained a much better insight into what would be required to accomplish such a challenging and hazardous project successfully.

Discussions and correspondence with Dr. Lyon and Dick Boyle in late 1968 and early 1969 concerning their efforts to gain support within the navy for such a survey by one of the new *Sturgeon*-class Arctic submarines indicated that approval by the CNO for such a mission as early as the summer of 1970 was a real possibility. Up to this point I had been a minor participant in these endeavors. I now realized that if I wanted to take part, I would have to do everything possible to be sure that my submarine command following the completion of my tour at the war college would be a fully operational *Sturgeon*-class nuclear attack boat ready in all respects to undertake the mission. For this to occur, however, I would have to be not only selected for the rank of full commander but also placed in the forefront of the prospective commanding officers in the submarine force considered sufficiently experienced and best qualified to lead such an expedition.

My first priority was to get myself ordered back to sea for three months during the summer of 1968 so I could hone all my submarine skills. Thanks to a former submariner, Captain Gene Henry at the war college, I was assigned to the new nuclear attack submarine USS *Greenling (SSN-614),* commanded by Guy Shaffer, to take part in a forthcoming four-month cold war mission. Among other things, I requalified for and stood command watches, rotating with the commanding officer and the executive officer, Don Shelton, on a four-hours-on, eight-hours-off basis during a special operation for which *Greenling* and her superb crew were awarded the Navy Unit Commendation.

On my return from sea in mid-October of 1968, I learned that I had been selected for full commander. Remaining at the U.S. Naval War College as a staff member while awaiting orders, I began working hard to assist a director of war gaming, Captain Coleman Smith, in upgrading the capabilities of the war gaming department. My main effort was directed to helping the department begin working with Submarine Development Group Two, New London, in incorporating its more realistic sonar detection and counterdetection ranges, warship exchange ratios (number of warships/submarines destroyed by the attacking sub or ship before it, too, is destroyed), and weapons systems effectiveness results into all war college, fleet, and CNO war games involving submarines. By the early 1970s, in fact, all war games involving submarines were proving their value in the development and revision of the U.S. Navy's strategic and tactical plans for future contingencies. During this time, too, I won a War College scholarship to Brown University to pursue a doctorate in Chinese government and politics.

These professional efforts and a dash of luck eventually culminated in an unexpected and very brief telephone call from Admiral Rickover late one Friday afternoon in April of 1969. He informed me that I would receive dispatch orders to report several weeks later to his headquarters in the Naval Reactors section of the U.S. Navy Bureau of Ships in the old Main Navy Building in Washington, D.C. My assignment: prospective commanding officer of USS *Queenfish*.

I could not have been more delighted. My opportunity had come, and it was now time to drop everything I was doing and prepare for submarine command. The really hard work was about to begin.

Starting in the late 1950s, Admiral Rickover and his staff had developed a three-and-one-half-month course of rigorous study designed to prepare each PCO for the myriad responsibilities and challenges of commanding a nuclear-powered submarine or ship. Successful completion of the course required complete mastery of every detail of all components: mechanical, fluid and electrical systems, radiological safety and controls, water chemistry, and operation of the engineering plant of the vessel the PCO was slated to command.

The overall objective, of course, was to be sure that each PCO gained in-depth knowledge and understanding of the engineering plant of his particular submarine (or ship) so that he would be highly unlikely to be confounded by any threats to her safe operation, in particular her nuclear propulsion plant. If any PCO were found to be seriously deficient in any aspect during the course, he would be immediately reassigned outside the submarine force. A serious illness or family problem could also spell the end of one's aspirations for nuclear submarine command. At the time I arrived at Naval Reactors, attrition was rumored to be running at one out of every four PCOs.

I began the course in late April of 1969 with an old friend from Pearl Harbor days, Bob Montross. We were soon joined by another good friend from submarine school and from Nuclear Power School, Tom Hopper. The three of us occupied a little room that had seen better days in the Main Navy Building on Constitution Avenue in Washington. I will never forget the worn linoleum floors throughout Rickover's portion of the building and the many strange "coffin-shaped patches" used to repair them. I was quite superstitious about inadvertently stepping on any of them, certain that it would bring instant bad luck!

In the core course we were required to memorize every detail of the Bettis training manuals and blueprints that covered the components and systems of the Westinghouse S-5-W nuclear propulsion plant, which would power the submarines we were to command. The knowledge we were expected to gain in each area, whether it be fluid or electrical systems or radiological control and water chemistry, was assessed at key points by written or oral examination or both. A less-than-near-perfect grade on any portion of the basically self-study course was not an option for one hoping to continue on the path to nuclear submarine command.

We were expected to be in our assigned study rooms from eight o'clock in the morning to six o'clock in the evening during the week and from eight o'clock in the morning to two o'clock in the afternoon on Saturdays. Most of us were at our desks well before six o'clock in the morning, studying late into the evening each day. For lunch we resorted to homemade brown-bags; for dinner we grabbed whatever fast food might be available nearby when we returned to our lodgings. I put a definite dent into the Alexandria, Virginia, chicken population, eating "Chicken Delight" for seventeen straight days. The overall schedule left no time for family, which had in most cases been left behind at our previous duty station to patiently await our return.

We were instructed to wear "tasteful" but conservative civilian clothes—coat and tie at all times—and given to understand that bowties or any sign of personal unkemptness could result in the Naval Reactors' equivalent of being struck by lightning when one least expected it. Another serious pitfall was talking even briefly with any one of the numerous attractive secretaries and active-duty Waves who seemed to proliferate around the Naval Reactors offices. If one were so unwise as to address her in a friendly fashion, she would probably be the first to report you. The first such offense was cause for an unpleasant session with our "guidance counselor" for the course at the time, Commander Bill Cowhill. The result of a second offense could only be imagined.

Every Thursday each of us was tasked with being the "inside man" to escort nuclear program candidates to and from Admiral Rickover's office and to remain during the interview to record the admiral's questions, the candidate's responses, and anything else of significance that occurred during the interview. All handwritten rough notes, including the pen or pencil impressions left on underlying pieces of paper, had then to be turned over to the admiral's senior staff assistant as soon as the admiral had finished with his interview.

A candidate might be subjected to as many as three or four interviews during the course of a day to test his mental agility and behavior under pressure. If an inside man was lucky, there would be only one interview. More often than not, any one of us might have to monitor as many as three or four candidates, losing most of our study time for that day.

I sat in on a total of fifteen interviews conducted by Admiral Rickover, and it soon became apparent that he was neither cruel nor capricious to any excessive degree. He seemed always to look for the composure that would be expected of a nuclear submarine officer and captain under both mundane and extremely trying situations. His questions probed deeply into the candidate's motivation for serving in nuclear submarines or ships and into his basic honesty, integrity, and ability to think and problem-solve when the stakes were high. Each interview was unique and seemed to draw on what the admiral had already learned about the candidate from his own inquiries and from the research of his staff. It was critically important that the candidate not be found to have reached any sort of personal growth plateau or, worse, already peaked in his academic or professional performance. Such a discovery could kill one's chances for the nuclear program.

Certainly one of the shortest interviews on record had to be the day I escorted a confident young Naval Academy graduating midshipman of excellent bearing into the admiral's office. Without a greeting or even a preliminary question, Admiral Rickover asked the midshipman, "Do you think you can make me angry?" The young man blinked, thought for just a second or two, and replied, "Yes, sir!" The admiral then said, "Go ahead!" The midshipman immediately approached the admiral's desk chaotically loaded with books, stacks of articles and papers, pencils, pens, and several partially filled cups of coffee of unknown age and, with his right hand and arm, swept everything off to hit the floor with great thuds and crashes.

Admiral Rickover made no attempt to stop him, but his face grew beet red, and he jumped up and down shouting. Now, I cannot say whether he was really angry, but I quickly grabbed the young man and pulled him as far away from the desk as possible. Rickover's senior secretary or executive assistant and two, possibly three, other female staff members rushed in and had their hands full trying to calm the admiral down. The most senior of the group shoved us out of the office and told us to stay out of sight. The midshipman was hurried to a vacant office or "holding" room, where I checked on him from time to time to see how he was doing as we awaited developments. We both learned late that afternoon, certainly to the candidate's complete astonishment, that the young midshipman had been accepted for Nuclear Power School.

I was paired a week later with a seemingly bright young man who struck me as being a mite too relaxed and at ease—what might be called "an attitude" these days. His first interview with Rickover was quite early in the morning, and it was brutally short. After the candidate sat down, unbuttoned his coat, and casually reclined in his chair, he and I were both immediately ordered out of the admiral's office. I was told to "shape him up" and "instruct him on how to answer questions!" So I took the young man aside and patiently explained that he should maintain a respectful and attentive posture in the presence of the admiral and be as brief as possible when asked a question. If the question required only a "yes" or "no," then it should be answered just that way.

We returned to the admiral's office two more times that day, each time getting thrown out for various reasons relating to a combination of the same candidate's relaxed demeanor and the seemingly provocative way in which he responded to the admiral's questions. For example, when asked what he had last read, the candidate responded, "*Catch-22*, sir." The admiral then asked, "How long did it take you to read it?" The candidate responded, "A month." "Oh!" Admiral Rickover said, with a perfectly straight face, "You are a fast reader!" The candidate responded with a self-satisfied nod of agreement.

It was a long and totally lost day for me, and I frankly could not understand why the process was being dragged out for so long. The candidate had acquitted himself thus far in an undistinguished manner at best, so it was hard to imagine what the admiral might have seen in him. We returned to the admiral's office at seven o'clock in the evening for a record fourth interview. The young man relaxed in his chair and once more unbuttoned his coat as he had done during each of the three previous interviews. The admiral looked at him in a deceptively friendly fashion and finally asked him why he wanted to join the nuclear power program. The candidate crisply responded, "Because I have always wanted to make a career of the navy!" "How long have you wanted to do that?" asked Admiral Rickover. "Since this morning!" responded the candidate. With that the admiral leaped to his feet and said, "Out! Out! Get that dumb SOB out of here!"

I rushed the young man out of the office and turned him over to one of the admiral's support staff. As I walked backed to my desk, I shook my head, not having the slightest inkling why the admiral had spent so much time with this particular candidate.

A third interview in which I unexpectedly found myself intimately involved occurred several weeks before my graduation from the PCO course. Admiral Rickover had been interviewing a raft of candidates with advanced degrees during late July 1969 for possible assignment to his staff or to one of the Naval Reactor's shipyard field offices. With a massive buildup of U.S. armed forces in Vietnam in progress, he did not lack for candidates who would do anything to avoid being drafted.

On this particular morning the admiral was interviewing a candidate who held a doctorate from a major university and whose purported area of expertise and occupation had much to do with the motivation of personnel. The interview proceeded in an almost ho-hum manner, and I was having no difficulty keeping up with my note taking when suddenly I heard the admiral say to the candidate, "I am having a great deal of trouble motivating this PCO!" I looked up, puzzled, and discovered that Admiral Rickover was pointing at me. My heart jumped. "What is going on?" I asked myself. To my knowledge no PCO had ever been directly involved in an interview. The candidate turned in his seat, looked at me arrogantly, and in a very condescending manner asked me, "What is your problem?"

Knowing that my prospective command, if not my entire submarine career, was suddenly on the line, I instinctively responded with "Low pay!" "Long working hours!" "Lack of recognition!" "Slow promotion!" "Family separation!" "Too much time at sea!"

The admiral waited for the candidate to respond, but he visibly paled. He opened his mouth and shut it several times without offering a single word. Growing impatient, Admiral Rickover yelled at the candidate, "Say something! Motivate him, motivate him!" I waited like a cornered animal for what might come next, but the candidate remained as mute as if he had been struck by a two-by-four. Exasperated, the admiral abruptly stood up and, with a colorful insult pertaining to the candidate's "credentials," ordered us out of his office. I later passed the admiral in the hall, and although we did not speak, his eyes seemed to twinkle, and he came as close to a grin as I had ever seen him.

Besides the interviews and an occasional encounter with him in the hall, the PCOs (several different groups of two or three) had to meet with the admiral as a group for about an hour or so every Saturday morning. These supposed "group sessions" could be grueling in their own way, especially if he did not care for the answer to a question he posed. "Why aren't more of the nuclear-trained engineering personnel taking the new bonus offered and reenlisting in the navy?" he asked (a question that no PCO knew how to answer and hence could only guess at). I quickly learned that it paid to position oneself to the admiral's right so as to be the first to be called on. The last PCO called on generally caught the most abuse for "not being able to think for himself" or worse.

Our final examination came in late July of 1969, consisting of a seven-and-one-half-hour written test; several lengthy "spot check" oral exams by experts in radiological control and water chemistry, such as Murray Miles, a key member of Admiral Rickover's staff; and a final session with the admiral in which it was wise to keep very calm and cool. Each of us then received an oak "wedge" (a small wedge-shaped piece of polished oak) with a bronze plaque inscribed with the Breton seaman's prayer, "Oh God, thy sea is so great and my boat is so small."

7
Taking Command of *Queenfish*

I reported aboard *Queenfish* in Pearl Harbor in mid-August of 1969. After a thorough turnover and inspection both in port and underway, I relieved Captain Jack Richard as commanding officer on 12 September. Although Jack seemed happy to have me succeed him, he jokingly remarked that there was nothing worse than having his former executive officer conduct an administration inspection of his former submarine and commanding officer.

Words could not describe my joy on finally returning to, and taking command of, what I had always felt was truly "my boat." I knew *Queenfish* to be superbly constructed, having seen Newport News build her almost from the keel up. But I also had gained a close, hands-on familiarity with her hull, her major components and equipment, and all her key systems—nuclear, mechanical, electrical, and hydraulic—during their testing and operation both in port and at sea. I believed I knew the boat like the back of my hand. Such intimate knowledge of her "bones and guts" and of her maneuvering, handling, and depth-keeping characteristics, gained during my previous time aboard her at sea, were soon to prove vital in pushing the submarine to the limits of her capabilities and in dealing with occasional engineering problems and casualties.

Behind me were more than twelve years of sea experience encompassing eleven special operations, two Arctic operations, and many lengthy deployments in the Pacific, Atlantic, and Mediterranean gained on board *Greenfish, Seadragon, Skipjack, Greenling,* and, as her precommissioning executive officer, *Queenfish.* My personal philosophy of command had evolved and been shaped by the superb personal examples, training, and mentoring of the best of the attack submarine captains with whom I served: Jack Knudsen and "Tiger Al" Davis; George Steele; Les Kelly, Shep Jenks, and Paul Tomb; Jack Richard; and Guy Schaffer.[1] Each helped me to develop and mature as a submarine officer and potential commanding officer. Through them I came to understand and appreciate in depth that a frontline attack submarine will never be ready in all respects to accomplish an assigned mission unless boat, crew, and captain have been finely honed at sea and molded into an aggressive team with high morale and near-perfect communication.

I certainly found this to hold true whether the mission be cold war reconnaissance and intelligence gathering, a scientific and exploration operation, or readiness for an actual war patrol. The commanding officer's responsibility was a neverending one. It required his constant day-to-day attention to the details and effects of repairs and modifications on the capabilities and performance of his submarine and continuing close contact with both crew and boat. This was particularly true when experienced crew members left, new ones joined, and the resultant subtle changes in crew personality and overall boat capabilities began to be felt.

The entire submarine, with all her components, systems, and equipments, had to be brought to, and maintained at, a level of material, operating, and sound-quieting condition such that her myriad intelligence and scientific data collection and war-fighting capabilities could be fully realized and steadfastly relied on. Her radiated noise—broadband, narrow, and transient frequencies—always had to be significantly less than that of the surrounding sea state or of any potential adversaries. A submarine must at all times remain undetectable and undetected no matter what the mission. This point cannot be overemphasized.

In addition, every officer and enlisted crew member had to be prepared, trained, and formally qualified for optimum and safe execution of all duties and responsibilities assigned, both specified and implied, at sea and in port. All hands, moreover, had to be mentally and physically fit to withstand any and all operational and emotional demands and stresses made on them at sea. Ideally, each crew member should undergo medical and dental checks prior to any deployment or lengthy period at sea. The executive officer, chief of the boat, and senior hospital corpsman should also be tasked with ensuring, to the maximum extent possible, that no one departed with any personal or family problems or emotional and psychiatric disorders that might prevent him from performing his duties in a safe and responsible manner.

The premission preparation criteria briefly outlined above more than applied to the commanding officer, who was responsible for the safety and best possible performance of both submarine and crew. I knew from personal experience and from my father (former naval aviator; commander of two destroyers, a fleet oiler, a mine-sweeper squadron, and the Naval Ammunition Depot, Bangor; and veteran of both World War II and the Korean War) that it was imperative to be fully prepared in all respects for pursuing a mission aggressively and well.

I will never forget getting "my boat" underway for the first time as her commanding officer. On 13 September 1969, as we proceeded across Pearl Harbor Channel to load torpedoes from a weapons storage facility called West Loch, the quite sober realization hit me of what I had taken on. No longer could I escape my duty for even a few hours by going home at the end of the day or the weekend while we were in port or by permitting myself a deep or long sleep while we were at sea. The operation and safety of *Queenfish* and all that comprised her, including crew, twenty-four hours a day, seven days a week, came before anything else and fell on my shoulders alone.

As it happened, the trip across the channel and then getting under way in windy conditions to return to our assigned berth proved uneventful, and the confidence I had gained as her executive officer in my ability to handle *Queenfish* under all conditions quickly returned. But, lest I sound overconfident, halfway through a celebratory cocktail party, a call came to me from two persons who, without identifying themselves, reported that "you just had a fire on your boat, skipper, but don't worry, everything is ok, the flooding put it out." I confess I bit, and my heart was in my mouth. The anonymous callers turned out to be two old friends, Doug and Peggy Stahl. Some joke! I know of at least one new captain whose crew, just hours after he had assumed command in Pearl Harbor, did in fact inadvertently flood his new submarine's forward torpedo room, including six torpedoes, to a level of well over four feet.

Queenfish was soon to have her work cut out for her, for just a week or so preceding my assumption of command, the CNO came through with his approval of the first survey of the vast and uncharted waters of the Siberian continental shelf. This survey was to be conducted by *Queenfish* on a high-priority basis, beginning July 1970. I now had about ten months to ready both submarine and crew for deployment to the Arctic Ocean.

Intense and demanding workup operations during the late fall of 1969, followed by almost two months on a cold war mission in the icy waters of the northern Pacific beginning in late January of 1970, provided ideal opportunities for coalescing both officers and men of an already first-class team into one that would be more than equal to the mission that lay ahead. We had trained hard since I took command, and we were ready.

8

Mission Underway

En Route to the Arctic at Last

All of us on board *Queenfish* had fully appreciated our extraordinary good fortune in having been chosen to conduct the first hydrographic survey—acoustically tracing and recording a particular water-depth contour of high navigational interest—across the entire pack-ice–covered Siberian continental shelf. We all knew that an incursion into these vast, extremely mysterious, and totally uncharted waters was the opportunity of a lifetime—one that would test our collective capabilities and experience to the fullest. We were aware, as well, that *Queenfish* stood to bring back new knowledge that would be of enduring interest and value to mankind. The scientific and geological data collected would be unprecedented. The possibility even existed that we might discover new islands or a new landmass.

Initially we planned to collect ice-thickness data along the same route followed by *Nautilus* twelve years earlier, the result of a proposal submitted to the Arctic Submarine Laboratory and the Office of Naval Research as an add-on to our main mission. The idea was to analyze and compare both data sets to determine any changes that might have occurred in the vast Arctic Ocean sea ice during the interval between the two voyages.[1]

The expedition would require us to remain submerged the entire length of the survey. This was necessary not only to prevent detection by unwelcome or unfriendly eyes but also, and more importantly, to navigate safely through an extremely hazardous, ice-covered shallow-water environment. We would be generating our own oxygen while continuously removing carbon dioxide, carbon monoxide, hydrogen, and hydrocarbons in order to remain completely divorced in all respects from the outside atmosphere.

USS *Queenfish* backed clear of her berth at the submarine base, Pearl Harbor, shortly before noon on 6 July 1970 for the long transit to Seattle. From there we planned to head up to British Columbia, through the Gulf of Alaska, the Aleutians, the Bering Sea, and the Bering Strait en route to the Arctic Ocean and the North Pole. We departed to the spirited accompaniment of a U.S. Navy band and the vigorous waves and loud cheers of families and loved ones. We were off at long last.

The relatively short 2,420-nautical-mile transit to Seattle and the Pacific Northwest was spent exercising the crew in a rigorous series of drills to further sharpen our ability to handle the myriad emergency situations that could arise at any time while at sea. These situations included fire, flooding, loss of depth and steering control, loss of propulsion, power plant and radiological casualties, emergency surfacings, man-overboard drills, and unplanned excursions beyond test depth. We would in addition refine our plans for the more advanced under-ice operations training that would be conducted from Seattle en route to the Bering Strait.

During *Queenfish*'s stop in Dabob Bay and Nanaimo, British Columbia, from 13 through 17 July, a number of special cold regions–related acoustic and weapons tests were carried out, followed by a final load-out of stores and supplies at the Naval Weapons Station, Bangor. The crew was pleased to learn that provision had been made for liberty in Seattle and Victoria, British Columbia, prior to leaving for the Arctic on 21 July.

During the transit to Seattle, we also used the time to verify the existence on board of all supplies and lubricants that would be necessary for the operation of the boat in low-temperature conditions. This was particularly true for *Queenfish*'s periscopes, masts and antennas, diving planes and rudder, and rotating components of all under-ice sonar equipments. We had to make doubly sure that adequate spare parts were on board, properly stowed, and logged for ready access to support all of *Queenfish*'s equipments, systems, and components in the event that we would be at sea longer than planned. These time-consuming but vital final predeployment checks served to identify and requisition, by urgent message, a number of critical parts and spares discovered to be either missing or considered prudent to overstock.

Finally, a number of important initiatives were taken to enhance the crew's already high morale during the months to come. All on board who desired it would receive advance pay in Bangor, before reaching Seattle, so that it could be sent

Figure 8.1 USS *Queenfish* alongside pier at U.S. Naval Ammunition Depot, Dabob Bay, Washington. (Courtesy of the U.S. Navy)

home and used to pay bills. Standing very high on the list of desirables was, without a doubt, a very careful review by the supply and commissary officer (Lieutenant Junior Grade Grant Youngman), the chief of the boat (Senior Chief Torpedoman Kenneth Ickes), and I of the food stores and freeze-box load for the Arctic voyage.

It is a truism that the level of crew morale and performance during any lengthy submarine deployment is in direct proportion to the quality and availability at all times of the food served. It was unbelievable how irritated and upset crew members could become should any essential item like salt, sugar, or coffee run short. Variety, quality, and quantity were key, but submarine cooks also had to prepare meals every day that were the equal of those of the best restaurant chefs. The men on *Queenfish* could easily consume more than four thousand pounds of steak alone in just two months.

While making maximum effort to obtain the best steaks and ground beef available in the Pacific Northwest, the cooks off-loaded all the low-grade Swiss and Salisbury steak that we had not managed to get rid of in Pearl Harbor, plus several hundred pounds of rabbit meat that had recently been foisted off on Grant Youngman and our leading cook, Michael Knaub, as "being back on the menu by popular demand!" Spurred by the many complaints and sarcastic comments of our chief petty officers en route to Seattle, I had threatened Youngman several times that if he did

Figure 8.2 Crew loading stores on board USS *Queenfish* at Dabob Bay, Washington. Sonar Technician Second Class Paul Speaker in foreground. (Courtesy of the U.S. Navy)

not find a way to replace the rabbit meat with something more palatable, the crew would make him eat all of it himself. Even lamb could suddenly be shunned by some submarine crews if a jokester decided to call it "goat," in which case it would stay in the freeze box for the rest of the voyage.

Next in food priority was ensuring we had all the ingredients on board for making superb bread and pastries; all the potatoes, rice, spaghetti, fruits, and vegetables necessary for a well-balanced diet; and all the coffee, sugar, and salt that a hungry crew could possibly consume during a lengthy voyage. Finally, because we would be in the Pacific Northwest for a week or so, I tasked Youngman and Knaub with obtaining several hundred pounds of fresh salmon, clams, and oysters just prior to departure and, oh, not to forget the capers, lemon, and hot sauces!

The crew's library was replenished with good books and games sufficient to amuse all on board for any length of time. Last but not least, and of keen interest to all, was our "movie load." We had two fully operational projectors on board, with all the spare parts to keep them running in both the crew's mess and the officers' wardroom every night of the expedition. The choice of which sixty movies to load was never left to chance. I had seen a lot of bad movies during my career in submarines, with the worst being Marge and Gower Champion in *Give a Girl a Chance*. So even though *Queenfish*'s movie petty officer was nominally in charge of the selection, the damage control assistant and auxiliary division officer, Tom Hoepfner, was instructed to accompany him to make absolutely sure that all movies obtained from the movie exchange ashore were first-run and up to crew standard. On the quiet, Tom was authorized to use a case or two of steak and some cans of coffee beans as necessary.

Queenfish's crew particularly liked good westerns, with *Shane* heading the list. The inadvertently funniest Western I ever saw was on board *Greenfish* in 1958. It was a Japanese production titled *The Outlaw of Yokohama Gulch.* The spectacle of short, bowlegged Japanese cowboys speaking with heavily accented, dubbed English kept the crew rolling in the aisles. Alas, that movie could no longer be found. Tom did a good job. Both Western and "leg and breast" fans were amply provided for, although there were many loud complaints later about J. Arthur Rank's production of *Hamlet,* which everyone found absolutely unintelligible.

We were fortunate in having Dick Boyle join us prior to departure from Pearl Harbor. In addition to his work at the Arctic Submarine Laboratory, Dick was a highly experienced former nuclear submarine officer. He had served on USS *Skate* during her historic 1958 voyage to the Arctic Ocean and was later commanding officer of the U.S. Navy's experimental, hydrogen peroxide–fueled submarine *X-1.* On *Queenfish*'s 1967 Davis Strait operation, we had become good friends. He was of immeasurable assistance to us during those final preparations and training from Pearl Harbor to Seattle and the subsequent transit to the Bering Strait and Chukchi Sea.

Sadly for us, Dr. Lyon had to remain behind in order to fight for an adequate budget for planned Arctic operations. In his place he sent a first-rate oceanographer, Dr. M. Allan Beal, senior science advisor at the laboratory, to join Dick. This was to be Dr. Beal's first Arctic submarine voyage. He was soon to prove a crucial addition to the *Queenfish* team.

Queenfish got underway from the Seattle city pier late on 21 July and headed for the Arctic on a beautiful Pacific Northwest summer afternoon. The sea was calm, the sky was a cloudless blue, and the snow-covered volcanoes on the horizon were a magnificent backdrop as the boat set a westerly course for the Strait of Juan de Fuca and the Pacific Ocean. We submerged well to seaward of the entrance to the strait shortly after two o'clock in the morning on 22 July. It was on this nighttime approach to the mouth of the Strait of Juan de Fuca that *Queenfish* had her unforeseen confrontation with the rogue wave that could have lost both Bob Baumhardt and James Petersen and ended the expedition before it had barely gotten underway.

The first leg of our voyage, covering nearly 2,420 nautical miles from the Strait

Figure 8.3 View of USS *Queenfish* ship's control panel and diving station. (Courtesy of the U.S. Navy)

of Juan de Fuca to the Bering Strait via the Gulf of Alaska, seemed endless. As occurred in all deployments, the first hours passed at a snail's pace as each of us adjusted in his own way to the reality that *Queenfish* was to be at sea for many more
weeks. Hardest of all was the realization that we would be completely out of touch
with our loved ones and friends.

Once again we had to get used to close quarters and the proximity of our fellow shipmates twenty-four hours a day. A good sense of humor with an attendant
ability to laugh at oneself, plus the capability to retreat into one's head for privacy,
were essential attributes for anyone pursuing a life in submarines. We also had to
readjust to a chilly air-conditioned–controlled interior temperature of approximately 60° F throughout most of the boat. This was a problem for those of us who
were used to southern climes or summer in the Seattle area or, like myself, had
extra-sensitive sinuses. But the myriad electronic systems and components had to
be kept well cooled at all times.

Queenfish's crew quickly settled into a submerged transit routine and began
to focus on the final training for the arduous two months ahead. Most of us had
known for almost a year that we would be headed for the Arctic Ocean and the

Figure 8.4 Bird's-eye view of special Arctic operations electronics equipment in USS *Queenfish* crew's activity space. (Courtesy of the U.S. Navy)

North Pole during the summer of 1970, but nothing more than that. Only the executive officer, Lieutenant Commander Lincoln "Linc" Mueller, the navigator, Lieutenant Commander Toby Warson, the engineer officer, Lieutenant Commander Ralph Beedle, Bob Baumhardt, and I knew prior to departure the true mission and full extent of the voyage.

As it turned out, the final weekend in Seattle was infinitely busier than originally planned. Chief Yeoman Robert Diehl, Linc Mueller, and I, with the "impressed" service of Admiral Rickover's Bremerton Naval Shipyard representative, Vic Larson, used three flexiwriters and wardroom proofreading teams over a forty-hour period to accomplish the onerous task of preparing and proofing nearly one thousand letters to be mailed from the North Pole for Admiral Rickover. The sample letter and list of names and addresses had been handed to me by Vic Larson just two days before our departure. The least we could do in grateful appreciation was to invite him to remain on board and help us.

Letter recipients ranged from the president and vice president of the United States, the secretaries of state and of defense, and every U.S. representative and senator to Admiral of the Fleet, the Earl Mountbatten of Burma, and Queen Frederika of Greece. Each letter had to be editorially and cosmetically perfect and signed by me personally on Rickover's behalf. In view of the letters' political importance, nothing would save me from Rickover's wrath should even one of them be later found to have even the slightest error.[2] The letters were further enhanced in value through the fortuitous find of special Arctic submarine stamps issued almost a decade earlier honoring the North Pole voyages of *Nautilus* and *Skate*. We were also authorized by the U.S. Postal Service to design and cut a special rubber *Queenfish*-at-the-North-Pole cancellation stamp to be used on each envelope the day we reached the North Pole.[3]

In parallel with the foregoing efforts was the important task of completing a "flag bag" of all fifty U.S. state flags. These would be part of *Queenfish*'s own public affairs initiative of photographing each crew member standing on the sea-ice–covered North Pole with his state flag. To our dismay, the U.S. Postal Service delivered only thirty-one of the fifty ordered several months before departing Pearl Harbor. *Queenfish*'s junior officers, Lieutenants Lars Hanson, Steve Gray, and Frederick Moore, solved this problem in fine fashion by making a chance acquaintance, over beers at a local waterfront pub, with a senior person associated with the Seattle World's Fair Center. As luck would have it, the center's beautiful fountain was surrounded by fifty poles from which flew all U.S. state flags. As if by magic, we acquired our full complement of flags. Although I asked no questions as to the exact origin of the nineteen, a string of irate messages from the Seattle Naval District commander soon enlightened us as to their source.

Within a couple of hours *Queenfish* was in deep water. The chief of the boat, Kenneth Ickes, informed all hands at breakfast that as soon as the off-going watch had eaten and the crew's mess had been cleaned and secured for sea, the boat would be put through a series of vigorous high-speed maneuvers, affectionately dubbed "angles and dangles." Ickes and Mueller had already warned the crew repeatedly during our last days in port to stow securely all personal possessions and all equipment and supplies for which their division or watch was responsible.

About midmorning, "battle stations" throughout the boat were manned with *Queenfish*'s most experienced and capable men on watch. After carefully ascertaining by periscope, ECM, and sonar that there were no surface or submerged contacts in the area, we began to exercise *Queenfish's* maneuverability to the maximum. Beginning with a sustained 10° down-angle (or "bubble") at ten knots, the boat was then abruptly brought to a 10° up-angle, followed by a rapid series of ever-increasing speeds and up- and down-angles as our 292-foot-long boat (plus 3 inches), displacing some 4,640 tons, hurtled faster and faster throughout our safe-operating depth range.

On reaching a speed of twenty knots, *Queenfish's* rudder was ordered shifted rapidly from right to left full, working a "fish-tailing" maneuver into the entire evolution. A cacophony of crashes, bangs, clunks, thuds, and loud curses was heard as *Queenfish* proceeded to a 30° down-angle, only to be immediately followed by a 35° up-angle. By the time we leveled off and resumed our original transit course, depth, and speed an hour later, it was pretty certain that everything not properly stowed would have been discovered.

While holding on for dear life, those crew members not manning a watch station were kept busy catching and attempting to quickly secure the items shaken loose as we progressed through the maneuvers. More than twelve years in submarines had taught me, among many other things, that a vigorous sequence of "angles and dangles" shortly after departing port and submerging was an almost foolproof way to uncover any unauthorized caches of alcoholic beverage that might have been secreted away. Everything that turned up was considered an anonymous "gift" to the captain, even Mr. Boston's Sloe Gin, and kept under lock and key until the end of the voyage.

During our first full night at sea, I took time to brief the crew in detail about the very special and demanding mission we were assigned to conduct: a hydrographic survey of the uncharted portions of the western Chukchi, the Laptev, and the East Siberian seas and the specific task of locating and acoustically tracing a "depth curve" that would permit safe submarine navigation within the perennially ice-covered seas of the Siberian continental shelf.

I made it very clear to all that *Queenfish* would operate so as to remain undetected, that she would remain within international waters, and that she and her crew would not be unduly risked during the operation. I concluded the briefing by explaining the scientific and potential military importance of what we were about to do. The oceanographic information to be collected would be of vital interest to the United States in the event that our forces might one day have to pursue and eliminate an enemy's submarines or conduct ballistic missile deterrent patrols within the Arctic Basin. No doubt was left in anyone's mind of the need to pursue *Queenfish's* assignment as aggressively as possible.

The crew put forward excellent questions, as one might expect from more than

Figure 8.5 (*Left to right*) Navigator and Lieutenant Commander Toby G. Warson, Chief Quartermaster Jack B. Patterson, and Lieutenant (Junior Grade) Grant H. Youngman during briefing for crew. (Courtesy of the U.S. Navy)

one hundred well-educated and experienced young submariners, many of whom possessed a higher education degree. The briefing was the beginning of many lively discussions that were to take place throughout the boat for the duration of the trip. In addition to the dangers of icebergs and very thick ice in shallow water, concerns were expressed about the possibility of encountering Soviet submarines. "Possible, but not probable, considering the remoteness of the area," was all I could answer.

As we continued toward the northwest the following day, Dick Boyle and Allan Beal began the first of a very well-presented series of daily lectures for all hands on the history of Arctic exploration and submarine exploration of the Arctic, Arctic Ocean oceanography and undersea topography, and the characteristics of the perennial sea-ice cover that we would be operating beneath during the months to come. The topics, questions, and follow-on discussions generally kept those crew members not on watch thoroughly occupied and entertained.

The advanced operational training conducted en route to the Bering Strait was to prove more difficult than expected, particularly for the control-room and

Figure 8.6 Lieutenant Commander Toby G. Warson briefing wardroom officers on high-latitude navigation through Arctic Ocean. (*Left to right*) Warson; Commander Alfred S. McLaren; Lieutenant Robert J. Baumhardt; Lieutenant Stephen V. Gray; Lieutenant (Junior Grade) William G. Blenkle; and Lieutenant Commander Walter A. Pezet. (Courtesy of the U.S. Navy)

engineering-space watch standers. *Queenfish's* program included drilling several times a day in well-worked-out simulations of both normal and emergency operational situations that would, or might, occur in the Arctic Ocean. These exercises covered effective handling of flooding and fire while submerged under thick ice; searching for a surfaceable polynya or lead; conducting vertical ascents and descents into and from open water or thin ice; performing a vertical surfacing with the reactor shut down; making a vertical ascent through sea ice of varying thickness; using the SPM beneath and within a polynya or lead; and practicing the special engineering plant lineups required for operating in proximity to the sea bottom.

Each control-room watch section, in addition, practiced the slow-speed depth control and all-stop hovering techniques that would be required to operate *Queenfish* safely throughout the Arctic Ocean, especially within the very restricted operational envelopes that would be imposed by shallow water and thick ice over the Siberian continental shelf. All benefited from the close study and integration of procedures and engineering system configurations, or lineups, developed by *Sargo* during her 1960 winter Arctic operation and from *Queenfish*'s earlier 1967 Davis Strait operation.

At every opportunity the sonar team, under James Petersen, began the process of carefully calibrating and recalibrating the overhead-ice-thickness-measuring and ice-obstacle-detection features of our AN/BQS-8 under-ice sonar suite.

The performances of the officers and crew watch standers during these drills left much to be desired at first. Plenty of excitement and comic relief were provided when, in a number of simulated emergency situations, the boat took unexpected up- or down-angles due to the ill-considered actions of watch team members. Their expertise became increasingly evident with each passing day, however, as each watch section cohered as a team. We were confident that *Queenfish* and her crew would be more than ready to meet the challenges of sustained under-ice operations by the time we reached the Bering Strait.

As we entered the Gulf of Alaska, the "midnight requisition" of nineteen state flags from the Seattle World's Fair Center finally caught up with us. A strong message from the Seattle Naval District commander demanded the immediate return of the flags. At our next opportunity to communicate, I relayed this message to our boss, Commander Submarine Forces Pacific, with a copy to the naval district commander, requesting help in "replacing" the flags that had been "borrowed" to remedy an urgent "public affairs need." The district commander's staff members had been sufficiently exercised over our transgression that they even tracked down my father, who had retired in the Seattle area from command of the U.S. Naval Ammunition Depot, Bangor, eight years earlier, to ask for his help. The brouhaha was eventually resolved during the months to come. How it worked out I do not know, but I was certain that I had not heard the last of it from my father.

9
A Brief on the Arctic Ocean
and Siberian Continental Shelf

Any understanding of the challenges and hazards that *Queenfish* and her crew, and I as commanding officer, were soon to face must start with an appreciation of the vast extent, severe climate, and great shroud of mystery that characterizes the islands and seas of the still largely unexplored but vitally important Arctic Ocean.

The ice-covered Arctic Ocean is the smallest of the world's five oceans, encompassing a surface area of some 5,426 million square miles—still more than six and one-half times the size of the Mediterranean Sea.[1] It is ringed by a considerable landmass, the continents of Europe, Asia, and North America and the huge island of Greenland, and is further restricted in size by the Greenland and Norwegian seas.

The bottom topography of the central Arctic Ocean is extraordinarily rugged, marked by deep basins and submerged mountain ranges. The deep-water portion of the ocean is the Arctic Basin, which is divided by the transoceanic, submerged Lomonosov Ridge into two main subbasins: the Amerasia (containing several "hollows" including the Canada Basin) and the Eurasia. The deepest part of the Arctic Ocean is in the Eurasia Basin, which at its deepest level plunges to 18,133 feet.[2] Partly bisecting the Eurasia Basin is the submerged Gakkel Ridge, formerly called the Nansen Cordillera, which separates the Nansen and Amundsen basins and which *Queenfish* explored on this expedition for its possible tectonic or volcanic activity.

Approximately 50 percent of the Arctic Ocean's floor consists of continental

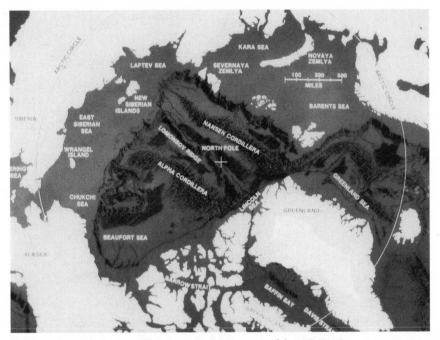

Figure 9.1 General bathymetry of the Arctic Basin. (Courtesy of the U.S. Navy)

shelf. By "continental shelf" is meant the relatively shallow undersea extension of the continental landmass whose width, from the coast to where the seabed begins to slope downward to the deep ocean, can vary enormously. The Arctic Ocean has the highest percentage of continental shelf of any ocean on the planet—stretching northward toward the pole from all three continents. The continental shelves surrounding the Arctic Ocean depths are covered by seven ice-mantled seas. From east to west they are the Chukchi Sea, the East Siberian Sea, the Laptev Sea, the Kara Sea, the Barents Sea, the Lincoln Sea, and the Beaufort Sea.[3]

The widest of all continental shelves in the world occurs off the coast of Siberia, averaging in breadth about 373 miles as it extends northward from the Asian continent, except around the Severnaya Zemlya Archipelago, where it narrows. Its northern boundary is the six-hundred-foot depth contour, beyond which is the Arctic Ocean. Its southern boundary is the Siberian coastline that extends thousands of miles eastward, from the northernmost point on the Asian continent, Cape Chelyuskin, due south of Bolshevik Island in the Severnaya Zemlya Archipelago to the Bering Strait.

Three shallow seas span the entire length of the Siberian continental shelf: the Chukchi, East Siberian, and Laptev. The most easterly, the Chukchi, encompasses

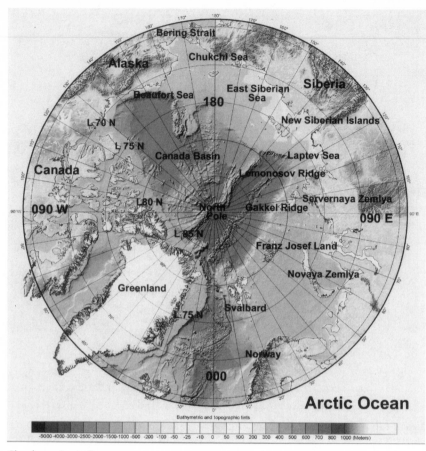

Chartlet 9.1 Arctic Ocean.

some 229,670 square miles with an average depth of 285 feet.[4] Its northern boundary extends from Mys, or Cape, Uering, on the east coast of Wrangel Island, longitude 177°-28' W, eastward along the Arctic Ocean edge of the Siberian continental shelf to the western edge of the Beaufort Sea at longitude 156° W. This longitude represents the eastern boundary of the Chukchi Sea and the dividing line between it and the Beaufort Sea to the east, which also happens to be the international date line that bisects the Bering Strait to the south. The Chukchi Sea is bound on the west by the Siberian coast and on the south by the Bering Strait. Overall, its central, northern, and northwestern regions were largely unexplored in 1970, although the seafloor of the eastern Chukchi was fairly well charted by that time.

As discussed in the following chapters, *Queenfish* entered the Arctic Basin via the eastern Chukchi Sea in order to intercept and begin retracing *Nautilus*'s 1958

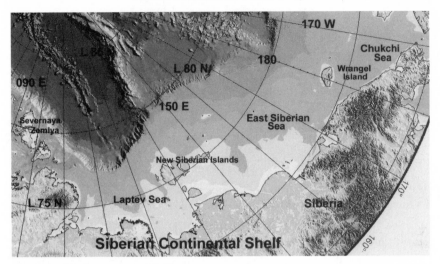

Chartlet 9.2 Siberian continental shelf.

track across the Arctic Ocean. She returned to the northwestern and western portions of the Chukchi Sea in order to complete her hydrographic survey of the Siberian continental shelf and finally exited the Arctic Basin via its most southerly reaches and the Bering Strait.

The largest and certainly the least known and most mysterious of the three seas is the East Siberian Sea, which extends northward from the Siberian coast along the eastern shores of the New Siberian Islands to the six-hundred-foot depth curve at the edge of the continental shelf. It then encompasses some 352,895 square miles of relatively shallow sea-ice–covered water eastward to Wrangel Island. It was not discovered until the seventeenth century and, with the exception of its most southerly regions, remained virtually unexplored as late as 1970 because of the closely compacted polar ice pack that covers it throughout the year. *Queenfish* found it to be the shallowest of the three seas, with an average depth of 190 feet.[5]

The most westerly of Siberia's shelf seas, and where *Queenfish* would actually begin her hydrographic survey, is the Laptev. Overall the best-charted of the three seas, it covers some 255,840 square miles of oceanic area from Cape Chelyuskin on the Siberian coast to the western shores of the New Siberian Islands. At the time of *Queenfish's* exploration and survey, very little was known about the physical oceanography and bottom topography of its central and northern waters, having been discovered only in the seventeenth century. It is, like all the shelf seas, relatively shallow, but its northern boundary extends into the deep basin of the Arctic Ocean, giving the Laptev an average depth of 1,896 feet. On the west its boundary is defined by the Severnaya Zemlya Archipelago, on the east by the East Siberian Islands, and on the south by the Siberian coast.[6]

As discussed in a forthcoming chapter, the Arctic Ocean has an important seasonal waterway that has played a prominent role in European exploration, trade, and politics—the Northern Sea Route (NSR). This waterway overlaps a significant portion of the famed Northeast Passage and traverses the southern portions of the three seas of interest to *Queenfish*.

A few words here about the climate in the polar regions. Almost the entire Arctic Ocean is above the Arctic Circle at latitude 66°-33′ N, plunging the region into near-total darkness for six months of the year and near-total daylight for the other six months. In winter, temperatures generally range from 28.4° F to –32.8° F, but they can be as low –63.4° F in the Laptev and East Siberian seas.[7] High winds and snowstorms largely determine the circulation and thickness of ice in the Arctic Ocean. But even during the harshest months, about 2–3 percent of the ocean is always open water in the form of lakelike polynyas and narrow openings called leads. These open-water areas are an important source of heat exchange between ocean and atmosphere, considered by most authorities today to represent the main process through which the world's oceans contribute to the balancing of the global energy cycle. They are certain to play an increasing role in Northern Hemisphere climate change as global warming progresses.

It is hard to believe, but the Arctic Ocean was largely unknown until well into the twentieth century. Postulations and speculations by various learned authorities and institutions, in view of what we now know, range from the bizarre to the ridiculous. In the late nineteenth century, there was the firmly held belief that the polar ocean was shallow, with a solid and immovable mantle of ice, the Paleocrystic Sea, which had covered the entire area since the beginning of time. Also current was the view that the pole was capped with a glacier-covered land called Crocker Land.[8] Others thought it a vast open sea encircled by heavy-ice pressure ridges wherein the North Pole was centered. It was thought, too, that the higher Arctic Ocean latitudes and North Pole might overlie a submerged continent.

In 1897 the great explorer Fridjof Nansen, in his voyage in the *Fram,* found that the Arctic Ocean was large and deep, and he confirmed the presence of a drift current carrying sea ice with it from north of the Bering Strait and Siberia across the Arctic Basin to between Spitsbergen and Greenland. His discovery had a great impact on scientific thought regarding the Arctic Basin.

Nonetheless, the state of knowledge about the physical oceanography of the Arctic Ocean remained so meager that, as recently as 1949, the American geographer K. O. Emery constructed a bathymetric chart of the Arctic Ocean from only

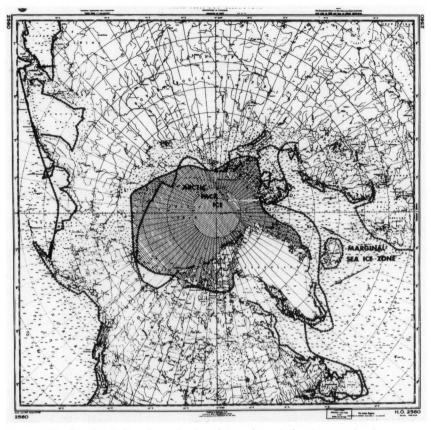

Figure 9.2 Graphic of typical maximum Arctic pack ice and marginal sea ice extent in winter. (Courtesy of the U.S. Navy)

152 depth soundings deeper than 3,280 feet—all that was available at the time. This chart showed only a single basin and was little different from Nansen's bathymetric chart compiled from his *Fram* expedition, published in 1904. At roughly the same time that Emery was writing, the Soviet High Latitude Aerial Expeditions made the significant discovery of a submerged mountain range extending from Ellesmere Island across the Arctic Ocean to the New Siberian Islands. This was the Lomonosov Ridge, which was soon determined to divide the central Arctic Ocean into the two major subbasins.[9]

As late as 1962, Hakkel' of the Soviet Union estimated that only ten thousand depth soundings had been collected in the entire Arctic Ocean. Today this number might be taken in the course of a single day at sea.[10]

Not a great deal more than this was known at the time of *Queenfish*'s depar-

Figure 9.3 Richard J. Boyle of Arctic Submarine Laboratory, San Diego, lecturing *Queenfish* crew on history of submarine Arctic operations. (Courtesy of the U.S. Navy)

ture for her 1970 Arctic expedition. It was thus quite fortuitous, and of considerable importance to the ultimate success of *Queenfish*'s mission, that our expedition had use of Dr. Beal's recently completed Ph.D. dissertation, "Bathymetry and Structure of the Arctic Ocean." The dissertation, completed in 1968, provided the first-ever and relatively complete picture of the bottom topography of the Arctic Ocean, constructed from some seven million newly released, precise depth soundings collected by four U.S. Navy nuclear submarines along nearly 24,840 miles of track during the pioneering years of Arctic Ocean exploration from 1957 to 1962. The data included not only *Nautilus*'s 1958 track along the route we would take to the North Pole but also depth soundings between the North Pole and waters north of the Severnaya Zemlya and across the northern Laptev Sea recorded during *Seadragon*'s 1962 expedition.[11]

Figure 9.4 Dr. M. Allan Beal, senior scientist, Arctic Submarine Laboratory, San Diego, lecturing *Queenfish* crew on Arctic Ocean oceanography. (Courtesy of the U.S. Navy)

No depth soundings or bottom topography information from any source was in existence in 1970 for the largely uncharted Laptev, East Siberian, and western Chukchi seas, however. In assembling what charts that did exist for these areas, *Queenfish*'s navigator, Toby Warson, and I were bemused by the antiquity and ambiguity of information on the British Royal Navy charts, dated 1867, and by the overall paucity of depth soundings for this critically important area.

Through the Bering Strait and into the Chukchi Sea

As we transited submerged through the Unimak Pass in the Aleutians and entered the Bering Sea on 26 July, Allan Beal, Dick Boyle, Toby Warson, and I pored over the charts and discussed the voyages of *Nautilus, Sargo,* and *Seadragon* between 1958 and 1962. All three submarines had transited fully submerged along a shallow route past St. Lawrence Island and Fairway Rock, proceeding between Little Diomedes Island and Alaska and through the Bering Strait into the Chukchi Sea.

As previously described, *Nautilus* went all the way to the Arctic Ocean via an ice-free Bering Sea in early August of 1958, but only after making an unsuccessful attempt two months earlier when heavy pack ice in the Chukchi Sea made it impossible to push farther. *Sargo*'s penetrations took place during the dead of winter, January to March of 1960, when thick sea ice in the Bering Sea could sometimes reach the bottom. *Seadragon* followed *Sargo*'s inbound route without difficulty during the summer of 1962. *Seadragon*'s exit routes from the Arctic Ocean southward through the Chukchi Sea and Bering Strait in September of 1960 and 1962 would be of particular interest to us during the outbound phase of our operation.[1]

Allan Beal and Dick Boyle were consulted each day concerning just where we could encounter ice north of the Bering Strait and what degree of severity we might expect in the Chukchi and Beaufort seas. Daily satellite information was not available in 1970 to answer such questions as the following: would the Arctic ice pack remain well to the north, in deeper water, as oceanographic experts in Washington, D.C., had assured me a month ago, or would we experience the same difficulties with an unusually extensive and compact ice pack farther south, as did *Nautilus*?

Figure 10.1 National Oceanic and Atmospheric Administration satellite view of the Bering Strait. (Courtesy of the National Oceanic and Atmospheric Administration)

The sighting of the truncated Fairway Rock—a small island south of the Bering Strait—early on 30 July was an exciting moment for us all. We had at long last reached the threshold of "the Pacific door" to the Arctic Ocean. It was sobering to realize that this expedition was going to call on every ounce of experience, judgment, and coolheadedness that we could muster from our collective years of submarine service. Toby Warson and his navigation team had a few minutes of anxiety when a strong current seemed to exert a suctionlike effect toward the island. Right rudder and a quick burst of speed took us safely by. Like our predecessors, we slipped north past Cape Prince of Wales, Alaska, through the Bering Strait, and into the Chukchi Sea.

At this point in our voyage, the important question of what constituted the Soviet Union's territorial sea limits came to the fore, and the subject is worth a brief digression. In 1970 there were absolutely no international treaties that applied to the Arctic and no Law of the Sea that applied to the Arctic Ocean and its adjacent seas. International agreement on the actual breadth of territorial sea limits was yet to be achieved. The existing First United Nations Convention on Law of the Sea (1961) did not adequately address the issue.[2]

As a result, a total of sixty-seven nations, including the United States, continued to observe the twelve-mile limit, measured seaward from the low-water mark along a nation's coast as noted on large-scale charts officially recognized by coastal states. A few nations still adhered to the older six-mile limit, although eight nations, including the Soviet Union, insisted on a two-hundred-mile limit. These varying claims of territorial waters were addressed again in the United Nations in 1967 and were to lead to a Third United Nations Convention on Law of the Sea in 1973. Final agreement and ratification of a territorial sea limit of twelve miles and a twenty-four-mile contiguous zone did not occur until 1994, however.[3]

Meanwhile, in 1968 the Soviet Union issued an edict concerning the continental shelf of the USSR that fixed its seaward boundary beyond the outer limit of Soviet territorial seas up to a depth of six hundred feet. This edict implied that Soviet permission was required to explore and conduct research on the continental shelf areas claimed. It was not recognized by the United States, of course, and, interestingly, it was not officially enforced by Soviet authorities (as was a similar edict for the White Sea and Sea of Okhotsk) until 1984, when the USSR established a two-hundred-mile Economic Exclusion Zone (EEZ) and attendant jurisdiction with regard to maritime scientific research work within their EEZ.[4]

So where did this thicket of interpretations leave *Queenfish* in late July of 1970 as we entered the Chukchi Sea and the Arctic Ocean? Our orders from Admiral Walter L. Small, Commander Submarine Forces Pacific, were clear-cut and unambiguous: the United States recognized a twelve-mile territorial limit only. Accordingly, we on *Queenfish* were directed to respect the twelve-mile territorial limit at all times while conducting our hydrographic survey. We were strongly advised, in addition, to be conservative in our estimate of navigational accuracy and add an additional two nautical miles to the twelve-mile limit we observed.

As we proceeded a few miles north of the Bering Strait in the Chukchi Sea, *Queenfish* ascended to periscope depth. Warson and his able team of quartermasters clamored to take a series of visual departure fixes for latitude and longitude in order to update the SINS.[5] The moment for viewing was opportune. Visibility in this normally fog-covered area was clear enough to see not only the Alaskan and Siberian coasts but also Fairway Rock, Big Diomedes Island (Soviet), and Little Diomedes Island (U.S.). Our newest qualified chief of the watch, Fire Controlman First Class Perry Kuhn, passed the word over the sound-powered phones to all compartments, inviting one and all to come to the periscope stand in the control room to witness this unusual and seldom-seen sight.

Navigation fixes completed and the last "periscope tourist" satisfied, *Queenfish* returned beneath the surface and resumed transiting north at a keel depth of one hundred feet and a speed of eight knots.[6] Shortly thereafter we crossed the Arctic

Chartlet 10.1 The Bering Strait and Chukchi Sea, 30 July to 2 August 1970.

Circle at latitude 66°-33′ N, entered the "Realm of the Ice King," and began retracing *Nautilus*'s 1958 route through the Chukchi Sea. It was quite a thrill to pass through this most significant latitude, crossed by so many Arctic explorers before us, especially because it was the first time for most crew members. Mike Knaub and his superb bakers prepared a delicious cake of gigantic proportions, elaborately decorated to honor the occasion. We all partook of it throughout the day and well into the mid-watch, when the last of it disappeared into the engineering spaces.

We passed latitude 69° N early on 31 July on a northeasterly course as we continued retracing *Nautilus*'s route. Ice forecasts received via radio indicated that we could expect to see brash ice (fragments of broken floes) around latitude 70°, some sixty miles farther north.[7] I instructed our three engineering officers of the watch, Lieutenants Fred Moore, Bill Blenkle, and Lars Hanson, to begin monitoring main seawater suction injection temperatures and to notify the officer of the deck when these temperatures approached the freezing point of seawater, somewhere between 29° and 31° F, depending on water salinity. This would be a sure indicator of sea ice in the near vicinity.

Allan Beal had advised us earlier that the overall extent and thickness of the Arctic ice pack would probably be greater than normal this summer because the past winter had been sufficiently severe to have caused a half-month's delay in opening the Soviet Northern Sea Route. He further advised us that we should expect to encounter heavier-than-normal deep-draft ice floes much farther south in both the Chukchi and Beaufort seas. Needless to say, the adverse effects of an unusually harsh winter on the extent and roughness of the sea ice throughout the Siberian continental shelf several weeks hence were soon to preoccupy my thoughts.

Dick Boyle added to this litany of bad news by privately informing me that one of my officers had failed both the knowledge and operational examinations on *Queenfish*'s AN/BQS-8 under-ice sonar suite. He was the only one to have done so among both officer and sonar watch standers. I was extremely disappointed and concerned, for the individual in question was soon to take his station as one of my key watch officers. He was among those tentatively slated to pilot *Queenfish* on the hydrographic survey. It was a serious setback. I asked Boyle, who had been a watch officer on *Skate*'s 1959 Arctic voyage, to monitor this officer's watch section and provide whatever backup assistance was deemed necessary.

A command watch consisting initially of Linc Mueller, Ralph Beedle, and myself was established in the control room as *Queenfish* approached latitude 70° N. A three-section AN/BQS-8 under-ice sonar watch, made up of our most experienced sonar technicians, also went into effect, providing continuous manning of the IBD.[8] The IBD was located portside aft in the control room, which would be serving as our primary station for safely piloting us through deep-draft ice.

Additional watch standers (quartermasters or sonar technicians) were assigned, as well, to monitor the associated top sounder used to measure ice draft, or ice thickness under water, and the fathometer for depth of water beneath the keel. Both equipments continuously recorded their results in feet on paper chart rolls.

All BQR-7 long-range passive sonar and BQQ-5 passive sonar watch standers were directed to listen carefully for any possible sea-ice noises, such as the grinding, clashing, and smashing of ice together and immediately report them to the officer of the deck. Finally, we shifted to an "Ascent to Periscope Depth" procedure that directed that the thicker-barreled No. 2, or navigation periscope, be used for conducting underwater searches for sea ice and other obstacles such as drifting logs on the sea surface prior to *Queenfish's* ascension to periscope depth.[9] When the sea surface was determined to be clear, the narrower-barreled No. 1, or attack periscope, was then to be used during the actual ascent to periscope depth and initial "close aboard," surface, and aircraft searches.

The ever-vigilant and competent Ralph Beedle, a former U.S. Naval Academy All-American fencing champion, reported during the late afternoon that main seawater suction injection temperatures at our present transit depth of 100–120 feet had now decreased to 32° F. When *Queenfish* was estimated to have just crossed latitude 70° N, I took the conn (maneuvering control of the submarine) and made a careful search for ice overhead and on the surface above and ahead of our bow. As soon as the surface above us was determined to be clear, I ordered the diving officer to proceed to periscope depth. During the course of several rapid periscope searches for air and surface contacts, what appeared to be scattered ice on the horizon, beginning some five thousand yards to the northwest, came into view.

As we continued to close the ice, we saw a considerable number of house-size bergy bits of several thousand tons each, some of them as high as twenty to thirty feet and ranging in color from an almost "dirty ice" black to a very pristine bluish white.[10] The former were probably rotting or mushy land-based or fast-ice remnants, the latter the remains of still-hard glacial or multiyear sea ice. Dr. Beal's warning notwithstanding, sea ice of such magnitude this far south was an unwanted sight. The edge of the pack itself might be just over the horizon.

Queenfish resumed transiting to the northeast at a keel depth of 120 feet and speed of six knots. We soon began passing beneath large ice floes whose drafts or keels penetrated as much as thirty-five feet below the surface. I repositioned myself behind the AN/BQS-8 under-ice sonar operator and assumed the conn from the officer of the deck just in time to pilot the boat beneath a surreal underwater topography of rugged, deep-draft ice that completely blanketed the sea. The seemingly endless procession of jagged icy talons along our underwater track thrust sufficiently deep to pose a serious collision hazard to *Queenfish*. The situation called for immediate and often dramatic avoidance action. Because the ice stalactites were not detected until they had closed to less than fourteen hundred yards from *Queenfish's* bow, as much as 20° rudder might be required to slip around and safely pass them.

Added to the overall threat to safe navigation along our northward track were

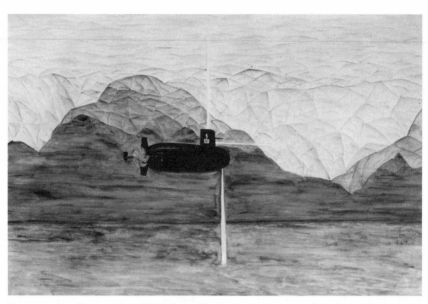

Figure 10.2 Artist's conception of USS *Queenfish* piloting under Arctic pack ice during the summer of 1970. (Courtesy of the U.S. Navy)

Figure 10.3 Iceberg detector presentation of deep-draft ice ahead of USS *Queenfish* in the Chukchi Sea. (Courtesy of the U.S. Navy)

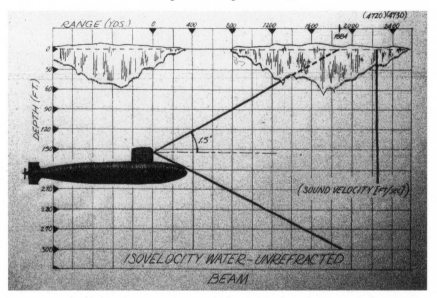

Figure 10.4 Path of iceberg detector acoustic rays under ideal (isothermal) acoustic conditions. (Courtesy of the U.S. Navy)

the increasingly shallow water depths, compelling *Queenfish* to hug the bottom or seabed in order to clear deep-draft ice along our route. Fortunately for us, the eastern Chukchi seafloor was fairly flat and well charted.

Bob Baumhardt had noted that seawater temperature had increased from 32° to 43° F during our last ascent to periscope depth and then returned to 32° when *Queenfish* returned to her earlier transit depth. It thus became apparent that the steadily increasingly negative temperature, or sound-velocity profile (SVP), that Bob had observed from periscope to transit depth was probably the reason that IBD ranges on deep-draft sea ice directly in our path were much shorter than the originally predicted minimum range of 2,500 yards.[11]

This phenomenon meant, in effect, that the only returning acoustic signals, or echoes, appearing on the IBD scope would be those from deep-draft ice so close to *Queenfish* that the IBD's outgoing echo-ranging signals would be reflected from the ice before the signals had a chance to curve downward sufficiently to pass beneath—without detecting the deep-draft ice in our path. We soon realized that, depending on the change in the speed of sound in response to change in seawater temperature, reliable IBD acoustic ranges on deep-draft ice in our path could be anywhere from just five hundred yards to not more than fourteen hundred yards, with an average of eight hundred. Everything depended, in other words, on the

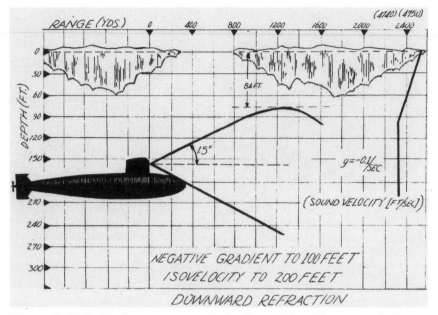

Figure 10.5 Path of iceberg detector acoustic rays under adverse conditions (temperature decrease with increased depth) in Chukchi Sea. (Courtesy of the U.S. Navy)

relationship of the velocity of sound at the surface to the velocity of sound at the depth of our under-ice sonar transducer. It was an unpleasant surprise, although it would not have been if we had done our acoustic homework more thoroughly.

Queenfish could not afford to graze even slightly the ice overhead or the seabed that was already so close to our keel. One or the other could damage the boat's control surfaces and propeller blades, requiring us in all probability to abort the expedition and proceed as best we could to the nearest U.S. port for repairs. As the grossly understated saying goes, "A collision at sea can ruin the entire day."

It soon became necessary for *Queenfish* to hug the bottom to as close as thirty feet while we constantly maneuvered her to avoid the deep-draft ice above and along an intended shallow water track. We were literally sandwiched between thick ice and the bottom. This situation was to continue for several extremely tense and exhausting hours. *Queenfish* was definitely receiving a nerve-racking baptism, the first of many hostile environments and threats to navigational safety that she would encounter on the expedition.

By early evening, improvement in overall water depth in the Chukchi Sea provided a little more maneuvering room as we continued to vary our course as necessary. As soon as it became evident that the ship control party (diving officer of

Figure 10.6 Lieutenant Karl Thomas (Tom) Hoepfner, *Queenfish*'s diving officer, checking velocity of sound in water prior to estimating maximum range of iceberg detector. (Courtesy of the U.S. Navy)

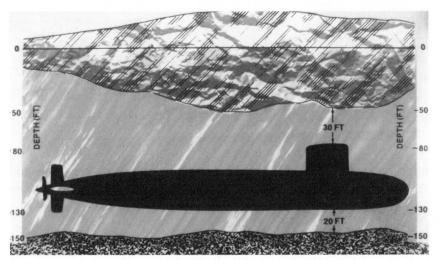

Figure 10.7 Artist's concept of USS *Queenfish* hugging bottom to avoid thick ice above it in shallow Chukchi Sea. (Courtesy of the U.S. Navy)

the watch, helmsman, and planesmen) was relatively comfortable operating close to the bottom (forty feet between the boat's keel and the seabed), speed was increased to eight knots where possible. Three and one-half hours later, to the relief of all, the top sounder indicated no ice overhead, and *Queenfish* entered an area of continuous open water. The decision was then made to "plane up" to the surface and broach to a keel depth of fifty feet to see whether we could spot the ice line, or edge, of the Arctic ice pack ahead.

A quick search on No. 2 periscope revealed no ice line, or any ice in sight, and the boat returned to periscope depth. We continued transiting in ice-free water to the northeast, increasing speed to ten knots, on the advice of Toby Warson, so as to remain ahead of our "plan of intended movement," or PIM. Toby, a 1959 U.S. Naval Academy graduate, was a tall, ruddy, well-built man who had played tackle on the academy's football team and been its heavyweight boxing champion for several years. He was definitely not a man with whom one wanted to get into an argument. As Toby pointed out, we were certain to be slowed by heavy ice as the evening progressed. The protective periscope fairing was raised to keep No. 2 periscope from "chattering" (vibrating) and to shield it from small fragments of ice.

Shortly before midnight on 31 July, Toby reported that the latest satellite navigation fix showed *Queenfish* to be at latitude 70°-49′ N, longitude 166°-50′ W.[12] In the meantime, Bob Baumhardt and Dick Boyle came up with a revised estimate of the effect of the continued severe negative temperature gradient, from 45° F at 50 feet to 32° F at 120 feet, on the maximum effective range on deep-draft ice of our iceberg detector. Their best estimate of only 450 yards was disconcerting. It meant that our next under-ice piloting episode in the shallow water of the Chukchi was certain to be more dangerous, particularly if we were to encounter even deeper-draft ice floes. It was our strong hope that we would soon reach the southern boundary of the Arctic ice pack where the temperature gradient, and velocity of sound in water, would become isothermal, or the same, from the surface to the deepest depth at which we expected to be operating, thus lengthening our detection ranges to deep-draft ice in our path.

We began a routine of broaching up to fifty feet every half hour to check seawater temperature and search for the ice line with No. 2 periscope fully raised so as to gain maximum height-of-eye above the sea surface. It was not long before we began to see an ever-increasing number of ice floes and bergy bits on the horizon. Was this the edge of the pack ice or just another band of heavy ice? Increased ice meant that it would soon be time to descend below the surface and resume dodging deep-draft ice while hugging the bottom.

About 1:40 a.m. on 1 August, Toby Warson reported that we had passed latitude

71° N. Because water depths were becoming steadily shallower, a command decision was made to change course to the northwest where there should be deeper water. Although this meant an abrupt departure from *Nautilus*'s 1958 track, there was a need to increase *Queenfish*'s underwater maneuvering envelope between the seabed and deep-draft ice overhead before the concentration of sea ice drove us completely beneath the surface again.

I was pleased to note that Bob Baumhardt, one of our best officers of the deck, had just come on watch. Open water toward the northwest was rapidly disappearing as the ice field became more compact, and he was directed to take the boat down to 120 feet, decrease speed to five knots, and resume our "under-ice-in-shallow water" operations routine. Bob, a former enlisted submariner, had gained his commission via the Navy Scientific Education Program and Marquette University. A most mature and competent naval officer, he possessed a calm nature and an unusual degree of situational awareness, which repeatedly proved its value in previous operations. Our best diving officer of the watch, Grant Youngman, was also to be on watch with Bob. *Queenfish*'s ship control teams had now all been "blooded." I therefore informed them that I had every confidence they could safely operate *Queenfish* as close as twenty feet from the bottom if need be. A collective low whistle was their reaction.

As *Queenfish* proceeded beneath the ice at five knots to a keel depth of 125 feet, just 30 feet above the seabed, the top sounder chart indicated, to our consternation, that we had just passed beneath a number of heavy ice floes whose drafts approached 35 feet. The floes probably cleared the top of *Queenfish*'s sail by less than thirty feet, yet not a single one had been detected by the forward-scanning IBD. Wow! Bob Baumhardt and Dick Boyle quickly reminded me that the continuing negative sound velocity profile could result in IBD detection ranges on deep-draft ice directly in our path to be not more than three hundred to four hundred yards. There was even more incentive for us to hug the bottom.

Opportunity to remedy this rather tricky situation soon presented itself. Sonar Technician First Class Frederick Miller, our AN/BQS-8 Arctic sonar suite expert, had been experimenting with the polynya delineator "up mode" of the IBD and found that it might help us out. The "up mode" was normally used to delineate the far edge of an ice-surrounded polynya as we approached the center of open water in preparation for a vertical ascent within it. Miller found that the up mode's initial upward angle of active sound transmissions, or echo ranging, from the IBD's sail-mounted transducer resulted in an overall increase of the curved path followed by these acoustic signals or rays. It meant they would end up traveling a longer distance horizontally before curving downward in response to a negative temperature profile and ultimately beneath a deep-draft ice keel in the path of the transiting submarine. The net effect was an increase in effective detection range.

Not only was this occurring, but during the past thirty hours we noted that "bell-like" tones, or echoes, from deep-draft ice in our path could be detected aurally several hundred yards in advance, or greater than the range indicated on the scope by the IBD's returning echo. The serendipitous effect of both these discoveries was to provide a welcome gain of approximately five hundred yards or more to the IBD's effective range of detection—shades of old destroyer days![13]

Even so, the response time of the ship control party, from the initial detection of deep-draft ice in our path to the maneuvering of *Queenfish,* was seldom more than five minutes. This second ordeal of transiting under ice in the shallow Chukchi Sea was to prove every bit as tense and demanding as the previous one. The IBD operator had, if anything, to be even more alert to any ice that might present a collision hazard. I, in turn, had to immediately maneuver *Queenfish* well clear and then, as soon as it was safe to do so, move back to our original course. At times it became necessary to order maneuvering (the engineering officer of the watch in the maneuvering room aft) to increase or decrease the submarine's propeller revolutions by a few turns, thus ensuring the maintenance of sufficient speed, or steerage way.

As before, I frequently found that we required as much as 20° port or starboard rudder. The diving officer of the watch had to supervise members of the ship control party very closely and help them maintain the very finest in "zero bubble" depth control as we maneuvered to avoid a seemingly endless procession of deep-draft ice keels.[14]

Just in case, having learned from studying USS *Skate*'s experience during her 1962 Arctic expedition, when she bent several propeller blades in a collision with ice and successfully straightened them with a "homemade" clamp so that the boat regained almost full speed without excessive vibration, we had a similar large clamp made up, stowing it below decks for quick assembly and mounting on a bent propeller blade to gradually tighten and straighten it.

Toby Warson remained close by and, together with Clarence Williams, kept me informed of depth beneath the keel as well as ice clearance overhead. They assured me repeatedly that overall water depth was gradually increasing and that the portion of the Chukchi Sea through which we were transiting was known to be relatively flat. Never far from my thoughts was what *Queenfish* was likely to face within the more expansive and totally unexplored ice-covered and shallow Laptev and East Siberian seas.

The top sounder recorder and IBD indicated that we had entered another ice-free area, but we were not certain how extensive this next open-water area might be. The decision was made to remain submerged. We had departed from, and fallen behind, our PIM and needed to make up time. Accordingly, course was changed back to a northeasterly one, approaching *Nautilus*'s 1958 departure point north of Point Barrow, Alaska. I returned the conn to Bob Baumhardt and took a catnap nearby.

After a surprisingly quiet and ice-free hour, I reviewed the chart with Warson and directed Baumhardt to slow the boat to less than four knots in order to clear baffles toward deeper water.[15] If there were no contacts on sonar, he was to decrease depth to one hundred feet and raise No. 2 periscope for a careful search for sea ice overhead. Following a thorough search, Bob lowered the periscope and reported no ice in sight. Although he could still see the surface, the water was very murky, with myriad jellyfish of various sizes and some sort of seaweed everywhere he looked.

I relieved Bob of the conn. Reversing course with 20° rudder toward the ice-free direction from which we had just come, I raised No. 1 periscope. Confirming that it was clear overhead, I ordered, "Six-five feet smartly!" Grant Youngman, who was still on the dive, replied, "Six-five feet smartly, aye!" and zipped us right up. He leveled *Queenfish* off at the ordered depth and reported that he had done so. There was no ice in sight. I lowered No. 1 periscope, raised No. 2, and ordered a depth of sixty feet, followed by fifty-five feet. Again there was no ice, not even on the horizon. Amazing! It would seem that we had passed through several bands of heavy sea ice as we transited through the Chukchi Sea in a northeasterly direction but had yet to reach the ice line or southern edge of the perennial Arctic ice pack. I turned over the periscope and conn to Bob Baumhardt. He was directed to remain at periscope depth and, because there were no visual or ECM contacts (that is, radar signals from aircraft, ships, or shore), to increase speed to twelve knots as soon as he had raised the protective periscope fairing sufficiently to prevent chatter.

Bob's relief as officer of the deck, Tom Hoepfner, soon reported that sea ice was detected on the horizon to the northeast. I confirmed Tom's sighting and saw what appeared to be strong "ice blink" above the horizon to the north and northwest.[16] Dick Boyle was invited to take a look. He confirmed my sighting and conclusion that, at our present height-of-eye range to the horizon of approximately eight thousand yards, the ice blink denoted considerable sea ice ahead. He and Allan Beal agreed that, with no contacts of any sort in our vicinity that might detect and report our presence, it might be prudent to surface the submarine briefly in order to get a very good "high look" through the periscopes at what might well be the edge of the Arctic or polar ice pack before we proceeded farther north submerged. As we conferred, Senior Chief Electronics Technician Richard Dietz, on duty as machinery watch supervisor, reported that main seawater injection temperatures had dropped significantly during the past half hour and were now at 29° F. This was the sign we had been looking for. The Arctic ice pack was very near.

After slightly changing course once more to confirm that there were no submerged contacts lurking in our baffles, Tom Hoepfner was directed to make an "airless surface." He immediately ordered speed increased to ten knots and directed the diving officer of the watch, Steve Gray, to "surface without air." With both sail and stern planes on full rise, *Queenfish* planed up rapidly. As soon as it seemed she was broached and that depth was holding, Steve ordered the low-pressure blower started so as to begin removing seawater from the main ballast tanks. This procedure saved air from the high-pressure air banks for the time when it might really be needed for a major emergency.

Once I was certain that *Queenfish* was holding on the surface and in a stable condition, I gave Tom permission to open the lower hatch to the long vertical trunk through the sail to the bridge above and to send Clarence Williams to crack the trunk's upper hatch in order to equalize *Queenfish*'s internal pressure with that of the outside atmosphere. I quickly followed Williams and Hoepfner to the bridge as soon as the loud hissing of air had ceased, confirming that the boat's interior and atmospheric pressure were equalized and that it was thus safe to open the upper hatch fully.[17]

The view from the bridge was spectacular. A vast field of ice spread between *Queenfish* and the horizon some ten thousand yards to the north. Toby Warson subsequently reported that a search with No. 2 periscope, at an even greater height-of-eye than before, confirmed the existence of compact sea ice stretching from the northwest to the northeast of our position. At about eight o'clock on the morning of 1 August we were just north of latitude 72° N and at longitude 168°-03′ W. It appeared we had reached the edge of the permanent Arctic Ocean ice pack at last.

Queenfish was almost thirty miles south of where *Nautilus* had encountered the ice pack on this same day twelve years earlier.[18] This more southerly sighting and the bands of heavy ice that we had just navigated beneath tended to confirm Allan Beal's prediction that the extent and thickness of the Arctic Ocean ice pack would be considerably greater this year than last.

While on the surface, I followed the excellent example set by my former commanding officer, George Steele, on reaching the ice edge at the beginning of *Seadragon*'s 1960 North Pole voyage.[19] At my direction, Linc Mueller and Kenneth Ickes arranged for each crew member to come on deck for a few minutes to view and contemplate the monumental size of the Arctic ice pack, which *Queenfish* and they would be operating under during the next month or so. Judging from their ex-

Figure 10.8 Edge of Arctic ice pack as observed in Chukchi Sea from USS *Queenfish* on 1 August 1970. (Courtesy of the U.S. Navy)

pressions and questions, they took the lesson to heart and put in their best watch-standing performances in the coming days.

It might be useful here to describe the nature of the Arctic ice pack in more detail. First of all, the Arctic ice pack is an extremely complex mixture of many different types and thicknesses of ice and open-water areas, whether lakelike polynyas or narrow leads, that characterize it. In scientific parlance this is referred to as its "thickness distribution."[20] Ice thickness is the total thickness of sea ice as opposed to ice draft, which is that portion of the sea ice beneath the surface of the sea.

During any given year, the perennial Arctic Ocean ice pack, which includes the Chukchi and six additional peripheral continental shelf seas, will expand from 2.7 to 3.5 million square miles in the early fall to almost 6.2 million square miles by late winter. The ice-thickness distribution characteristic of the entire Arctic Ocean, or a particular geographical area within it at any given time, comprises basically the following: (1) the mean draft below the surface and/or overall thickness; (2) the percentage of different ice types such as first-year (less than 6.6 feet thick), multiyear (6.6 to 13.1 feet thick), and deformed (greater than 13.1 feet thick) ice in combination with the number of deep-draft independent keels (greater than 29.5 feet thick) present; and (3) the percentage of open water that falls within the category of "surfaceable areas" (level and less than 6.6 feet thick).[21]

The term "thickness distribution" thus serves as the best way to describe the severity or roughness of the pack ice encountered in any given location.[22] The thicker and more varied the ice, the rougher.

Although the overall mean thickness of the Arctic ice pack may range from less than 9.8 feet to more than 13.1 feet on a day-to-day and interannual basis, the ice-thickness distribution is extremely dynamic and will vary widely both seasonally and geographically throughout the Arctic Ocean. This is due in large part to the strong winds of the Arctic Basin as a whole, which keep ice floes within the pack in continuous motion. Strong winds cause individual ice floes to break up and move away from each other, creating open-water areas, or to build thicker (or deformed) ice and deep-draft keels when they crash into and override other floes. Ice-thickness distribution can also be affected by currents, upwellings, and tidal actions.[23] In summary, *Queenfish,* or any submarine operating beneath the Arctic ice pack during August and September of 1970, could expect to find 60 percent of the pack ranging in thickness from 6.6 to 13.1 feet, 10 percent to be greater than 29.5 feet thick, 25 percent to be less than 6.6 feet thick, and the remaining 5 percent to consist of open water and refrozen leads and polynyas.[24]

A little over an hour after our first viewing of the Arctic pack, we submerged to 120 feet, in water depths of 150 to 180 feet, continuing to head slowly north at just four knots. Following consultation with Toby Warson, Allan Beal, and Dick Boyle, I decided to alter *Queenfish*'s course to one that would take us several miles outside the western edge of the "Moving Haven" that surrounded our plan of intended movement.[25] The purpose was to reach a deeper 210-foot depth contour and then change course to the east to intercept *Nautilus*'s 1958 track north of Point Barrow, Alaska. Once overall water depth increased enough to permit a safe clearance of at least thirty feet beneath one-hundred-foot-draft ice, we would increase our speed from four to six knots.

I resumed piloting *Queenfish* using the IBD presentation of deep-draft sea ice in our path, with James Petersen now operating the AN/BQS-8 under-ice sonar. Because seawater temperature was essentially isothermal at 29° F from the surface down to our operating depth of 130 feet, we predicted, and were delighted to see, that the IBD was now providing ranges on the order of sixteen hundred yards to deep-draft ice keels in our path. Clear, bell-like tones alerted us, as before, to the existence of heavy deep-draft ice several hundred yards in advance of its initial appearance on the IBD scope.

Nevertheless, we once again found it necessary to take *Queenfish* to within thirty feet of the bottom in order to pass safely beneath, or maneuver around, a steady procession of ice with keels of increasingly deep draft. It was extremely critical that the boat's overall fore-and-aft trim, or "bubble," be maintained as close to a level 0° as possible. At all costs, we must prevent the rudder from striking and possibly dragging along the bottom or, even worse, hooking and becoming entangled in the ice overhead from either too much up- or down-angle on the boat.

Queenfish's diving officers of the watch and planesmen showed themselves to be more than equal to the task from the moment we passed beneath the ice edge and ran up against deep-draft ice. Their proficiency in maneuvering *Queenfish* in these stressful circumstances steadily improved with each passing hour. Very much on all our minds, particularly Dick Boyle's and Allan Beal's, at this time was that *Nautilus* had had to turn back in mid-June of 1958 following two close encounters with massive deep-draft ice floes, with one of them missing the boat's sail by only five feet. I would not have hesitated to make the same decision as Captain William Anderson if we had found ourselves in similar circumstances.[26]

On the other hand, we all knew that *Queenfish* would not be given another opportunity later on in the year. A delay of just one month would be considered by Dr. Lyon and my military superiors to be too late in the season for a lengthy first-ever exploration of the Siberian continental shelf. We were mindful as well that a number of senior submarine officers of influence in Washington, D.C., were not convinced that it was safe for a single-screw submarine to operate in shallow water under ice in any circumstances, for if the propeller was damaged, we would not have a second one to fall back on. This was going to be *Queenfish's* one and only chance to make it through the ice-covered northeastern Chukchi Sea. There was no question in our minds that we had to succeed.

This final phase of our transit through the Chukchi Sea was to prove every bit as strenuous and tiresome as we feared. We were heartened, therefore, when the sound velocity profile became slightly positive during the late morning, lengthening IBD ranges on deep-draft ice in our path to anywhere from eighteen hundred to twenty-four hundred yards. At this point I decided it best to alter course to the north in order to intercept the 240-foot bottom contour before turning east. This soon enabled us to operate at a keel depth of 140 feet while gradually increasing the distance to the seabed beneath.

During the six hours that followed, we were forced to maneuver around a surprising number of very large deep-draft ice pressure ridges, or "bummocks," whose drafts approached seventy feet beneath the sea. Interestingly, we found that ice of such severity faded from our IBD presentation at ranges of 350 to 375 yards as we closed and passed beneath. The ice floes were also considerably larger, with some exceeding 250 yards in length. Overall water depths continued to increase steadily, finally enabling *Queenfish* to achieve sufficient clearance beneath the endless blanket of deep-draft ice overhead to make avoidance maneuvers less necessary.

By late afternoon on 1 August, the overall operating environment beneath the ice pack was so much improved that I was able to turn over the command watch to Ralph Beedle and retire to my cabin just aft of the control room for a much-needed shower and a few hours' sleep. Conditions remained much the same for the next four hours, until Ralph called me to report that *Queenfish* had just passed beneath a series of extremely deep ice keels whose drafts exceeded ninety feet, the deepest thus far. This got me out of bed in a hurry. Ice of this magnitude had not been predicted for this area by either Waldo Lyon or Walt Wittmann, an oceanographic expert with the U.S. Navy's Oceanographic Office in Washington, D.C. Was it a fragment of an ice island? We never knew and were not to see anything like it for several more days.[27]

As bad luck would have it, *Queenfish's* AN/BQS-8 top sounder drive motor failed shortly before midnight, after having run continuously since just north of the Bering Strait. It had been fully operational and completely reliable until now and during the times when it was most needed for measuring and recording ice clearance overhead as we carefully navigated through the shallower waters of the Chukchi Sea. We would soon need it again for the precise and continuous recording of ice draft directly above *Queenfish's* sail when we resumed retracing *Nautilus's* 1958 track and during surfacings within open water or thin-ice–covered leads and polynyas. Bob Baumhardt and Sonar Technician Frederick Miller assured me that the device would be repaired and back within an hour. In the meantime, course was adjusted to the north to remain in deep water. Our plan was now to cross the six-hundred-foot depth curve before turning east to intercept *Nautilus's* 1958 route northward to the North Pole along longitude 155° W.

Queenfish reached the six-hundred-foot depth curve during the early morning hours of 2 August and was at long last at the northeastern edge of the Chukchi Sea shelf. Our keel depth was 250 feet beneath the sea surface. Water depths beneath the keel were almost three hundred feet. Course was changed to due east or 090°, and speed was increased to fifteen knots.

We had made it through safely. We could now afford to stand down somewhat from what had been a relentlessly demanding "under-ice-in-shallow-water routine." I had Linc Mueller pass the word to all hands that there would be a twenty-four-hour break from all drills and lectures, giving everyone a well-deserved rest from one of the most stressful experiences that any of us had ever endured.

There was no doubt in my mind that *Queenfish's* crew members were in top form for dealing with what were certain to be similar or worse conditions along the Siberian shelf. The severe operational demands and constraints imposed on them during the past thirty-two hours had helped to determine who among the officers and enlisted watch standers was best prepared to respond to unusual or threatening operational situations.

A sure indicator for any commanding officer that a key watch stander might be of special concern is the continuous presence in their near vicinity of several experienced off-watch senior petty officers. This has probably been true since the earliest days of submarining. I anticipated having to make a few critical shifts in personnel and to conduct additional training before we could attempt our first real surfacing within an ice-surrounded polynya or lead on our way to the North Pole.

First Surfacings in the Arctic Ocean

En Route to the Geographic North Pole

Queenfish had reached the northeastern edge of the Chukchi Sea continental shelf and the deep water of the Arctic Ocean shortly after midnight on 2 August. We were now proceeding at almost twenty knots to a point north of Point Barrow, Alaska, whence we would resume retracing *Nautilus's* 1958 route across the Arctic Ocean along longitude 155° W northward to the North Pole and then southward along longitude 25° E to latitude 83° N. The route would entail continuous recording of the under-ice topography and overall water depths along the same track and speeds that *Nautilus* had followed twelve years earlier.[1]

With the top sounder just reported by the sonar officer to be "fully repaired and continuously measuring ice draft overhead," *Queenfish* was ready in all respects to make her first surfacing in the Arctic Ocean. Quartermaster of the Watch Louis Soukey was instructed to be particularly alert for, and to immediately report, any polynyas or leads of 150 yards or greater in length that were sufficiently ice-free in which to conduct a safe vertical ascent.

The command watch officer and the officer of the deck were instructed to "execute" on the first such open water. "Execution" on a polynya or lead consisted basically of reversing course through the use of a Williamson Turn and then decreasing speed and depth in order to reach an "all stop and hovering" position from which to make a vertical ascent into the center of the polynya or lead directly above the submarine.[2] It was to become a standard under-ice operational procedure during the weeks ahead.

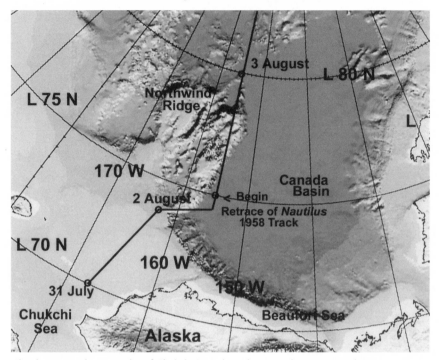

Chartlet 11.1 Northeastern edge of Chukchi Sea to latitude 80° north, 2 August and 3 August 1970.

Two hours into the morning, Quartermaster Soukey suddenly yelled, "Polynya, over 150 yards long!"

"Left fifteen degrees rudder!" responded the officer of the deck, Lieutenant Commander Walter "Bud" Pezet, who added, "Diving officer, make your depth one-six-zero feet. Maneuvering, make turns for four knots," followed by "Chief of the watch, call away the polynya-plotting party!"

"Call away the polynya-plotting party, aye sir," answered Senior Chief Torpedoman Kenneth Ickes.

The order was passed via sound-powered phones to all compartments, and polynya-plotting stations were quickly manned in the control room. In the meantime, Bob Baumhardt, who had relieved Pezet as officer of the deck, ordered, "Right fifteen degrees rudder!" and began maneuvering *Queenfish* to complete the circular Williamson Turn and return to the center of the open-water area that we had just passed beneath.

The quartermaster of the watch, who had just plotted the polynya on the dead-reckoning tracer, or DRT, now turned the plot over to the polynya-plotting officer,

Figure 11.1 Typical surface of Arctic ice pack. (Courtesy of Alfred S. McLaren)

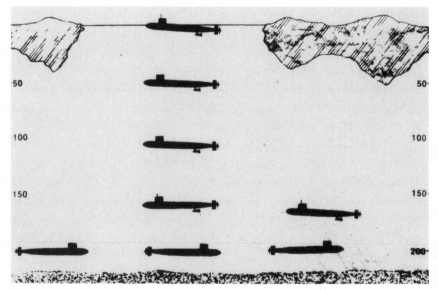

Figure 11.2 Artist's concept of *Queenfish*'s maneuvers prior to conducting vertical ascent to surface or periscope depth in Arctic Ocean. (Courtesy of the U.S. Navy)

Bud Pezet, who soon called out, "Officer of the deck, recommend steer course one-seven-zero to intersect the polynya!" as he began coaching him back to a best estimate of the polynya's center. "Polynya now bears one-six-eight, range two hundred yards," he next said, adding, "Recommend steering one-six-six and slowing to minimum turns!" Pezet, a tall, well-qualified submarine officer who had recently obtained a master of science degree in oceanography from the U.S. Navy Postgraduate School, Monterey, was slated to relieve Toby Warson as both navigator and operations officer during our return voyage home.

During the final approach to the polynya, *Queenfish*'s depth was gradually decreased to 160 feet. The polynya would in all probability be surrounded by a conglomerate of thick multiyear and deformed deep-draft ice normally expected in this area. I had been in the control center the entire time and now took the conn.

"Polynya center now bears one-six-three, fifty yards to go!" reported Pezet.

"Ice thickness fifteen feet!" reported Quartermaster Soukey from the top sounder recorder.

"Ease up to one-two-zero feet!" I ordered, then "Helm, come left to one-six-three degrees!" and "Maneuvering, make turns for three knots, lower and test the secondary propulsion motor!"[3]

"Come left to one-six-three degrees!" responded the helmsman, then "Steady one-six-three degrees, sir!"

"At one-two-zero feet!" reported *Queenfish*'s diving officer, Tom Hoepfner, followed by "Ice thickness ten feet," from Soukey.

"Polynya bears one-six-zero degrees, forty yards to go," from Pezet.

"Very well," I responded and ordered, "Maneuvering, make minimum turns."

"Thirty yards to go, ice overhead is in motion!" reported Pezet. "Recommend steer one-five-seven!"

"Helm, come left to one-five-seven!" I replied, following with "Maneuvering, all stop!"

"One-five-seven, aye sir!" responded the helmsman, then "Steady one-five-seven, sir!"

Maneuvering was then ordered to shift propulsion to the SPM.

We continued to coast toward a position directly below the polynya's center. From this point on, only the SPM would be used as a thruster to maneuver the ship. Sonar Technician First Class Frederick Miller, now using the polynya detector or "PD UP" mode of the iceberg detector, reported, "Open water ahead!"

The thickness of the pack ice overhead began to decrease dramatically as *Queenfish* drifted slowly forward in an essentially neutrally buoyant condition. Quartermaster Louis Soukey reported, "Open water overhead!"

"Train the SPM to one-eight-zero!" I ordered, intending to use it to kill all forward way (motion).

"SPM at one-eight-zero!" reported Hoepfner.

"On SPM!" I ordered, quickly followed by "Off SPM!"

The burst of reverse thrust from the SPM brought *Queenfish* to a complete stop within a large polynya that appeared more than adequate in size for our first surfacing in the Arctic Ocean, at latitude 73°-40′ N, longitude 164°-04′ W.

I gingerly raised No. 2 periscope to search for ice overhead and in our near vicinity. We were dead in the water. Depth control of our 4,640-ton submarine was now a matter of moving very small increments of water to and from sea to adjust *Queenfish's* ballast carefully as she hovered beneath the polynya. The top sounder watch continued to report open water overhead, and I completed a periscope inspection of the polynya above us.

Because all appeared clear of ice overhead, the main propeller shaft was ordered stopped and the main propulsion clutch disengaged. This permitted the engineering watch standers to spin independently the two main propulsion turbines, now no longer connected to the main shaft via a reduction gear, as necessary in order to prevent "bowing" of their blades due to uneven heating when not in motion. Even more important, it ensured that we would not move within the polynya and possibly collide with surrounding ice as the result of unexpected main propeller rotation.

Lowering the periscope, I ordered, "Vertical ascent to the surface!"

"Vertical ascent to the surface, aye!" Hoepfner echoed.

The vertical ascent into the polynya was accomplished by deballasting or pumping water to sea from *Queenfish's* internal variable ballast tanks. Hoepfner then reflooded the tanks to achieve the desired rate of rise to the surface. He soon reported, "Rate of rise, ten feet per minute!" During the next few minutes our rate of rise increased and then gradually decreased to zero as *Queenfish* approached and leveled off on the surface of the polynya.

Hoepfner ordered the chief of the watch to use the low-pressure blower to remove seawater from the main ballast tanks. As the boat settled and seemed to hold on the surface, I very gingerly raised No. 1 periscope and reported, "Periscope clear!" as the head window cleared the water and I commenced a rapid series of aircraft and close-aboard (near obstacle) surface searches.

"We are holding on the surface!" Hoepfner soon reported.

Permission was given, once the low-pressure blower had been secured, to crack the upper hatch to the bridge and equalize the difference in pressure between the boat and the outside atmosphere. Once this was accomplished, the officer of the deck was permitted to open the upper bridge hatch and proceed to the bridge.

All seven transducers, from No. 1 near the bow to No. 7 near the stern, of the upward-beamed fathometer array had indicated no ice directly above. It became painfully obvious, however, that *Queenfish*'s rudder and stern area had somehow managed to strike and break through more than fourteen inches of first-year ice along the polynya edge directly astern of us.[4] Several alarmingly large blocks of sea ice had been lifted well clear of the water in the process. Our first surfacing was far from an unqualified success.

Concerned and somewhat chagrined, I ordered a thorough examination, both under water and topside, of *Queenfish*'s rudder and propeller. As soon as it was safe to go on the main deck, our scuba divers, led by Quartermaster First Class Clarence Williams, suited up and then closely examined the rudder, stern planes, and all seven propeller blades. To our profound relief, Williams reported that although the anchor light atop the rudder had been cleanly sheared off, neither the propeller nor the rudder or stern planes was damaged. This close call made it necessary to revise our ascent procedure so that all future vertical ascents would be made with a slight "up bubble," keeping both rudder and propeller as far beneath the surface as possible and thus away from any ice that might suddenly appear.

We remained within the polynya for several hours as Chief Radioman Mike Hein and his team of radiomen, John Nice and Dennis Kawakami, succeeded in sending off our first check reports from the Arctic and copied two assigned radio broadcasts, or "skeds." At the same time, a series of navigation fixes (satellite or NavSat, Omega, and Loran C) obtained by electronic technicians Gordon Branin and Joseph Boston confirmed that we had almost reached the six-hundred-foot depth contour. Particularly impressive was that both the SINS and hand dead-reckoning (DR) position estimates were within a mile of our position determined by the more-accurate NavSat system. Toby Warson and his team were congratulated on a job well done.

Although it was generally overcast and chilly, we took the opportunity while surfaced to put Chief Photographer's Mate Charles Wright into a life raft along with two scuba divers and send them off to take photos of *Queenfish*'s first surfacing within the Arctic Ocean. Wright, a combat photographer on special assignment, had joined us in Seattle following an action-filled tour in Vietnam. His often hair-raising tales made us grateful that we were in a submarine in the Arctic and not on patrol in the very shallow waters off North Vietnam.

While we were still on the surface, the bow compartment deck hatch was opened

Figure 11.3 *(Left to right)* Quartermaster First Class Clarence F. Williams and Commander Alfred S. McLaren sitting on chunk of ice covering *Queenfish*'s rudder following first surfacing in Arctic Ocean ice pack. (Courtesy of the U.S. Navy)

to permit Allan Beal, Dick Boyle, and Bud Pezet to go topside to collect environmental and physical oceanographic data. We then called up the crew in small groups to observe and photograph their first polynya and the spectacularly chaotic surrounding icescape. We were now in polar bear country. An armed polar bear watch was posted, and everyone was on the alert. Bets were made on who would be the first to see "Nanook of the North." Old Arctic hands such as Master Chief Electrician's Mate Mike Kotek and Chief Hospital Corpsman Andrew Gunn, who had been with me on *Seadragon* in 1960, regaled their less-experienced crew mem-

Figure 11.4 Polar bear watch while *Queenfish* surfaced in polynya in Canada Basin (*Left to right*, Commander McLaren and unidentified crew member). (Courtesy of the U.S. Navy)

bers with stories of gigantic, ravenous polar bears covering their black noses as they stalked and swiftly closed in on their prey: how far they could smell, from what distance they could pounce during the final stages of an attack, and how fast they could run and swim. "Remember," Kotek warned, "you won't be able to see them until they open their mouths!" This last comment caused several of the crew to take a hurried look and escape below decks.

Satisfied with all aspects of our first excursion into an Arctic Ocean polynya, the decks and sail area were quickly cleared. All deck hatches were shut and secured, the SPM was retracted and rehoused, and *Queenfish* was restored to a full rig-for-dive condition. Bob Baumhardt initiated a stationary dive beneath the surface by ordering Grant Youngman, who was acting as diving officer of the watch, to "open main ballast tank vents aft!" Grant in turn ordered the chief of the watch, Kenneth Ickes, to "open the after vents!"

Figure 11.5 *(Left to right)* Engineer Officer Ralph E. Beedle and Commander Alfred S. McLaren on ice pack in Arctic Ocean. (Courtesy of the U.S. Navy)

Confirming through No. 2 periscope that the after group of main ballast tanks was venting and that *Queenfish*'s stern was sinking well clear of the ice, Baumhardt then ordered the forward main ballast tank vents opened. As soon as they were reported open, Youngman ordered the chief of the watch to flood variable ballast tanks with approximately three thousand pounds of water from the sea, and we descended very smoothly beneath the surface.

At 150 feet I ordered maneuvering, "Engage the main propulsion clutch! Answer all bells on main engines!" The engineering officer of the watch, Fred Moore, immediately responded, "Main propulsion clutch engaged, answering stop!" Having confirmed from a series of depth soundings that we had plenty of water beneath us, I ordered, "Ahead two-thirds [ten knots], make your depth three-nine-zero feet!" Once Youngman acknowledged the order and *Queenfish* was well clear of ice overhead and on her way to deeper depth, I turned over the conn to Bob Baumhardt, who was instructed to proceed on the navigator's recommended new course of 083° and to increase speed to "full" (now slightly less than twenty knots, due to some hull fouling, or vegetation, picked up in Seattle).

After transiting some 120 miles, we reached the Barrow Sea valley used by *Nautilus* to enter the Arctic Basin in early August of 1958 and entered the Beaufort Sea. *Nautilus*'s 1958 point of departure was achieved shortly thereafter, at latitude 74°-23' N, longitude 155° W, during the early afternoon of 2 August 1970. *Queenfish* then changed course to 000° or "due north" and commenced retracing *Nautilus*'s route as closely as possible as we measured and recorded the under-ice topography overhead with our 205 kHz upward-beamed acoustic profiler, or top sounder. A depth of 390 feet had been chosen to ensure that *Queenfish* would pass safely beneath even the deepest-draft pack ice or errant iceberg in the Arctic Ocean on her way to the North Pole, some 937 miles distant.[5]

Water depths steadily increased during the next several hours as we left the steep continental slope and entered the portion of the Canada Basin called the Abyssal Plain, where water depths exceeded ten thousand feet.[6] We located and made a vertical ascent into a second, very large polynya without incident shortly after the evening meal that day.

Critical to the overall success of our mission during this surfacing was to perfect our technique for ascending into and descending from polynyas and leads so that important appendages such as the propeller, rudder, diving planes, antenna, masts, and periscope stayed clear of the ice. In order to minimize further our detectability to others, we also endeavored to accomplish all vertical ascents and stationary dives in thirty minutes or less. Although I was sorely tempted to test *Queenfish*'s capability for breaking through thick ice, as *Whale* and *Pargo* had done through as much as three feet of ice the previous year, we dared not unduly hazard any part of the boat this early in the mission.[7]

In the event of poor underwater visibility, drifting sea-ice overhead, subsurface currents, or significant changes in water salinity or temperature, we would, of course, take whatever time was necessary to accomplish each evolution in the safest manner possible. We had to arrive at the Laptev Sea and the beginning of our Siberian shelf survey in perfect condition and readiness for what was certain to be a demanding and dangerous under-ice environment.

Our position by satellite having been determined to be latitude 75°-39' N, longitude 155°-05' W, *Queenfish* made a stationary dive and resumed the transit north. Once at ordered depth it became mandatory, considering we were operating in seldom- or never-visited waters, to maintain depth, course, speed, and zero bubble using minimum diving-plane and rudder movement and main-turbine throttle control.[8] This was necessary for making accurate recordings of both ice drafts overhead and water depths and of other basic physical oceanography information such as temperature, salinity, and dissolved oxygen. No other scientific data platform was capable, in 1970, of obtaining the high-quality scientific data that *Queen-fish* would be collecting during this unique voyage of exploration—data that we knew would be of interest and potential use to U.S. military and scientific communities.

As we proceeded deeper beneath a vast and increasingly compact Arctic Ocean ice pack, the main event each day became the location of open water of sufficient size in which to surface and accurately fix our navigational position. We continued the process of carefully measuring and recording the physical environment on, above, and under the surface that had been initiated on entering the Chukchi Sea.

Shortly after midnight, early on 3 August, *Queenfish* achieved a position one hundred miles ahead of our PIM. As we traversed the eastern portion of the East Wind Ridge between latitudes 76°-30' and 79°-45' N, the depths beneath our keel continued to be greater than three hundred feet, although we were alert to the possibility of suddenly encountering an uncharted seamount or shoal area.

We were now well ahead of our planned track. There was time enough to give each of the three watch sections, or ship control teams, an opportunity to make their first vertical ascent into open water, followed by a stationary dive. Beginning with the morning watch, the command watch officers assigned to each section were told that they would be fully in charge of the vertical ascent and stationary dive conducted by their section. The most experienced, Ralph Beedle, had the additional task of examining Lieutenant William Enderlein for final qualification as diving officer of the watch.

Chief of the Boat Kenneth Ickes, Senior Watch Officer/Navigator Toby Warson, Allan Beal, Dick Boyle, and I observed and evaluated each team's performance to see which team-member changes were necessary to strengthen a section or position and determine what additional training was indicated before *Queenfish* reached the Siberian continental shelf.

We were now in the Canada Basin between latitudes 72° and 82° N.[9] The ice conditions in which to test and evaluate each watch section could not have been better. We did not realize it at the time, but *Queenfish* was in the greatest amount of open water, the thinnest ice, and the fewest number of thick-ice ridges that she would ever encounter during the rest of the trip.

As the day progressed, each watch section demonstrated its prowess. Two of the three sections located suitably large polynyas along our track north and made almost textbook-perfect vertical ascents followed by equally excellent stationary dives. Lieutenant Enderlein qualified as diving officer on the first vertical ascent and stationary dive to be conducted and proudly took his place on the watch bill.

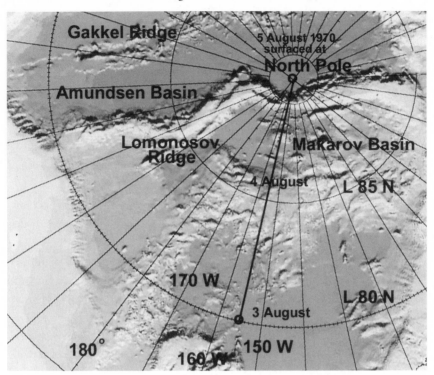

Chartlet 11.2 Latitude 80° north to North Pole, 3 August to 5 August 1970.

During the early afternoon following a second surfacing, we took photographs of the surrounding ice pack under nearly ideal lighting conditions: a pale blue sky with wisps of feathery cirrus clouds, dark blue water within the polynya, and myriad shades of white throughout the vast ice pack. It was an enchanted landscape, with sparkling ice crystals scattered throughout. It certainly brought home the truth of what the famous Arctic explorer Vilhjalmur Stefansson had intimated when he joined Captain Steele and a group of *Seadragon*'s officers for lunch in 1960 about the compelling nature of the Arctic's beautiful colors and their effect on an explorer. His remarks roughly translate to "Once you have seen them, you are never satisfied or really happy until you have seen them again." With great reluctance we departed the surface and continued north.[10]

The third watch section's attempt to conduct a vertical ascent during the late afternoon was not a great success. The top of the sail struck ice, which had not been detected directly above us, causing *Queenfish* to lose both bubble and depth control for several minutes as the boat bounced off a quite massive ice keel and momentarily headed downward at a steep angle.

The unexpected ice collision and the slowness of the subsequent recovery action were largely a problem of command and coordination created, in large part, by the least proficient of our command watch officers. I discussed with him at some length later that day what went wrong and decided to give him one last chance before reordering the watch bill. It was clear to me, however, from the facial expressions and body language of my fellow "observers" and several senior petty officers "who just happened to be in the control room" that they had already cast their vote. The day's events provoked lively discussion during the evening meal in the crew's mess and, as would be expected, some pretty rough ribbing of members of the third watch section.

August 4 was spent almost entirely in carefully retracing *Nautilus's* 1958 track. From approximately latitude 80° N on, the ice overhead became progressively thicker and more compact, with fewer surfaceable polynyas and leads.

In the early afternoon, about an hour after a superb lunch that featured thick rare steaks specially prepared by Commissaryman Second Class Artemio Gapasin, all seemed sufficiently calm for me to take a catnap. I was soon to be rudely awakened from a deep sleep, however, by Dick Boyle and Senior Chief Sonar Technician James Petersen, who requested that I come to the control room immediately. As I hurried to it I learned that although *Queenfish* was transiting at a supposedly safe depth of almost four hundred feet, clear, bell-like echoes had been detected for some time from something massive that was dead ahead of us. Whatever it was, it was now presenting a very bright return on the IBD presentation, not more than five hundred yards from us. Could it be an iceberg? Impossible! Had I not recently been assured by experts in Washington, D.C., that "there are no icebergs in the Arctic Ocean"? Was I not told on several occasions that the only report of such was by a Soviet aviator in the late 1930s, who claimed he saw "hundreds of icebergs" at latitude 78° N, south of Franz Josef Land?[11]

As soon as I arrived in the control room, the command watch officer, the one whose vertical ascent had struck ice the previous day, informed me that although bearing to the "target" had been steady for some time, he had not slowed or altered course because he was certain that the bell-like tone was an "acoustic anomaly" and that we would pass well below "whatever" appeared to be in our path.

One look at the sonar presentation reminded me instantly of a similar incident back in 1967, when we were first testing *Queenfish's* under-ice sonar suite en route to the Davis Strait, and we passed just seventeen feet beneath a large iceberg.

I immediately took the conn and ordered, "Emergency deep! Emergency deep!"

The officer of the deck, Steve Gray, ordered, "Full dive both planes!" and "Ahead full!" Both planesmen shoved their control columns fully forward, and *Queenfish* rapidly descended below four hundred feet at a healthy down-angle. In less than a minute what was most certainly a gigantic iceberg passed overhead. Our hearts almost stopped when Dick Boyle and Senior Chief Sonar Technician James Petersen simultaneously yelled, "Thirteen feet! We had just cleared one portion of it by only thirteen feet!" We hated to think what could have happened if another portion or spur of it had penetrated even deeper.[12]

As the iceberg receded astern, I ordered in sequence, "Zero bubble!" "Ahead one-third!" "Right fifteen degrees rudder!" and "Sonar, check baffles to starboard!" As we slowed and changed course to starboard, Sonar Technician Paul Speaker, listening on our AN/BQS-6B passive sonar, reported, "Loud fizzing noises emerging from the starboard baffles!" Those fizzing or "seltzer" noises, which originate from the release of entrapped air bubbles from a melting iceberg, were first noted during *Seadragon's* investigation of the underside of icebergs in 1960.[13] I remembered, as a diving officer of the watch during that voyage, that the "fizzing" could be heard as far as seventy miles away. It was strange that our passive sonars had not detected them sooner. Was this due to speed, depth, or possibly operator inattention? The seltzerlike noise increased as we decreased depth and changed course to pass the iceberg, at approximately latitude 85° N, longitude 155° W, off our starboard side.

Thinking that it would be worthwhile to take a few minutes to confirm visually and photograph the very large iceberg we had just underrun, we looked for, soon found, and executed on a relatively narrow lead that appeared of sufficient length to accommodate us. It was a tight fit, but with Youngman on the dive and Baumhardt as officer of the deck, we made a rapid and successful vertical ascent to the surface in spite of the fact that the ice overhead was moving in a westerly direction.

Unfortunately, a quick periscope search did not reveal the errant iceberg, because we had surfaced in a blustery snowstorm that reduced visibility to less than one hundred yards. I decided, therefore, to remain surfaced only long enough to copy our radio broadcast and get a navigational fix without sending anyone to the bridge or on deck.

As we lay to on the surface, Bob Baumhardt, on No. 2 periscope, called my attention to what appeared to be an exceedingly large flat ice floe fairly close aboard to the west, possibly thirty feet higher than the surrounding ice pack and several times longer than *Queenfish.* I had never seen anything quite like it. As Chief Charles Wright photographed it, Allan Beal and Dick Boyle were called to take a look. Both pronounced it an ice island. This, too, was not expected in our present location, considering how far we were from the Ward Hunt Ice Shelf on Ellesmere Island in the northeastern Canadian Arctic islands from which it must have

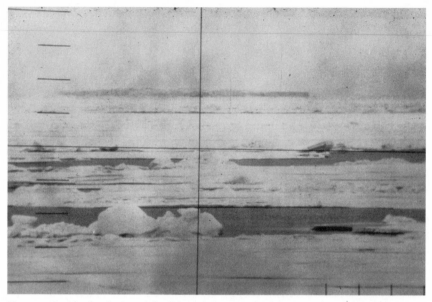

Figure 11.6 Ice island on horizon sighted through periscope from open water lead in which *Queenfish* just surfaced en route to the North Pole. (Courtesy of the U.S. Navy)

originated. August 4 had turned out to be a quite unprecedented, excitement-filled day.

A few among the crew began to wonder what else might be discovered or, more properly, stumbled on. The betting money was on an uncharted island or even part of a previously undiscovered submerged continent—not beyond the range of possibility considering how little of the Arctic Ocean had been explored up to 1970. Either was about the last thing that any Arctic submarine crew would want to encounter while running at full speed submerged.

A stationary dive took us beneath the ice once again, and we resumed the careful retracing of *Nautilus*'s 1958 track. On the basis of his latest fix, Toby Warson reported that we should reach the North Pole by late afternoon of the next day. With respect to daylight, of course, time of day becomes irrelevant in high Arctic latitudes during the summer months. The sun is always above the horizon at this time of year and circles through 360 degrees every twenty-four hours.

My most immediate problem at this stage of *Queenfish*'s voyage was what to do with the command watch officer who had had two really bad days and in whom I no longer had confidence. I met with him in my stateroom, and we both agreed that, in view of what would be demanded of a command watch officer during the next several weeks, particularly over the Siberian shelf, he was not sufficiently pre-

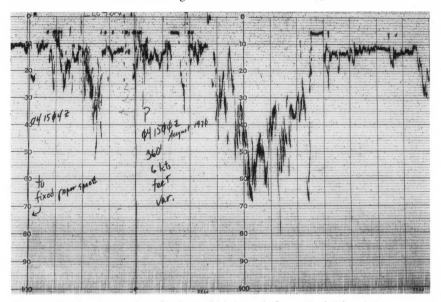

Figure 11.7 Top sounder recording of under-ice thickness or draft near North Pole, 4 August 1970. (Courtesy of the U.S. Navy)

pared to continue in that position. This was not so much his personal fault as it was the less-than-optimum detailing by the Navy Bureau of Personnel and the officer's lack of any prior nuclear attack submarine experience. I was as disappointed as he was, but the problems that ensued had now put into question the safety of boat and crew.

We passed latitude 85° N shortly after dinner that evening. We were now less than three hundred miles from the North Pole. Toby Warson and Dick Boyle mentioned at that time that the depth soundings recorded by the precision depth recorder since *Nautilus*'s track had been picked up in the Beaufort Sea did not always correspond closely with the soundings taken by her in 1958. The reason for this may have been that either she or we were slightly off the 155° W meridian to one side or the other. In any case, there was no basic disagreement with *Nautilus,* particularly with respect to just where the shallow water areas were in the Chukchi Sea.

We greeted the morning of 5 August with high anticipation. The previous night, Santa Claus had magically slipped aboard *Queenfish* and made a brief appearance, letting it be known that he was anxious to return home. He charged us with replacing his "missing" candy-striped pole that marked the exact location of the North Pole.[14]

Our first task was to locate the geographic North Pole precisely and then pass directly beneath or above it and surface as close to it as possible. To the best of my knowledge, only four of us had ever been to the North Pole: Dick Boyle, as a young officer on *Skate* and later as a civilian scientist on *Seadragon* and *Whale;* Chief Hospital Corpsman Andrew Gunn; Senior Chief Electricians Mate Mike Kotek; and me. All of us had been there together on *Seadragon* in 1960.

We were to experience some additional moments of excitement before we achieved the pole. After quietly transiting through waters whose depths had exceeded five thousand feet for the past three days, with a significant portion being more than ten thousand feet, no one in the control room, with the possible exception of Dick Boyle, was prepared for an extremely steep-sided Lomonosov Ridge during the early afternoon beginning at latitude 88°-50' N. The seabed rose so rapidly toward us that I instinctively ordered "all stop," changed course with full rudder to starboard and away, and directed the diving officer to bring us up to two hundred feet smartly. The peak or shallowest depths above the relatively flat and narrow ridge passed less than fourteen hundred feet beneath our keel within minutes and continued this way for the next forty minutes or so.

Recovering our composure, we returned to our original course, speed, and depth toward the North Pole. *Queenfish* was in deeper water within the hour, this time within the Amundsen Basin, where water depths exceeded thirteen thousand feet. A number of officers and senior petty officers wandered up to the control room to see what had caused the excitement. We all shared a good laugh at the realization that we were still quite "goosey" from our recent harrowing experiences with very shallow depths in the Chukchi Sea. With the North Pole now little more than thirty miles away, we resumed preparations to pass directly over it and then to find a nearby polynya in which to surface.

A little more than three hours later, at 5:11 p.m. on 5 August 1970, *Queenfish* became the seventh nuclear submarine, out of a total of ten U.S. Arctic submarine voyages up to that time, to reach the geographic North Pole. We obtained a sounding of 13,560 feet as our best estimate of the depth at the pole, essentially identical to that previously obtained by *Nautilus, Skate, Sargo, Seadragon, Whale,* and *Pargo.* Some of us said a silent and humble prayer for earlier explorers who had lost their lives during their arduous attempts to achieve what we had just accomplished so easily. Foremost in my mind at this time was Lieutenant George Washington DeLong, leader and commander of the ill-fated *Jeannette* North Pole expedition of 1879–81.[15]

We located a small polynya, and *Queenfish* maneuvered into a hovering position directly beneath its center. With Tom Hoepfner, the ship's diving officer on the dive, we conducted a flawless vertical surfacing at 5:32 p.m. into a largely ice-free expanse of open water beneath an exquisitely blue sky like the one we had on 3 August. Toby Warson and his navigation team soon reported that fixes from both satellite and Omega confirmed *Queenfish* to be within 550 yards of the geographic North Pole.

The day remained beautifully clear and sunny, with lighting conditions ideal for recording the historic event. Little did we know that we would experience only one more such day during the entire voyage. That we were ultimately to be graced with only three clear, sunny days in the more than thirty spent in the Arctic Ocean caused me later to wonder how either Frederick Cook or Robert Peary, using just a handheld sextant and manual dead reckoning while traversing a constantly moving polar ice pack, could possibly have claimed with any certainty that they had reached the exact North Pole in 1908 and 1909, respectively.[16]

Santa Claus (Chief Quartermaster Jack Patterson) disembarked with great ceremony, in company with the crew member selected to be the first to set foot on ice at the pole, Storekeeper Seaman James Kennedy. Toby Warson joined Santa Claus, and together they planted a most impressive red-and-white striped pole as close as possible to the exact North Pole. Chief Radioman Michael Hein sent a check report announcing our arrival to our boss, Rear Admiral Walter Small, Commander Submarine Forces Pacific, in Pearl Harbor.

A flagpole was raised nearby, and the Stars and Stripes of the United States of America was broken for all to see and honor. Newly qualified submariners Electronics Technician James Harrick, Sonar Technician Paul Speaker, Radioman Michael Keck, and Yeoman Lawrence Invie were awarded their hard-earned silver "Dolphins," fully initiating them as members of a select and close-knit brotherhood that began in the early days of our country with the Revolutionary War submarine Bushnell *Turtle* and the Civil War submarines *Hunley* and *Alligator*. This ceremony was followed by a raucous and impromptu snow fight—or rather snow bombardment—of the new Dolphin wearers.

The next event was photographing each crew member with his state flag at the North Pole. The combination of fifty state flags, 117 men and officers to be photographed, and a limited quantity of acceptable-looking foul-weather jackets and sexy white "submarine sweaters" turned this event from an allocated one hour into a more than six-hour operation. It was much like suiting up young children to go outdoors to play in the snow and then bringing them back into the house a short time later to undress them and then doing the same with yet one more group of children. Compounding it was an exhaustive and ultimately fruitless search for the

Figure 11.8 Commander Alfred S. McLaren, commanding officer of USS *Queenfish,* on bridge while surfaced in Arctic ice pack. (Courtesy of the U.S. Navy)

Mississippi state flag. Although we had our suspicions, we were never able to determine just who had purloined it. I took the occasion to have the chief of the boat, Kenneth Ickes, make sure that Radio Seaman Steven Apple, who always managed to wear his hair longer than navy regulations allowed, received a special haircut before his picture was taken with his state flag.

Each of the flags was subsequently presented to the appropriate state governor "on behalf of the U.S. Navy and its Submarine Force." Lieutenant Tom Hoepfner was later to have the honor of presenting the Georgia state flag to the then governor and later president, Jimmy Carter.

Figure 11.9 Commander Alfred S. McLaren and Santa Claus (Jack B. Patterson) at North Pole, 5 August 1970. (Courtesy of the U.S. Navy)

In the meantime an open galley of steak and eggs fried to order plus freshly baked bread and a magnificent North Pole cake prepared by the leading commissaryman, Michael Knaub, and his assistant cooks, William Dunford and Allan Peña, kept us well fortified throughout the day.

We put a team of scuba divers led by the senior diver, Toby Warson, into the 29.5° F water to photograph the underside of the ice at the North Pole. The excellent series of pictures they took illustrated very well how the high winds that char-

Figure 11.10 USS *Queenfish* surfaced at North Pole on 5 August 1970. (Courtesy of the U.S. Navy)

Figure 11.11 USS *Queenfish* surfaced at North Pole on 5 August with hull number 651 pasted on sail. (Courtesy of the U.S. Navy)

Figure 11.12 Commander Alfred S. McLaren, commanding officer, USS *Queenfish,* holding Hawaiian state flag at the North Pole. (Courtesy of the U.S. Navy)

acterize the entire Arctic Basin and myriad water currents of various strengths cause ice floes of varying sizes and thicknesses to raft one on top of another to create "deformed ice" with thicknesses of up to 165 feet.[17]

Later analysis of the ice pack within eight miles of the North Pole revealed the mean ice thickness over the pole to be 13 feet, with more than 30 percent of it being deformed ice of greater than 13 feet in thickness and another 62 percent between 6.5 and 13 feet. The thickest ice approached fifty-eight feet. It should be noted that open water has consistently been reported in the vicinity of the North Pole ever since *Nautilus* first achieved it in 1958, and 1970 was no exception. Indeed, *Queenfish* sighted at least three large open-water areas near the pole.[18]

Queenfish was ready to return beneath the sea shortly before midnight on 5 August. Removed were the special paper "651" hull numbers and the Battle Efficiency "E" with two hashmarks placed on each side of the sail that had been tacked on for the photography session. Our remaining hours on the surface were spent thoroughly examining every inch of our topside areas, both main deck and sail, to make sure nothing would rattle, break open, or break loose during the lengthy period we would remain completely submerged. Particular attention was paid to

Figure 11.13 Lieutenant Commander Toby G. Warson, scuba team chief, on completion of dive under ice at North Pole on 5 August 1970. (Courtesy of the U.S. Navy)

hatches to mooring-line lockers on the forward and after decks. Each hatch was secured as tightly as possible by inserting rubber between mating surfaces or tack welding. The worst thing that could happen would be for a mooring line to stream out of an after-deck locker and get entangled in our propeller, the stern planes, or deep-draft ice overhead.

Contemplation of this grim possibility persuaded us to move all our mooring lines below decks into an already-crowded submarine interior. Sonar Officer Bob Baumhardt and Chief Sonar Technician James Petersen, with help from the auxiliary division, did their usual thorough job of securing everything for sustained "silent running" under ice.

Once all was confirmed secured and all hatches were shut and dogged, all personnel went below decks, and *Queenfish* was rigged for dive. I granted our newest

Figure 11.14 Underside of Arctic ice pack at the North Pole on 5 August 1970. (Courtesy of the U.S. Navy)

Figure 11.15 USS *Queenfish* on the surface at the North Pole just prior to departing for Nansen Cordillera and Siberian shelf. (Courtesy of the U.S. Navy)

command watch officer, Bob Baumhardt, permission to make a stationary dive. There was a caveat, however. In preparation for the shallow waters of the Siberian shelf, he was directed to simulate a water depth beneath the polynya of no more than 180 feet. Steve Gray was on the dive, and the evolution was conducted flawlessly as he flooded water into the variable ballast tanks and began a downward descent, then pumped water out to regain neutral buoyancy overall. Baumhardt ordered maneuvering to raise and house the SPM and reengage the main propulsion as we descended through a keel depth of ninety feet. Main propulsion was briefly tested ahead and astern by the time we passed 120 feet. Baumhardt ordered, "Ahead two-thirds!" just before reaching 150 feet. Once we were leveled off and were steady at 150 feet, he ordered, "Ahead one-third, Maneuvering, make turns for five knots!" More than satisfied, I told him to ask the navigator for his recommended course, speed, and depth to now retrace *Nautilus*'s 1958 track south along longitude 25° E to latitude 86° N.

We all felt some pangs of regret and a strange emptiness as each of us on 6 August said a private good-bye to the North Pole. It was a high point of the entire voyage and certainly a peak experience in all our lives.

Exploring the Nansen Cordillera
for Volcanic Activity

After our highly satisfying visit to the North Pole, we submerged early on 6 August to 390 feet and resumed retracing *Nautilus*'s 1958 route south along longitude 25° E, which farther south passes through Nordaustlandet in the Svalbard Archipelago, beginning just above latitude 80° N. To our complete surprise, in less than an hour we were forced to maneuver to avoid an extremely deep-draft ice keel. It was in all probability an iceberg, located at latitude 89°-46′ N, another instance of where none should have been found. Allan Beal and Dick Boyle fully concurred with *Queenfish*'s latest watchword for this expedition: "Expect anything and assume nothing!"

We had originally intended to follow *Nautilus*'s route as far south as 83° N. We were also tasked, however, with checking for possible seismic activity along the Nansen Cordillera (today called the Gakkel Ridge, as mentioned earlier). The cordillera is a submerged range of mountains and V-shaped rifts separating the Nansen and Amundsen basins on the Eurasian side of the Arctic Ocean; it was then suspected to be tectonically active. The ridge is itself the northernmost extension of the huge Mid-Atlantic Ridge, running roughly from south to north in the central Atlantic and now known to be an area of considerable volcanic activity.[1]

About 130 miles wide, the ridge runs some eleven hundred miles from north of Greenland into the Arctic Ocean north of Svalbard and across the ocean bottom until it disappears into the continental shelf of the Laptev Sea. At its high point it stands about forty-nine hundred feet above the surrounding seafloor; at its low it is approximately eighteen thousand feet below the floor, which makes it the deepest

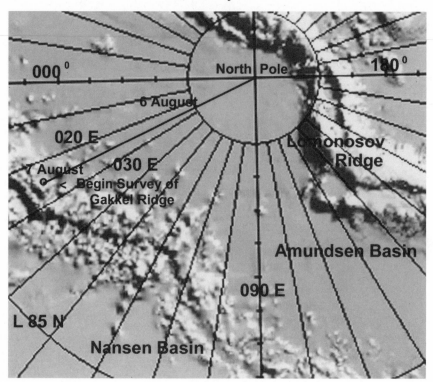

Chartlet 12.1 North Pole to Nansen Cordillera (Gakkel Ridge), 6 and 7 August 1970.

rift of the entire Arctic Basin.[2] Within the cordillera lies a narrow band of earthquake epicenters. The Nansen Cordillera was and continues to be of great interest to the scientific community.

Because we expected to reach the cordillera beginning at latitude 87° N, Allan Beal and Dick Boyle both agreed that we should begin to survey it at that point. We would, at the same time, continue retracing *Nautilus's* route until we reached its southernmost boundary and then change course to the northeast to begin the second leg of the survey.

When Dick and I briefed the crew early that evening on what was planned in the vicinity of the cordillera the next day, the more imaginative men expressed some concern that *Queenfish* might be passing directly over "underwater volcanoes" that could erupt at any time. Although there was an element of truth in this, their worries provoked some hilarity among our older, more seasoned sailors.

At latitude 87°-11' N during the late morning of 7 August, and again on reaching approximately 87° N, where we began our hydrographic and acoustic survey of the

Nansen Cordillera, *Queenfish* passed under a lengthy series of ice keels thrusting downward as much as 110 feet beneath the sea surface. We soon concluded that the massive ice floes we were underrunning might well be ice islands that could be as much as twenty-one miles long and twelve miles wide. If so, we wondered whether any were among the four drifting polar research stations manned by Soviet scientists in the Arctic Basin. Recently established on ice islands Severnyy Polyus, SP-19 (North Pole 19) and SP-20 (North Pole 20), these stations were collecting and frequently transmitted meteorological, aerological, and hydrological information in support of Soviet northern-area weather forecasting.[3]

We continued across the cordillera to latitude 84°-08′ N, longitude 25°-39′ E, at which point we officially terminated the retracing of *Nautilus*'s 1958 track and changed *Queenfish*'s course as planned.[4] We spent the remainder of the day conducting an alternating series of northeasterly and southeasterly hydrographic and acoustic survey passes across the axis of the Nansen Cordillera.

Our subsequent analysis of the bottom topography confirmed the presence of a deep rift valley with sufficient acoustic activity within the seismic frequency range as to suggest that it might be volcanically active. Several things are now known about the Gakkel Ridge: first, it not only is volcanically active but in all probability contains multiple hydrothermal vents, although this has not been verified visually; and second, it is the deepest, most remote, and slowest-spreading (up to 0.39 inches per year) portion of a global mid-ocean ridge system that is more than thirty thousand miles in length.[5]

We departed the Nansen Cordillera during the early evening of 7 August and set course for the northwestern corner of the Laptev Sea, beginning preparations for the hydrographic survey across the entire Siberian continental shelf. We would start with the Severnaya Zemlya (in English, "Northland") Archipelago, which defines the western boundary of the best-charted of the three seas, the Laptev.

To our knowledge no ship, icebreaker, or submarine, with the possible exception of a Soviet nuclear submarine, had ever traversed the Laptev, East Siberian, or northwestern Chukchi seas along the particular depth contour that *Queenfish* was tasked with tracing and recording. The ice-covered waters around the archipelago and throughout the Laptev Sea itself had never been surveyed to any extent as far as we knew, and the latest navigational charts we had on board provided only rough estimates of water depths.

We thus had no idea just what to expect in the way of undersea navigational hazards or from the sea-ice cover. It was truly a vast unknown. Where would shoal and shallow areas be found? Would we stumble on any previously undiscovered islands? Would the bottom topography be flat and relatively predictable like the eastern Chukchi Sea, or would it be irregular and unpredictable? Where would we encounter the maximum concentrations of ice? How thick would they be? Would the western Laptev contain icebergs from the glaciers of Severnaya Zemlya? Might there also be icebergs from Franz Josef Land as well? How large and how many would they be? Would we suddenly come on hazardous underwater pingos projecting upward from a shallow ocean bottom, many of which probably overlie thick permafrost?[6]

Finally, weighing heavily on our minds was the memory of our exciting experiences with the Arctic ice pack in the Chukchi Sea the previous week, when *Queenfish* was first confronted with the harsh realities and many dangers of operating in shallow water under a heavy mantle of sea ice.

13

The Northeast Passage and the Development of the Northern Sea Route

Essential for any student of the Siberian continental shelf region is to have a basic understanding of the often tragic history that attaches to this part of the world, which has only grown in geopolitical and economic significance over time. It is therefore worth devoting a few pages to review the most salient events that made this so, because all were to influence the preparations for, the parameters of, and the actual conduct of our expedition.

Being well above the Arctic Circle, with its severe climatic conditions and perennially thick pack ice, this unrelentingly cold and forbidding environment has sounded the death knell of an untold number of explorers throughout the centuries, from Viking times to the present. From the sixteenth century on, it attracted Western explorers and mariners searching for the fabled "passage to Cathay" and the riches of the Orient—what came to be called the Northeast Passage.[1] In the twentieth century, the region was of vital strategic and economic importance to Soviet Russia, centering on the opening up and maintenance of the Northern Sea Route. The entire area remains a high priority for the post–cold war Russian republic, a concern that has undoubtedly been further stimulated by the unrelenting progress of global warming in the Arctic regions.

The Northeast Passage and the Northern Sea Route are often confused with one another but are actually distinctive parts of the same geographic area. The Northeast Passage extends from the Greenland Sea through the Barents, Kara, Laptev, East Siberian, and Chukchi seas.[2] The NSR overlaps a major portion of the Northeast Passage, exclusive of the Greenland and Barents seas, and was the entry point for all Western explorers in their search for the Northeast Passage. *Queenfish's* hydrographic survey concentrated on only the least accessible and hence previously uncharted portions of the three Siberian shelf seas that are encompassed within both the Northeast Passage and the NSR but are to the north and farther offshore from the NSR.

The Kara, Laptev, East Siberian, and Chukchi seas of the NSR are linked by some fifty-eight straits that pass through three archipelagos: the Novaya Zemlya, Severnaya Zemlya, and New Siberian Island groups. The NSR is, therefore, for all practical purposes, a series of shipping lanes from west to east. It stretches from the Kara Gate Strait between the Barents and Kara seas south of Novaya Zemlya to the Bering Strait between Alaska and Siberia. Its northern boundary roughly coincides with the edge of the Russian two-hundred-mile EEZ in the Arctic Ocean.[3]

Unlike other major world sea routes, therefore, no single shipping lane defines the NSR per se. The exact length of the shipping lane to be traversed on any particular day, season, or year depends on the location of shoals and the prevailing ice conditions in various locations along the route and can range from 2,205 to 2,906 miles.[4]

At the time of *Queenfish's* 1970 survey, the Soviet Union had only one nuclear icebreaker, the *Lenin,* in operation. The NSR shipping season was, as a result, several months shorter than it is presently, when as many as six Russian nuclear icebreakers are available to keep the route open for shipping and military traffic.[5]

Finally, it is important to note that the envelope of possible shipping lanes spanning the entire length of the NSR, which might have been claimed to be under USSR legal jurisdiction in 1970, was more southerly and considerably narrower than it is in the first decade of the twenty-first century.

Although other explorers may have preceded him, the first recorded voyage in these Arctic waters was that of the Norse Viking explorer Ottar, who in the ninth century rounded Norway's North Cape and, heading eastward, reached the White Sea. Another seven centuries were to pass, however, before the English began their own search for a "passage to Cathay" by way of the seas of northeastern Europe. This was in 1553–54 with Willoughby's, Chancellor's, and Durfooth's British Northeast Passage Expedition in the *Bona Esperanza, Edward Bonaventure,* and *Bona Confidentia.*[6]

This first English expedition was followed by a long succession of English and Dutch exploration and trading expeditions that continued to search for a sea route via Arctic waters to the Orient. Led by such noted explorers as Pet and Jackman, Brunel, Barents, Nai, Ysbrantszoon, and Hudson, these expeditions were all unsuccessful and frequently ended in tragedy. Beginning at roughly the same time, numerous Russian hunters and seamen also began sailing the coastal waters of the Kara, Laptev, East Siberian, and Chukchi seas in search of fur sources.[7]

Greatly alarmed by an ever-increasing number of English and Dutch voyages into waters north of Russia, and fearing intrusion into Russia's future exploitation of Siberian resources, Tsar Mikhail Fedorovich in 1619 banned all foreign shipping in these waters east of the White Sea. This ban applied to Russian shipping until the first steps were taken to lift it in 1753.[8]

English and Dutch exploration along the Northeast Passage eventually ended in the late seventeenth century with de Vlamingh's Dutch Whaling and Exploring Expedition, which crossed the Kara Sea in 1664, and Wood and Flawes's failed British Northeast Passage Expedition in 1676.[9] Up to this time no voyages in search of a viable Northeast Passage were ever to reach as far as the Laptev Sea, where *Queenfish*'s survey began in 1970.

During the next two centuries, numerous Russian Cossack expeditions continued landward and to the south along what was eventually to become the Northern Sea Route. Their primary purpose was to conquer and colonize new territory, but they were also intent on finding new sources of fur. Russian hunters and merchants sought, at the same time, to establish sea routes over which to transport valuable sables, walrus, and mammoth ivory from northern Siberia to marketplaces in Russia. Tsar Petr I and later the Russian government organized at least three expeditions during this period, the first in 1720, the second in 1765, and the third in 1766, for the specific purpose of finding a northeast passage.[10]

These expeditions, plus the Russian Great Northern expeditions between 1733 and 1742 and various Russian exploring expeditions that took place during the same period, finally led to the discovery and exploration of the most southerly areas of the Laptev, East Siberian, and Chukchi seas. Discoveries that were particularly relevant to *Queenfish*'s exploration of the Laptev, East Siberian, and Chukchi seas are discussed in chapters to follow.[11]

The Swedish geologist Adolph Nordenskiöld was the first to discover, in 1878–79, a northeast passage from the Barents Sea to the Bering Sea in his steamship *Vega* via the southerly offshore waters of the Siberian coast. Nansen's voyage in the *Fram* then followed, over a three-year period beginning in 1893, and was the first to travel to the New Siberian Islands via the Barents, Kara, and southern Laptev seas, whence it made a slow, irregular drift back to the northern Barents Sea frozen fast in the ice in a failed attempt to reach the North Pole via the newly discovered Transpolar Drift Stream.[12]

Exploration continued in the twentieth century with the Russian ships *Taymir* and *Vaygach*, commanded by Boris Vilkitsky and Petr Novopashennyy, respectively, making a first east-to-west transit in 1914 and 1915 during the fifth and sixth seasons of the Russian Arctic Ocean Hydrographic Expedition. Their ultimate objective was to open up a northern sea route to regular shipping. Of equal if not higher priority, as a direct result of the bitter lessons of the Russo-Japanese War of 1904, was the development of such a route for more rapidly transporting Russian warships and armed forces to the Pacific if needed in the future.[13]

Roald Amundsen, conqueror of the South Pole and the Northwest Passage through the Canadian Archipelago, was next to try his hand at an east-to-west voyage from the Barents Sea to the Bering Sea. His ship *Maud* was twice frozen in the ice like Nansen's *Fram*, first off Cape Chelyuskin from September 1918 to August 1919 and again, just five hundred nautical miles short of his final goal of the Bering Strait, from September 1919 to July 1920.[14]

Under Stalin, the Soviet Union formed the Committee of the Northern Sea Route (Komseveroput or KSMP) for the express purpose of developing the Northern Sea Route into a navigable route over which it would be possible to travel from Arkhangelsk in the White Sea to Vladivostok in the Soviet Far East in one season. This goal was subsequently achieved by the Soviet icebreaker *Sibiriakov*, commanded by Captain Vladimir Voronin during the summer of 1932, but not without difficulty. Heavy ice caused severe damage to the boat's propeller blades in the East Siberian Sea, and the propeller shaft snapped off in a collision with an ice floe one hundred miles north of the Bering Strait. The icebreaker managed to complete the journey through the Bering Strait on jury-rigged sail power only.[15]

Komseveroput was replaced in early 1933 by the Main Administration of the Northern Sea Route, or Glavsevmorput (GUSMP), created under the leadership of the famous scientist and explorer Otto Shmidt for the express purpose of exploring and developing the Soviet Arctic.[16] A second Soviet expedition to transit the Northern Sea Route was subsequently undertaken during July of 1933 in *Chelyuskin*, commanded by Vladimir Voronin under the overall leadership of Shmidt, with more than one hundred passengers and crew members on board. The almost total unsuitability of the ship for Arctic waters made this ill-advised voyage one of the most harrowing and monumental failures of all Soviet expeditions, yet also one of its most successful Arctic rescues.[17]

Chelyuskin succeeded in crossing the Kara and Laptev seas but was slowed by heavy ice in the East Siberian Sea. She then threaded her way through and emerged into the northwestern Chukchi Sea, only to become icebound by mid-October some one hundred miles north of the Bering Strait.[18] The pack ice initially carried her eastward, toward the strait, and *Chelyuskin* actually entered the Pacific Ocean on 4 November.

Disastrously, within a few miles of safety, a sudden reversal of the pack ice carried *Chelyuskin* back to the northwest and well out of reach of rescue by a Soviet icebreaker. *Chelyuskin* proceeded to drift around the Chukchi Sea until February 1934, when the ship's hull was suddenly punctured by the pack ice. The passengers, necessary equipment for surviving on ice, and all but one crew member were off-loaded before the *Chelyuskin* sank just two hours later in the northwestern Chukchi Sea some 155 miles from Cape Shmidt. All 104 survived a severe winter on ice. After carving a total of thirteen makeshift airfields out of a snow-blanketed ice floe, they were eventually air rescued between 5 March and 13 April 1934, following twenty-eight heroic attempts by Soviet-piloted *Antinov-4*s.[19]

The USSR's determined efforts to develop a viable NSR in spite of *Chelyuskin*'s spectacular and well-publicized failure were finally rewarded by the successful transit, during a single season, by the icebreaker *Litke* from Vladivostok to Murmansk in 1934 and by the *Vanzetti, Iskra, Anadyr,* and *Stalingrad* under icebreaker escort in 1935.

By 1936, a total of fourteen ships had successfully navigated the entire route. After an unusually severe winter and cold spell beginning in late spring of 1937 and lasting through the summer and early fall, twenty-six ships, including eight of the Soviet Union's nine icebreakers, became entrapped in ice along the NSR. Needless to say, no successful transits of the route occurred that year.[20]

Ensuing political difficulties and the effects of Stalin's great purge during 1938 led to Dalstroi, the secret police's Main Administration for Construction in the Far North, taking control of GUSMP, with its responsibilities restricted to transport along the NSR. Otto Shmidt resigned as head of GUSMP in early 1939 and was immediately replaced by an Arctic hero of equal stature, Ivan Papanin.[21]

GUSMP recovered its reputation in 1939 with ten ships making complete transits of the entire route and the new icebreaker *Stalin* accomplishing the first one-season round trip of the NSR in history. The next year, 1940, went equally smoothly and further validated Papanin's claim in late 1939 that the year was the Arctic's "first year of truly normal commercial exploitation." The pre–World War II era of the NSR ended during the summer of 1941 with the completion of a west-to-east transit in just twenty-two days by Nazi Germany's commerce raider *Komet,* commanded by Captain Robert Eyssen.[22]

Under GUSMP's supervision, forty-one convoys transited along the NSR during World War II. Of the 792 ships that made up these convoys, only 62 were lost.[23] Single-season shipping through all or portions of the NSR steadily increased in the years that followed, through the late 1940s, 1950s, and 1960s, and became almost routine for USSR merchant, scientific, and warship traffic. Icebreaker escort and assistance were frequently required, however, especially through the Kara Gates, the Vilkitsky Strait, the East Siberian Sea, and the Chukchi Sea.

The advent of the world's first nuclear icebreaker, the *Lenin,* in 1960 gave the USSR the capability not only to increase the speed of escorting ships through the NSR but also to begin lengthening the shipping season along high-priority sections of it.[24]

By 1970, GUSMP had compiled a most impressive record in establishing the NSR as an increasingly viable seaway, especially with regard to the number of successful transits of the entire route in a single season. All the aforementioned transits, however, were only accomplished during the summer and early autumn months and, it should be stressed, only through the most southerly waters of the Laptev, East Siberian, and Chukchi seas.

At the time of *Queenfish*'s 1970 expedition, the entire NSR still remained virtually impassable for surface ships during the remaining three seasons and completely so during any season in the more northerly pack-ice–covered waters of the Laptev, East Siberian, and Chukchi. *Queenfish* was shortly to demonstrate that a nuclear submarine would have the capability to navigate these more northerly waters safely and securely year-round for many years to come.

Finally, of significance in 1970 was the fact that, although right of innocent passage through Soviet territorial waters had been denied an American icebreaker in 1967, the Soviet government had never denied that its Northern Sea Route was a seaway open to other nations. In fact, the USSR had even offered to open the entire route to foreign shipping in 1967 for a fee that would include the necessary icebreaker and navigational services.[25] The government even announced that use of the NSR could save up to thirteen days' transit time for shipping between Hamburg and Yokohama.

It would seem that the Soviet Union at this time was of two minds. On the one hand, the empire wanted to open the NSR to foreign shipping for development and revenue purposes; on the other hand, it wanted to maintain very strict control on national border security. This dichotomy remains unresolved to the present day.

14
To Severnaya Zemlya and the Beginning of the Shelf Survey

Having finished our survey of the Nansen Cordillera, we set *Queenfish* on a southerly course for Komsomolets Island, northernmost in the Severnaya Zemlya Archipelago. Visibility permitting, we would make landfall on its most northerly point, Mys (Cape) Arktichesky, some five hundred miles distant. We made two more vertical ascents into large polynyas en route, one in the early evening of 7 August and one shortly after midnight on 8 August, to obtain navigation fixes and copy our scheduled radio broadcasts. The ice surrounding each polynya was noticeably rougher than that encountered within the Canada Basin earlier in our voyage.[1] The number and size of pressure ridges sighted as a consequence of strong wind-induced rafting of one ice floe over another told us much about the severity of the weather in the Eurasia portion of the Arctic Basin.

Stationary dives into simulated shallow water followed each ascent in order to give the watch sections additional practice. The ice-covered shallow water environment promised to become even more extreme than that encountered in the Chukchi Sea.

Queenfish managed to catch the top of her rudder under a heavy-ice pressure ridge at the very edge of the polynya during the first surfacing in spite of indications from the aftermost top sounder transducers, No. 6 and No. 7, that the water directly above was clear of ice. A brief stationary descent freed the rudder with no damage noted. The boat then proceeded farther into the polynya, and the surfacing continued without difficulty. It was subsequently determined that, in the initial stages of the ascent, interference from a combination of a slight up-angle and bub-

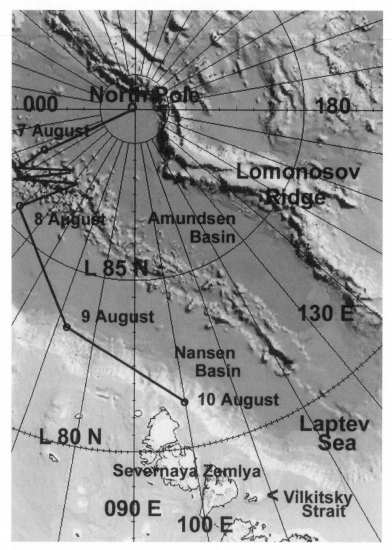

Chartlet 14.1 North Pole to Severnaya Zemlya, 7 August to 10 August 1970.

bles from the two oxygen generators (which made our internal breathing oxygen through electrolysis of sea water) caused false all-clear readings from the two transducers on the top sounder recorder. We had learned yet one more important lesson before tackling the Siberian shelf.

As incredible bad luck would have it, during the first ascent there was excessive noise in the direct current, or DC, end of the No. 2 ship's service motor generator (SSMG), one of two SSMGs (the other being No. 1 SSMG). The problem occurred when we experimented with using the electrical propulsion motor, powered directly off the DC bus, to drive the main propeller shaft at very slow speed as an alternative to using the SPM to maneuver the boat when the water depth on the Siberian shelf might be too shallow to safely lower and use the SPM. The No. 2 SSMG had to be shut down.

On inspection, the engineering department reported that the SSMG's lube oil appeared black and broken down, possibly due to overheating. The ever-resourceful Ralph Beedle went aft to the engineering spaces to evaluate the situation. He soon requested permission to flush out and replace the bad oil with new lubricant. If the bearings showed they were not damaged, this would probably solve the problem, he stated. He advised, however, that if we later determined that the bearings required replacement, *Queenfish* had a problem. In spite of our careful checks at the outset of our expedition, no spare bearings had been authorized or carried on board. Because the two SSMGs supplied power to all electrical loads on the DC bus, including keeping the Gould 132 cell emergency battery charged, the loss of one motor generator would be more than sufficient rationale for aborting the expedition.

It was a major setback, one that could threaten the overall safety of the ship in our present circumstances. The No. 2 SSMG, being on the starboard side, might be required for propulsion if *Queenfish* needed to shut down the port side of the main propulsion plant for any reason, such as serious material casualty, major repair, or emergency bottoming in shallow water under ice. Even worse, if *Queenfish* had the great misfortune to lose both SSMGs, we would lose all our navigational systems, as they, too, were powered from the DC bus, and our emergency battery would not be able to sustain us, even in severely reduced electrical load condition, for much more than two days. We would, therefore, be forced to go to periscope/snorkel depth or surface in the worst possible environment in order to run the emergency diesel engine to recharge the battery and keep it fully charged.

I was faced with an agonizing decision—one that only I, as commanding officer, could make and for which I bore full responsibility. It was either a critical "Go" or a very crushing "No go." Should we continue on to fulfill the main purpose for which we had come to the Arctic Ocean, or should we depart the Arctic Ocean as expeditiously as possible for the nearest emergency port, such as Adak in the Aleutians?

Ralph Beedle reported later that evening that a team of engineers and electricians led by Chief Machinist Mate Harry Tample had done everything possible to restore the SSMG to full operation, including replacing the lube oil. The SSMG appeared to run satisfactorily. Although a slight noise in the bearings could still be heard, Tample's engineers considered that the SSMG would be safe to use for short periods of time in the event of an emergency. Ralph concurred and so advised me. On the basis of their assessment, I made a command decision to continue on to the Laptev Sea.

Shortly after midnight on 8 August, *Queenfish* located and prepared to make a vertical ascent into a very large polynya. The water beneath this polynya was unlike any we had seen in the deep Arctic Basin—extremely murky and saturated with plankton, very small jellyfish, and numerous brown "hairy" diatoms. Visibility under water was so poor, in fact, that it was initially impossible to see the ice through the periscope and then not until we were very close to the surface. We had to make a slower and particularly well-controlled ascent of approximately ten feet per minute until we were certain that *Queenfish* was centered beneath the polynya with no ice above any part of the boat, particularly the stern area. Tom Hoepfner personally took the dive during the ascent and demonstrated how well automatic depth control performed in this situation.

But then Sonar Technician Second Class Paul Speaker, manning the AN/BQS-6B passive sonar, threw out a big wet towel when he reported that the automatic depth-control system emitted more noise than the manual system normally used, making us more detectable to potential adversaries. Speaker had a superb, if not extremely unusual, background for a sonar technician. He was a cellist with a master's degree from the Juilliard School of Music and had played with Mantovani's orchestra for five years before joining the navy. His wife had a similar musical background, and the two played for the Honolulu Symphony whenever *Queenfish* was in port. Speaker's music training and capabilities may explain why, next to Chief James Petersen, he had the best ear of all *Queenfish*'s ten sonar technicians for detecting and classifying external acoustic emissions of tactical and/or strategic interest.

The polynya in which we had just surfaced was surrounded by numerous heavy pressure ridges with icebergs in view on the horizon to the south. There was a dark gray fog, called a "water sky," along the southern horizon, a good sign of open water. Toby Warson and his navigation team obtained an excellent series of satellite and Omega fixes and determined that we were now at latitude 84°-18′ N, longitude 58°-10′ E. Toby further reported that the nearest land was Rudolph Island, which was almost 150 miles to the south of us. Rudolph Island, named after the crown prince and son of Emperor Franz Josef of the Austro-Hungarian Empire, is the most northern of 191 islands in the Franz Josef Land Archipelago.

The archipelago was accidentally discovered by SS *Tegetthoff* on 30 August 1873 when its glaciated mountainous regions suddenly emerged from the fog. *Tegetthoff,* of the Austro-Hungarian Polar Expedition led by Julius Payer and Karl Weyprecht, had become icebound some nine days earlier. The archipelago was subsequently explored during the course of three expeditions from this star-crossed ship during 1873 and 1874.[2]

Queenfish returned several hours later to the depths beneath the ice pack after receiving two important radio broadcasts. The last one provided the latest ice-line report and indicated that we would be clear of the pack during our penetration into the southern Laptev Sea. This was welcome news and confirmed a Naval Oceanographic Office's prediction in a prevoyage briefing.

Shortly before midnight, at latitude 84°-20′ N, longitude 061°-45′ E, we might have passed beneath an iceberg or ice island whose draft exceeded 120 feet, but the IBD failed to provide either an audio detection (bell-like tone) or a visual indication. Only a bright ice ring, or a band of increased brightness of circular scope, appeared at approximately twelve hundred yards, whose exact meaning was not clear to either of our under-ice sonar experts, Senior Chief Sonar Technician James Petersen or Sonar Technician First Class Frederick Miller. Could this be a new deep-draft ice phenomenon of some sort, and what might it suggest about further encounters?

We made a vertical ascent into a large polynya during the early morning of my thirty-eighth birthday, 9 August, using a slow ascent through even murkier water than we had the previous day. The ice overhead presented only indistinct shapes and shadows until the No. 2 periscope head was less than one hundred feet from the surface, which was only revealed by slight ripples in the water and somewhat greater light transmission. Quartermaster Louis Soukey reported that, en route to the polynya, we had passed beneath several long ice "skylites" of approximately three to five feet in thickness. It was reassuring to know that *Queenfish* could have surfaced within these refrozen, formerly open-water polynyas in the event of an emergency.

Our position was now latitude 84°-5.5′ N, longitude 71°-30′ E, which put us due north of the Kara Sea and the 430-mile-long Yamal Peninsula on the northwest Siberian coast far to the south of us. More water sky to the south and southwest was sighted along with one big iceberg, three small icebergs, and ten house-size bergy bits. The big iceberg was approximately five thousand yards to the southeast of us. We estimated its height at sixty-five to seventy feet, which meant that its draft beneath the sea might be as deep as three hundred feet.

Once again I could not help but chuckle with Allan Beal, Dick Boyle, and Toby Warson at the Arctic Ocean experts who had briefed us before we departed Seattle, especially those who assured us that "there are no icebergs in the deep Arctic Basin" and that "you need never fear suddenly encountering one." We were approaching that region and had already found three. In all probability they were from Franz Josef Land, although the wind-driven Transpolar Drift Stream that travels from east to west north of Siberia could have carried some that had calved from the glaciers of Severnaya Zemlya.[3]

Following an hour and a half on the surface, we used a stationary dive into a simulated shallow-water depth of 180 feet to return beneath the ice pack. Both Grant Youngman and Tom Hoepfner had experimented with flooding in only a slight amount of seawater to gain negative buoyancy, versus the standard three thousand pounds used earlier in the voyage. The result was better depth control and bubble during the descent and more time to execute the remaining steps of the procedure. The shallow-water stationary dive procedure called for rigging in the SPM as soon as a downward movement was achieved, engaging the main propulsion clutch at ninety feet, and then increasing speed on the main engines sufficiently to enable the diving planesmen to reach and level *Queenfish* off at a depth of 150 feet and maintain depth, and zero bubble, just 30 feet above the seabed.

All engineering officers of the watch and maneuvering room watch standers were reminded that all ordered "bells," or speeds, were to be answered smartly and without regard to cavitation during all future polynya surfacing and dive operations. The procedure concluded with a reduction in speed through the water to seven knots or less depending on bottom and ice conditions.

Satisfied with this last dive, I ordered the boat rigged for deep submergence and directed the command watch officer, Toby Warson, to increase speed to nineteen knots and proceed to a keel depth of 480 feet to better avoid the icebergs we were certain to encounter in increasing numbers as we approached northern Severnaya Zemlya. We were soon to pass yet one more very large iceberg to starboard that emitted very loud, distinct, bell-like echoes. The BQS-6B passive sonar operator on watch, Charles Clifton, also reported strong "fizzing noises" from the iceberg when the active echo-ranging IBD was secured momentarily.

As we proceeded to deeper depth, seawater temperature was noted to remain essentially the same, or isothermal, from the surface to a depth of four hundred feet. Beginning about four hundred feet, however, one of the sonar watch standers reported a drop in seawater temperature, from 34° F to 31° F. I decided to continue on to a depth of seven hundred feet in order to record the sound velocity profile more fully in this area. The change in temperature coincided with a significant increase in sound velocity, from 4,735 feet per second to almost 4,900 feet per second. This was in all probability due to increased salinity resulting in an increase in overall water density. Because we were still in the Nansen Basin, where water depths approached ten thousand feet, it would have been extremely interesting to have had an expendable device launched from the torpedo-tube-like "garbage gun" in the crew's mess to measure water salinity and temperature to deep depth.

Speaking of the garbage gun, from which the cooks ordinarily discharged garbage and trash in weighted unmarked burlap bags every few days, *Queenfish* ceased to use it and "red tagged" it beginning this day, 9 August.[4] Henceforth we would keep all garbage on board, stowed and frozen in large empty coffee cans in vacant areas of our two freeze boxes or, in the case of nonorganic trash, wherever we could safely stow it, until we had completed the entire hydrographic survey and were safely out of the Arctic Basin. We could not afford to have anything hang up on the outer door that would prevent it from being completely shut and thereby risk *Queenfish's* watertight integrity. Fortunately, the commissary officer and our cooks had observed the crew's eating habits and calculated just the right amount of food needed for each meal, so there was very little garbage to dispose of. In addition, before we left port in both Pearl Harbor and Seattle, we had taken great care to offload all nonprotective outer packaging and cardboard boxes.

Ice thickness overhead steadily decreased throughout the day, with fewer deep-draft keels and more areas of open water. We executed on a polynya more than five hundred yards long early in the evening and conducted a stationary ascent through the murky water to periscope depth. Although the skies were overcast, the air was unusually transparent, providing excellent visibility. We found ourselves surrounded by a vast expanse of thin, rotting ice, sharply defined in beautiful tones of white, gray, and blue. For ninety minutes we hovered at periscope depth to copy our scheduled radio broadcast and obtain a series of navigational fixes. Our position was now latitude 81°-05' N, longitude 98°-36' E. The nearest land was Komsomolets Island, in the Severnaya Zemlya Archipelago, just forty-five miles to the southwest. To avoid drawing unwanted attention to ourselves, we hovered beneath the surface with just the periscope showing above water. This became standard procedure for *Queenfish* for the remainder of the voyage.

We resumed our transit south at a depth of 390 feet, fifteen knots. Course was later changed to the southwest early on 10 August as *Queenfish* proceeded toward latitude 81°-17' N, longitude 100°-25' E. At that point the plan was to ascend to periscope depth and make landfall on the northern coast of Komsomolets Island. We expected to see icebergs calved from the glaciers of Severnaya Zemlya Archipelago along this course. The decision was made, therefore, to remain at 390 feet, slow to eight knots, and remain outside of the 600-foot depth curve until we returned to periscope depth and had accurately fixed our position in relation to Komsomolets Island. The wisdom of this course of action soon became evident when

Queenfish passed beneath several hundred yards of ice whose keels exceeded eighty feet in draft. We reached the six-hundred-foot depth curve during the next two and one-half hours, changed course toward the southeast, decreased depth, and began searching for a suitable polynya in which to make a vertical ascent to periscope depth.

We found a large polynya during the early morning hours of 10 August and estimated that we were now where Mys Arktichesky, the northernmost point on Komsomolets Island, could be seen to the southwest.[5] *Queenfish* had traveled almost six hundred nautical miles since departing the North Pole. We were all quite excited at the prospect of finally seeing the Severnaya Zemlya Archipelago and beginning our hydrographic survey of the Siberian continental shelf.

The vertical ascent to periscope depth took us through extremely murky green water into a polynya that was surrounded by thin first-year ice of no more than three inches in thickness, with only one large pressure ridge, almost twenty feet high, nearby. A periscope search revealed no icebergs or any other contacts. Although visibility was not the best, we did sight a large landmass on the distant horizon, its upper altitudes heavily shrouded in fog. Subsequent satellite navigational fixes through No. 2 periscope's antenna confirmed us to be approximately twenty-eight miles from our expected landfall and fixed our position at latitude 81°-05.0′ N, longitude 99°-56′ E.

Komsomolets Island, 3,785 square miles in size, is the third largest in the Severnaya Zemlya Archipelago. Two-thirds of it is covered by glaciers. It was first explored and named by G. A. Ushakov and N. N. Urvantsev during their 1930–32 Severnaya Zemlya expedition, considered one of the greatest geographical events of the twentieth century.[6] Allan Beal, Dick Boyle, Toby Warson, and I were extremely disappointed that poor visibility prevented us from spending several hours paralleling the coast of this fascinating and rarely seen island and photographing what was certain to be stark, severely frigid, 2,500-foot mountainous Arctic terrain.

The Severnaya Zemlya Archipelago, all of 14,171 square miles, is the last major landmass on earth to have been discovered. Its existence was not even suspected until the southern coast of its second largest island, Bolshevik Island, was sighted in 1913 by Boris Vilkitsky during the aforementioned Russian Arctic Hydrographic Expedition of 1914–15 by the survey ships *Taymyr* and *Vaygach*. Vilkitsky surveyed the east coast of what he thought was either an archipelago or a single landmass, up to its most northerly point, Mys Arktichesky. Heavy fog to the north apparently precluded for centuries the archipelago's earlier discovery by such explorers as S. Chelyuskin in 1741 during the Russian Great Northern Expedition and Adolph Nordenskiöld when he anchored for several days in August 1878 off Cape

Chelyuskin during his historic first transit of the Northeast Passage on *Vega* in 1878–79.[7]

We were in the Laptev Sea, and the first-ever survey across the entire Siberian continental shelf was about to begin. We could hardly contain our excitement as *Queenfish's* crew settled down to the task of carefully and accurately tracing and recording depth contours and gathering oceanographic information. Most, if not all, of the crew understood that we were now embarking on an exploration of one of the least known oceanic areas of the world and were thus in the process of making history—an achievement for which we might never be publicly recognized.

The East Coast of Severnaya Zemlya and the Vilkitsky Strait

We reached the northern Laptev Sea—the More Lapteryka—on 10 August 1970 and came to periscope depth in international waters some thirty miles off Komsomolets Island. The Laptev Sea, originally named the Nordenskiöld Sea and renamed after Dmitri and Khariton Laptev of the Russian Great Northern Expedition, 1736–42, was the most explored of the three seas that *Queenfish* was to survey. Its southern and western areas had been regularly transited since the seventeenth century, following the sea's discovery by Ilya Perfirlyev and Ivan Rebrov of a Russian exploring expedition in 1634.[1]

The Laptev Sea extends from the Taymyr Peninsula and Severnaya Zemlya Archipelago in the west to the New Siberian Islands some 544 miles to the east. The northern boundary starts at Mys Arktichesky, the northernmost point of Komsomolets Island, and proceeds eastward to the crossing point of longitude 139° E, east of the northern tip of Lotel'ny Island, and the edge of the continental shelf at latitude 79° N. The southern boundary runs eastward along the Siberian coastline from the head of Khatanga Bay to Mys Svyatoy Nos.[2]

The width of the sea along latitude 75° N is 460 miles. Its breadth from Mys Chelyuskin to the Dmitry Laptev Strait in the south, which connects the Laptev Sea with the East Siberian Sea, is 720 miles. Although we had no idea of this in 1970, it is now known that about 66 percent of the Laptev Sea is less than 328 feet deep; water depths in the southern and southeastern areas, which make up 45 percent of the total area, range from 32.5 feet to 164 feet.[3]

An Arctic continental shelf sea, the Laptev is frozen for much of the year. Dur-

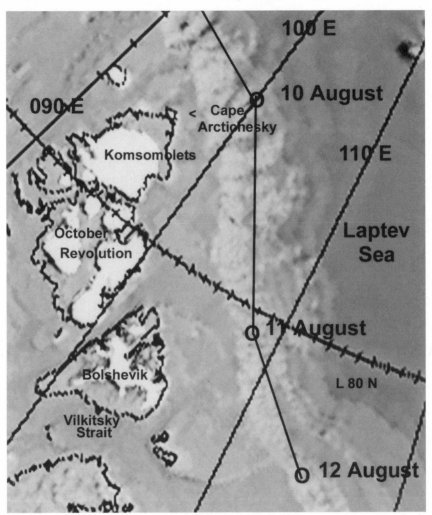

Chartlet 15.1 Severnaya Zemlya, 10 August to 12 August 1970.

ing the five warmest months of the year, the northward-flowing Lena River, which is one of the longest rivers in the world at more than twenty-eight hundred miles, discharges an average of 575,620 cubic feet of fresh water per second into a huge 270-mile-wide delta. This delta occupies some eleven thousand square miles and projects into the center of the southern Laptev Sea. As a result, the sea gets most of its water from the Lena and is thus a significant source of fresh water flowing into the Arctic Ocean.[4]

In view of heavy fog ahead, we returned beneath the surface several hours later.

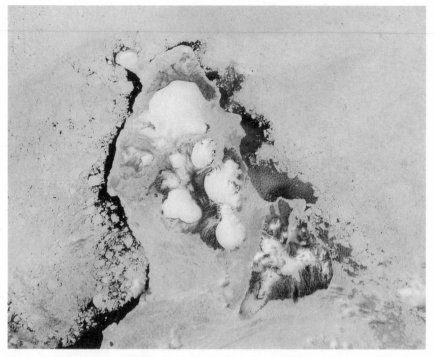

Figure 15.1 National Oceanic and Atmospheric Administration satellite view of Severnaya Zemlya and western Laptev Sea. (Courtesy of the National Oceanic and Atmospheric Administration)

Queenfish descended to three hundred feet, increased speed to ten knots, and spent the next fourteen hours surveying the edge of the western Laptev continental shelf on a meandering southeasterly course that roughly paralleled the Severnaya Zemlya Archipelago. A quick vertical ascent to periscope depth during the late morning placed us within a large polynya surrounded by heavy brash ice.[5]

Our hope of sighting the largest island in the archipelago, October Revolution Island, was frustrated by dense fog. Rising to a height of almost thirty-two hundred feet, the island was reported to be more than half-covered with spectacular glaciers that streamed down to the sea.[6] Disappointed, we returned to our previous depth and the survey. The six-hundred-foot depth contour we were tracing remained well clear of Soviet territorial waters. We noted, however, that the depths we were recording did not always coincide with those plotted on the latest corrected hydrographic charts provided to us for this area.

The formal watch-to-watch instructions that had been developed for conducting the hydrographic survey and collecting oceanographic data were now in effect, allowing for on-the-spot revisions if the operational situation demanded it. Two extremely important rules for maneuvering or piloting *Queenfish* safely on unexpectedly entering shallower ice-covered waters are worth mentioning. The first rule was to maneuver the boat immediately in the direction of deeper water if a rapidly shoaling bottom or if deep-draft ice keels made it impossible to remain within the prescribed "safe-operations envelope." The latter was initially established as a keel depth of forty feet above the bottom with a clearance of at least sixty feet from the top of the sail to the ice overhead. Once the boat regained her position within the prescribed safe-operations envelope and the overall operational situation was stabilized, she was then to return to the bottom contour being recorded, in course change increments of not more than 10°. The second rule was to keep the boat in a neutral trim, or buoyancy condition, at all times in the event it became necessary to stop suddenly—or kill all way—and hover.

The pack ice above us gradually thinned during the morning, with only a few deep-draft keels as deep as eighty feet beneath the sea. By midday, ice coverage overhead had decreased to less than 30 percent. Quartermaster of the Watch Clarence Williams reported later that afternoon that the top sounder recorder showed continuous open water for the past several hours, indicating that *Queenfish* might very well have emerged from beneath the Arctic ice pack. A check of the latest ice-line information received by radio confirmed that this could be the case, although we had not expected to emerge from beneath the pack until much farther south.

As early evening approached, *Queenfish* decreased depth to 160 feet and slowed to five knots in preparation for making a vertical ascent to periscope depth. Once steady at depth and speed, we changed course toward deeper water so that the passive sonar watch could search within our previous baffle, or stern area, for possible contacts. Now that we were in open water and well clear of the ice pack, we had to keep a sharp eye out for small fishing boats, Soviet frontier security vessels, large cargo ships, icebreakers, or even another submarine.

I stepped up to the periscope stand and raised No. 2 periscope to scan for ice and driftwood overhead. The seawater was a murky yellowish-brown, filled with diatoms, small white brine shrimp, and heaven knows what else. Underwater visibility was so poor that I was not certain I could see the surface.

As soon as sonar reported no contacts, I ordered, "All stop, make your depth one-two-zero feet!" followed by "Prepare to make a vertical ascent!" The diving officer of the watch, Grant Youngman, began pumping *Queenfish's* variable ballast tanks to sea, and the boat made a gradual ascent. As he reflooded the tanks to check the ascent and steadied on ordered depth, we found that visibility still remained too murky to determine whether the surface above us was completely clear of obstacles. I therefore ordered the diving officer to ease up to ninety feet. Grant trimmed the boat so that she slowly rose and then hovered perfectly at the new depth.

I made one more periscope inspection of the surface. Satisfied that it was safe to continue up to periscope depth, I lowered No. 2 periscope, shifted to No. 1, and called out, "Diving officer, make your depth six-eight-feet!" *Queenfish* rose very slowly but then stopped at seventy-five feet so abruptly that it seemed as if she had run up against a concrete ceiling. Grant pumped variable ballast to sea to continue the ascent, but the boat would not move even a single inch upward. "Grant, what is the problem?" I asked impatiently as soon as I heard that two thousand pounds of water had been pumped to sea with no effect. "I have no idea, Captain!" he replied. "I just can't seem to get her to rise any further!" The chief of the watch, Chief Sonar Technician Colorado Green, had in the meantime called all compartments to check for flooding or evidence of saltwater leakage into the boat. The reports from all compartments soon came back, "Negative flooding, negative leaks!" Grant had by now pumped more than five thousand pounds of water to sea.

The cause of *Queenfish's* inability to achieve positive buoyancy and continue her ascent to periscope depth suddenly dawned on us: the water directly above us was considerably fresher or less saline and therefore less dense because of meltwater from decaying sea ice, icebergs, and shore ice, augmented in all probability by freshwater runoff from melting glaciers.

I instructed Grant to continue pumping variable ballast tanks to sea. We eventually found that it helped to blow both sanitary tanks dry as well. When it began to look as if we should put a slight air bubble into the boat's main ballast tanks, *Queenfish* began to rise slowly. Grant reflooded variable ballast tanks as needed to check her ascent and leveled the boat off at sixty-eight feet. As the periscope gradually cleared the water several feet earlier, I whirled it around in a rapid but careful search for possible air and surface contacts and saw none. A subsequent search with No. 2 periscope and the ECM antennas confirmed that we were completely alone.

As soon as the boat was steady on depth and hovering, Grant reported that approximately thirty-three thousand pounds of saltwater ballast had been pumped to sea during the ascent from just ninety to sixty-eight feet. We soon realized that a freshwater lens was present near the surface in this area and that salinity had decreased from twenty-two parts per thousand at a depth of 120 feet to between six and eight parts per thousand during an ascent to within 20 feet of the surface.

We realized, too, that this same environmental condition would probably be encountered throughout the southwestern Laptev Sea and other open-water areas

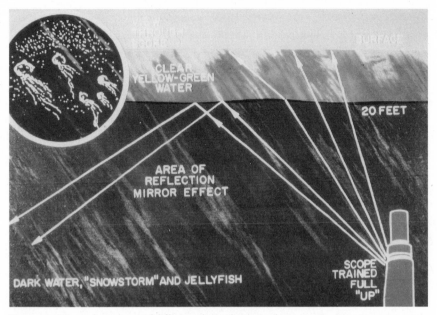

Figure 15.2 Water column layers of different salinity/density in the Laptev Sea on 10 August 1970. (Courtesy of the U.S. Navy)

across the Siberian continental shelf. Hence, *Queenfish* would need to deballast similar amounts of water each time she proceeded to periscope depth from deeper and more saline depths. This meant every day for the next two to three weeks. We had just learned the hard way that the additional time required to deballast/reballast during each vertical ascent and stationary dive would add as much as thirty to forty minutes to the process of completing an entire evolution.

Remaining at periscope depth, *Queenfish* proceeded in a southeasterly direction at a minimum speed of two to three knots. There was a fair amount of brash ice in every direction, so we stopped and hovered long enough to copy the next radio broadcast and fix our position by satellite. Visibility was less than five hundred yards in the heavy fog, although the sun was trying to break through at low altitude above the horizon. The nearest land was now Bolshevik Island, the second largest and most southerly in the archipelago some thirty miles to the southwest. We were unable to see it or any other part of the supposedly spectacular, glacier-covered archipelago, however. Chief Photographers Mate Charles Wright remarked in frustration, "It is not hard to understand why the Severnaya Zemlya Archipelago remained undiscovered until 1913!"

Returning to three hundred feet, *Queenfish* resumed her survey of the edge of the continental shelf off Bolshevik Island. We continued in a generally southeast-ern direction at ten knots, passing beneath alternating bands of brash ice of various thicknesses and open water. All watch sections were doing an absolutely superb job of keeping *Queenfish* right on depth, bubble, and course as we followed and re-corded the meandering six-hundred-foot curve.

Shortly after midnight on 11 August, we reached continuous open water and de-cided to make a vertical ascent to periscope depth to investigate. Tom Hoepfner took the dive in anticipation of encountering another low-salinity, freshwater layer near to the surface, and we slowly began our ascent through the murky, yellowish-brown soup. The surface could not be discerned through the periscope until the boat reached 120 feet and only then because of wind-generated ripples.

Tom did a terrific job of getting us to periscope depth, but only after pump-ing some forty-four thousand pounds of water to sea. Unbelievable! There was not much more he could have done short of putting a slight air bubble into our main ballast tanks, always a hard-to-control and noisy procedure and generally undesir-able because no submarine can afford to lose depth control when approaching the surface in ice-covered waters, much less be exposed to detection.

Steve Gray, *Queenfish*'s electronics material officer, took the dive once Tom had the boat in a stable hovering condition within plus or minus six inches. A quick search on No. 1 periscope showed us to be within a sizable area of open water, ringed with brash ice, all along the horizon to the southeast. We were elated. All of Bolshevik Island and its glaciers were visible to the southwest, with a large field of ice evident offshore.

No other contacts of any consequence were sighted through the periscope, with the exception of a solitary iceberg just four thousand yards to the northwest. The iceberg appeared to be approximately fifty-two feet high and drifting north. The sonar watch standers were surprised that it had not been detected passively, be-cause its draft beneath the sea had to approach three hundred feet. Was it possible that the surrounding air and sea temperature were so low as to preclude melting, with its attendant continuous release of entrapped air bubbles, producing the tell-tale fizzing or seltzer sound? If so, it would definitely be something else to keep in mind while operating in these waters.

A stationary dive, which required us to flood in all the water that had been pumped out earlier, was conducted as soon as Toby Warson and his team had fixed our position and the radio broadcast was copied. Once at three hundred feet, we resumed the survey in a southerly direction.

After passing beneath continuous open water for several hours, we made a verti-cal ascent to periscope depth shortly before breakfast. Once more we had to pump

Figure 15.3 Periscope view of glaciers on October Revolution Island in Severnaya Zemlya Archipelago, August 1970. (Courtesy of the U.S. Navy)

Figure 15.4 Periscope view of large iceberg in Laptev Sea. (Courtesy of the U.S. Navy)

a tremendous amount of water to sea, comparable to the last two ascents. An initial periscope search revealed an absolutely magnificent, bright sunny day devoid of any contacts or sea ice. The surrounding water was flat calm, and the resultant refraction was expected to provide some quite unusual sights. Indeed, a number of oddly shaped upside-down masses of ice appeared to be floating well above the horizon. The apparitions in view reminded me of a "twilight zone" day that I experienced in the Barents Sea under similar conditions seven years earlier when, as navigator on *Skipjack* (Jenks), I was trying to obtain a sun line without much success. What I saw instead was a procession of very distant ships floating inverted above the horizon with as many as four suns or "sun dogs" on entirely different bearings.

The glacier-covered land to the west was still Bolshevik Island, rising some three thousand feet above sea level. We could clearly see its coastline and massive glaciers advancing right down to the sea.[7] One glacier in particular presented a high, sheer, clifflike face and looked more than capable of calving icebergs whose heights above water might easily exceed one hundred feet. Chief Photographers Mate Charles Wright took a series of photographs of Bolshevik Island that later produced a magnificent panoramic view of its coast.

No surface or electronic contacts (radars) of any type were detected. *Queenfish* was now operating in essentially ice-free waters, so we decided to remain at periscope depth as long as possible to take advantage of the beautiful weather. We would maintain an "all-sensors"[8] search as we continued the survey southward at speeds of less than three knots so as to minimize any periscope wake, or "feather," and thus prevent chance detection by either air or surface traffic.

Assuming that the Laptev Sea continued to be ice-free to the south, we planned to remain well out in international waters as we proceeded in a southerly direction. We were heading toward, yet staying well to the east of, Starokadomsk and Malyy Taymyr islands and past the eastern approaches to the Vilkitsky Strait. If we did come upon an ice floe or two, we would change course toward the east and maneuver around it. Continuing southward until water depths decreased to our particular depth contour of interest, we would then follow its arc from a southeast-to-east-to-northeast direction across the southern Laptev Sea.

The remainder of 11 August was spent at periscope depth. Numerous large freshly calved icebergs were sighted, some as high as 150 feet above sea level. Those farthest from land appeared to be either aground in more than three hundred feet of water or moving slowly north in response to an offshore current.

Without knowing it, we might have seen tabular icebergs, or ice islands, from the very deep Marata Fjord that cuts into the southeastern portion of October

Revolution Island.[9] These ice islands would have been discharged into the Shokalsk Strait between October Revolution and Bolshevik Island to the south and then drifted eastward into the Laptev Sea. Marata Fjord and the Ward Hunt Ice Shelf off Ellesmere Island, Canada, are the only known sources of ice islands in the entire Arctic Ocean.[10]

The relatively deep bottom soundings recorded as we passed east of Taymyr Island and through the eastern approaches to the Vilkitsky Strait from the north coincided quite closely with those on the latest corrected navigational charts we were using. We knew, however, that the perennially ice-covered eastern and northernmost uncharted portions of the Laptev Sea, toward the New Siberian Islands, might be an entirely different matter.

About mid-evening the sky became very dark and overcast. The sea state rose to wave heights between two and three feet, and white caps developed as the wind steadily increased to fifteen knots. Perfect weather for operations at periscope depth.

Our survey led us past the eastern approaches into the famed Vilkitsky Strait, located between the southern coast of Bolshevik Island and the northernmost point on the Eurasian continent, Mys Chelyuskin, on the Taymyr Peninsula. This deepwater strait, named after Boris Vilkitsky, discoverer of Severnaya Zemlya in 1913, is the principal navigational passage between the Laptev Sea and the Kara Sea to the west. It was not determined to be fully navigable by ship until Nordenskiöld and Johannsen, in *Vega* and *Lena,* respectively, transited it en route to the Bering Strait and the Pacific on 10 August 1878.[11]

Interestingly, the only material in existence concerning submarine operations in Siberian waters was the *Office of Naval Intelligence Review*'s 1951 four-part series, "German U-Boats in the Arctic."[12] My officers and I had studied the material very closely to glean every conceivable lesson from the great number of patrols the German submarine force had conducted in these waters during each summer and early fall of 1941 through 1944.

As we surveyed the strait's eastern approaches at periscope depth throughout 11 August and into the early morning hours of 12 August, I recounted to those on watch some of the often hair-raising exploits of the brave German submariners who had operated in these waters some twenty-five years earlier. During an exceptionally mild-ice summer, three Type VIIC U-boats, *U-302* (Sickel), *U-354* (Herbschleb), and *U-711* (Lange) of Group Viking of the Thirteenth U-boat Flotilla, based at Trondheim, Norway, on patrol in the Kara Sea during late August 1943, trailed a Soviet convoy into the Vilkitsky Strait. *U-302* and *U-354* subsequently sank one ship each of the small convoy. A month later, *U-302, U-354,* and *U-601* (Grau) of this same group returned to patrol the western entrance of these straits in hopes of intercepting another convoy. During the following summer of a much less favorable ice year, three more Type VIIC U-boats of Group Gryphon of the Thirteenth Flotilla, *U-711* (Lange), *U-739* (Mangold), and *U-957* (Schaar), succeeded in reaching Cape Chelyuskin on 18 September 1944 while attempting to reach an assembly point for Soviet coastal convoys at Nordwik Bight to the east of Chelyuskin. Only heavy drift ice prevented them from going farther.[13]

Seasoned German Arctic U-boat veterans, including Hans-Günther Lange of *U-711*, who made the longest uninterrupted patrol in the Kara and "West Siberian" seas from 22 July to 30 September 1943, were a confident lot. They considered that "a submarine is never helpless in the ice because it can submerge, proceed under the ice, select an open area with the aid of its high-angle periscope, come to the surface, recharge the battery with the diesel engine, and submerge again." They also observed that "the sea is always calm in the drift ice even if a gale is blowing" and that "there are always clear lanes in the drift ice which permits boats to proceed." In spite of this, on 18 September 1943, *U-957* (Schaar), during the course of a submerged approach on the small convoy mentioned earlier, "found she could hardly use her periscope and had to steer by bearings taken with the sound detector."[14]

Despite all caution, the Germans' attack periscope was bent by the drift ice. The U-boat continued with the aircraft periscope, however, and reached a position for attacking, but missed one of the steamers. The torpedo detonated, probably hitting the ice, after which the escort vessels started a wild chase in the ice, in the course of which the second periscope was also bent. Completely blind, the boat retreated submerged. By trimming down the stern, the captain cautiously probed the underside of the ice with the bow from time to time. Eventually he surfaced in drift and pack ice and reached open water laced with drift ice near Russki Island off the western entrance to Vilkitsky Strait. The outer caps of the bow torpedo tubes were buckled.[15]

What subsequently happened to these pioneer Arctic U-boats, skippers, and crews that had penetrated so deeply and successfully into Soviet Arctic waters during World War II? *U-302* (Sickel) was sunk by hedgehogs (a type of thrown depth charge) from HMS *Swale* (Boyle) northwest of the Azores on 6 April 1944 with the loss of all hands. *U-354* (Sthamer), with a new captain on board, was sunk by depth charges from the British frigate HMS *Mermaid* (Mosse) northwest of Bear Island on 2 August 1944, also with the loss of all hands. Her captain during Arctic operations, Kapitänleutnant Karl-Heinz Herbschleb, survived the war. *U-601* (Hansen), also with a new captain on board, was sunk by depth charges northwest of the Lofoten Islands, Norway, by Catalina 'M' of No. 210, Royal Air Force Squadron, on 25 February 1944 with the loss of all hands. Her captain during Arctic operations, Kapitänleutnant Peter-Ottmar Grau, lost his life in 1944. On 25 June 1944, while he was captain of *U-1191* in the English Channel, the boat was sunk, with loss of all hands, by hedgehogs and depth charges from HMS *Affleck*. *U-711* was sunk by Avenger/Wildcat teams of the 846, 853, and 882 Naval Air Squadrons while she was moored at Harstad, Norway, on 4 May 1945. Thirty-two men of her fifty-one-man crew were lost. Her captain, Oberleutnant zur See Hans-Günther Lange, survived the war and later served in postwar Germany's Bundesmarine. *U-739* (Mangold) and her crew survived World War II. The sixth boat to penetrate the Vilkitsky Strait, *U-957*, was decommissioned in late October 1944 following severe damage from a collision with pack ice while en route to her patrol area earlier in the month. Most of her crewmen survived the war, as did her captain, Oberleutnant zur See Paul-Heinrich Gerhard Schaar, who later commanded the new Type XXI high-speed, deep-diving boat, *U-2551*, during the final months of the war.[16]

Certainly the one lesson that stood out from the rest was how vulnerable a submarine's periscopes and masts could be to even the slightest contact with ice. Even the smallest, most innocent-looking fragment of ice could destroy a periscope and should be considered very dangerous. I had the misfortune of learning this bitter lesson a few years earlier as navigator of *Skipjack* in the Barents Sea when an ice fragment banged the head window of the periscope, allowing water to seep in.

Here as an extra precaution, we normally used only our thicker No. 2, or observation, periscope and raised its protective fairing to prevent or reduce vibration when running at higher speeds near the surface. We were also now in a region where we had to keep an eye out for heavy tree branches and logs that were regularly discharged into the Laptev Sea from its five major tributary rivers: the Anabar, Khatanga, Olenek, Yana, and, mightiest of all, the Lena.

Solid ice was sighted ahead and to the east of us early on 12 August. Our last look at the Vilkitsky Strait in the distance showed it to be clear of ice, although visibility was gradually deteriorating as it became enshrouded by fog. Our survey of the eastern approaches to the strait indicated the existence of a deep passage within the strait, possibly as deep as 850 feet. It would seem that a submarine could pass through it with relative ease, without worry of either deep-draft ice or shoal areas within. It would, in fact, be possible to transit it and remain in international waters the entire time. I regretted very much that our operation order did not permit a quick round trip to the Kara Sea and back via the Vilkitsky Strait.

It was now time to proceed beneath the ice ahead and continue the survey southward. *Queenfish* headed down and leveled off at 150 feet. Sonar reported fizzing noises from two distant icebergs shortly after we reached depth. Both appeared to be within the Vilkitsky Strait to the west. Depth of water beneath us steadily decreased as we passed south of the eastern approaches to the strait and proceeded onto the continental shelf in the southwestern Laptev Sea. We had enjoyed a relatively easy and almost relaxed time during the past two days. We all knew that the time had finally arrived to begin the toughest part of the expedition.

16
Alteration of the Survey Plan in the Shallow Laptev Sea

After completing our hydrographic survey of the eastern approaches to the Vilkitsky Strait, we proceeded in a generally southerly direction at a keel depth of 150 feet, intending to survey as far south as possible in the Laptev Sea. We had yet to detect a single ship or aircraft of any type; we had not even seen marine life of any size. Our present position was approximately thirty miles north of the northeast coast of the Taymyr Peninsula, well within international waters open to all traffic, according to the international Law of the Sea then in effect.[1]

By early morning on 13 August, the depth of water beneath our keel had become so shallow that, as Chief Quartermaster Jack Patterson put it, "a submarine couldn't go much farther south without wheels or wings, much less come anywhere near Soviet territorial waters."

The rapidly shoaling sea bottom forced *Queenfish* to reverse course to port, toward the northeast, and then ease back to the depth contour of navigation interest. We soon began another short but intense period of under-ice piloting from the IBD display, which required everyone's full attention for most of the morning as we maneuvered beneath or around a considerable number of deep-draft ice floes, some of whose keels reached as deep as fifty-eight feet beneath the sea. Safe to say, the effect on our adrenaline was equivalent to downing an entire pot of coffee.

The planesmen exerted maximum effort to maintain *Queenfish* at zero bubble as we endeavored to stay at least thirty feet both above the bottom and below the ice. I remarked at the time that exploring shallow water under ice in a submarine was like exploring a subterranean cave in an airplane on instruments. This was

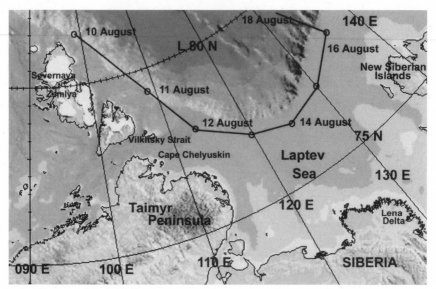

Chartlet 16.1 Laptev Sea, 10 August to 18 August 1970.

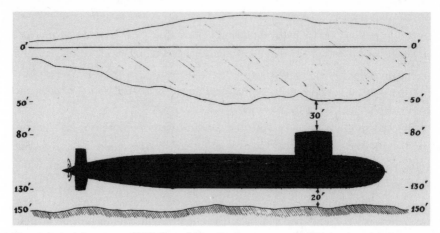

Figure 16.1 Artist's concept of USS *Queenfish* hugging bottom to avoid thick ice above it in Laptev Sea. (Courtesy of the U.S. Navy)

even worse than what we had experienced in the Chukchi Sea. The topographies of the underside of the ice pack and the seabed were increasingly irregular and unpredictable. We were caught between occasional upward-thrusting "stalagmites," which could well be pingos or underwater seamounts, and innumerable "stalactites" in the form of deep-draft ice keels projecting downward from a seemingly endless ice pack above. There was truly not a single instant when any of us could afford to let our attention wander. This kind of submarining was definitely a young man's game.

Sea-ice coverage gradually decreased with each passing hour, however, and by late morning it seemed to have completely disappeared. *Queenfish* gingerly returned to periscope depth and gradually adjusted course toward the southeast as we continued to follow the meandering depth contour. With the exception of half a dozen distant icebergs of differing shapes and sizes, no ice could be seen in any direction. It was a most welcome respite, enabling us to remain at periscope depth to catch our breath and accomplish some much-needed routine preventive maintenance that we had not dared to try while constantly maneuvering under ice in shallow water. It also permitted us to refine our navigational position and use all our visual and electromagnetic sensors to search for and record anything that might be of scientific interest.

The view through the periscope revealed an unusually gray, dismal, and altogether depressing day, similar to late autumn or early winter in northern New England when cold rain or snow is imminent. The sea was almost flat calm, mirroring a sky completely overcast with low, dark stratus clouds. Although visibility seemed more than sufficient for the detection and avoidance of logs and other floating debris in our path, one could not be completely sure, because the gray sameness of sea and sky made it difficult to discern a horizon or accurately estimate range on anything barely afloat. I had a nagging sense of foreboding as I continued to rotate the periscope in a close-in search for possible hazards in our path.

Suddenly, in less than a ship's length, Quartermaster of the Watch Clarence Williams reported that the bottom had jumped upward from 126 feet to 98 feet beneath the keel, some 28 feet shallower.[2] Startled, Ralph Beedle instantly maneuvered the boat to port with full rudder, almost immediately returning the depth beneath our keel to its previous range. Depth remained the same as he gradually maneuvered the boat back to starboard and our original southeasterly course.

The abrupt decrease in depth was a blunt reminder that *Queenfish* was in totally uncharted waters and that we would have to be alert continuously to the presence of shoals, seamounts, and more pingos. It was fortuitous that our navigation team was made up of such experienced and capable quartermasters as Clarence Williams, Louis Soukey, and Chief Jack Patterson. Still in training, the fourth man, Quartermaster Seaman Michael Falconer, was at the same time manning the diving-control planes, rudder, or both as part of a ship control watch team.

The quartermaster of the watch, or watch section navigator, bears an old and trusted position of great responsibility. He must, with the helmsman, have occupied one of the first watch stations aboard any ship. Certainly the ancient Egyp-

Figure 16.2 Quartermaster First Class Clarence F. Williams checking depth of water in Laptev Sea on precision depth recorder. (Courtesy of the U.S. Navy)

tians, Greeks, and Etruscans had them on every boat and ship, as did the Vikings many centuries later. As knowledgeable as most officers of the deck, especially on submarines, the quartermaster of the watch can be counted on to provide forceful backup for that officer in difficult navigation or maneuvering situations.

As the afternoon progressed, we observed that the continental shelf underlying this portion of the southern Laptev Sea remained irregular and somewhat rugged. It would therefore be less predictable in tight navigational circumstances than the relatively flat seabed of the northeasterly portion of the Chukchi Sea transited earlier. The bottom also appeared to be heavily silted, due in all probability to discharge from the Lena River delta more than three hundred miles to the south. This delta is huge, second in size only to that of the Mississippi River.[3] The underwater terrain could pose difficulties for our main seawater condensers in the coming days if unexpectedly thick ice forced us to hug the bottom in very shallow water.

Ice floes began to crowd the horizon as we continued in a generally southeasterly direction during the early evening. We soon reluctantly abandoned periscope

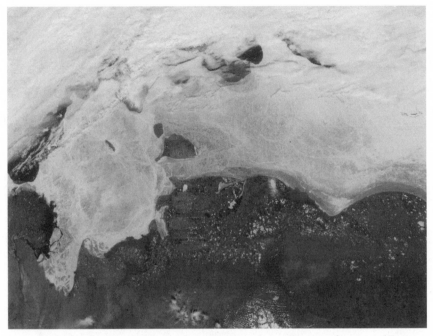

Figure 16.3 National Oceanic and Atmospheric Administration satellite view of Laptev and East Siberian seas. (Courtesy of the National Oceanic and Atmospheric Administration)

depth and dipped beneath a solid cover of rotting first-year ice less than a foot in thickness, which gradually thickened during the evening.

Each ship control watch team performed superbly during the long night that followed, particularly with regard to depth and bubble control.[4] As the ice continued to thicken and become more compact and open water leads and polynyas disappeared, I saw no signs of overconfidence among the crew. All personnel stayed calm in the unusually quiet atmosphere of the control room as each four-hour watch became more arduous and nerve-wracking. Many times it was necessary to maneuver *Queenfish,* and to hug the bottom to within twenty feet, in order to avoid colliding with the endless procession of ice massifs and deep-thrusting keels in our path. Bob Baumhardt, followed by Ralph Beedle, spelled me as "ice pilot" as the night dragged on and we continued to the southeast.

A continuous worry was the danger of suddenly encountering a grounded iceberg or two like those we had seen off Severnaya Zemlya. Outward-projecting spurs from beneath their waterlines would be a major hazard and especially difficult to detect. It was becoming obvious that such an irregular and unpredictable seafloor in uncharted waters was going to require some rethinking of our survey plan if we were to gain an extra margin of safety.

During the early morning of 14 August, Toby Warson, Ralph Beedle, Allan Beal, Dick Boyle, and I discussed these unrelenting challenges and other factors, such as the "emergency use only" status of No. 2 SSMG, and the risks these posed to *Queenfish* and her crew. What could not be ignored was that, if *Queenfish* should have the grave misfortune to become entrapped between a thick ice floe or floes and the bottom, we would have to develop our own means of freeing ourselves and getting to periscope depth or the surface.

On the positive side, we had well over one hundred days of stores on board and sufficient power from our nuclear reactor to meet our fresh water, electrical power, and atmosphere control needs indefinitely. On the other hand, any silting up of one or both main seawater condensers could seriously degrade the capability of our electrical and propulsion plant systems to sustain us for that length of time. Moreover, if we became encased in ice as a result of the high winds and severe temperature extremes in Siberian seas, it would probably take months for the U.S. Navy or any other navy to locate us, if ever. If we were found in time, there would be the added difficulty of trying to assist us in breaking free and clear.

In sum, there were just too many unpredictables in our present situation. Safety of ship and crew came first, especially on a mission like this one.

Accordingly, whenever the depth contour of interest led beneath heavily compacted conglomerations of thick first-year, multiyear, and deformed ice, we shifted our hydrographic survey to a deeper depth curve than the one originally planned.[5] The gain of water volume would give us more space in which to operate and hence a safer under-ice operating envelope for maneuvering *Queenfish*. It would, at the same time, enable us to use greater speed and rudder to avoid colliding with deep-draft ice or with a rapidly shoaling bottom. Finally, it would reduce the possibility of our having to shut down one side of the propulsion plant as a result of getting too close to the bottom and running the risk of sucking silt into one or both main seawater condensers.

Mine was a command decision that proved to be the right one for the success of the expedition. I confess, though, that it bothered me greatly as commanding officer of a frontline nuclear attack submarine to have to back off in any way from the pursuit of our primary objective.

The decision to survey a deeper depth contour whenever necessary was easier to live with, however, when we reminded ourselves that everything that *Queenfish* observed, collected, and recorded was unique and would add immeasurably to scientific and military knowledge. We would be the first ever to have explored and recorded the oceanography and underwater topography of the seas that we would be passing through.

By mid-evening on 14 August, the sea ice above us had become so thick and compressed that we shifted to the deeper depth contour in anticipation of encountering even thicker ice and shallower water during the night.

Shortly before midnight on 14 August, we passed over a depression, or "ice scour," in the seafloor thirty feet or so deeper than the surrounding bottom. We speculated that it might have been created by a deep-draft ice keel or an iceberg. After midnight the ice became thinner, to our pleasant surprise, and by early morning the next day, *Queenfish* was once again in ice-free waters. We planed up to 120 feet, confirmed there was nothing but open water overhead, and, using a vertical ascent, continued on to periscope depth.

During the ascent from 120 feet, seawater temperature increased almost 10° F, and salinity decreased from twenty-two to six parts per one thousand. With the decrease in water density, Bill Enderlein, one of the military riders whom I had qualified as a diving officer of the watch, found that he had to pump a total of thirty-three thousand pounds of water from variable ballast tanks to sea to get us to periscope depth in good trim. He accomplished it like a seasoned veteran. Bill's ability to learn quickly and his enthusiasm for the many duties assigned him throughout the voyage made him a particularly valued and popular shipmate.

A quick search at periscope depth revealed no contacts of any sort. I was pleased to note a 30° wedge of open water centered on an easterly bearing all the way to the horizon. There was also sufficient open water to the south to permit us to remain at periscope depth and return to surveying the shallower depth contour with which we had been originally tasked.

On achieving the desired depth contour shortly before breakfast, *Queenfish* changed course to follow it toward the east and resumed the survey. The contour soon meandered back toward the southeast, however. After half an hour, the special secure depth sounder revealed another deep depression in the seafloor, this time approaching eighty feet in width and averaging some fifty feet deeper than the surrounding bottom.[6] There were no icebergs or deep-draft ice anywhere in the vicinity to explain it. We were still some three hundred miles from the Lena River delta and thus much too far north for the ice scour to be a northern extension of the river's innumerable tributaries or a strong discharge from them. Both scours were fascinating discoveries. Allan Beal, Dick Boyle, and I now wondered whether they might have been created by the movement of a massive glacier or huge iceberg through this area near the end of the last ice age more than ten thousand years ago, when sea levels were lower worldwide, or during the "Little Ice Age" that ended during the last century.[7]

We remained at periscope depth throughout the day until almost midnight on 15 August. This was definitely the most desirable way to conduct a hydrographic survey, because it enabled us to fix our position frequently, copy every radio broadcast meant for us, and conduct continuous "all-sensor" searches for anything that might be of scientific or military interest. We saw scattered bands of ice floes oriented in a generally north-south direction. When coming on one of these bands, we changed course either to the north or south, depending on the depth of water beneath us. As soon as a gap in the floe line was found, we slipped through the open channel and into the next expanse of open water to the east.

During the early morning hours of 16 August, *Queenfish* entered a continuous field of heavy ice extending from the northeast to the southwest and preventing us from advancing any farther south. We found it strange that sonar had been reporting a lot of "ice noise" to the west for the past fifteen minutes where the water was still open but none coming from the massive ice line ahead of us.

We descended to 180 feet and changed course toward the east in order to relocate and resume surveying the deeper depth contour. Water temperature had decreased dramatically from the surface down to 120 feet and then became essentially isothermal at 31° F. Sonar reported a significant increase in ice noise once we passed through 120 feet and literally pegged sonar's signal-to-noise meter to its maximum reading by the time *Queenfish* leveled off at 180 feet. Again, this was very strange. We had definitely not seen any icebergs, large ice ridges, or contacts of any sort while at periscope depth. As soon as we cleared baffles to port to investigate, the ice noise was discovered to be a steam hiss. Low-frequency diesel engine lines, or tonals, also began to print out on the BQQ-3 spectrum analyzer recorder.

The answer came shortly. Senior Chief Sonar Technician James Petersen reported from sonar that there were at least six valid ship contacts to the west, north, and northeast of us, sufficiently close to cause "spoking" on the AN/BQS-6B active sonar presentation.[8] Once having ascertained that all six were at least six thousand yards away and opening to the east, we cautiously made a vertical ascent to periscope depth shortly after noon to investigate. Grant Youngman was on the dive. Once again he had to pump more than thirty thousand pounds of water to the sea to bring *Queenfish* up to where the periscope just cleared the water and I could carefully examine the ships without fear of counterdetection.

The water en route was extremely murky, making it difficult to see the surface or any ice that might be above us. Fortunately, there was no ice in the immediate vicinity, and the heavy brash ice that ringed the polynya and extended in every direction provided excellent cover. Using periscope observations of not more than five to eight seconds each, I was able to see and identify all six ships as Soviet. They consisted of an icebreaker leading a tanker and four cargo ships on an easterly course that slowly weaved back and forth through the chaotic ice pack. I later spotted a helicopter that appeared to be conducting ice reconnaissance several thousand yards ahead of them. None of the little ships appeared to displace more than four thousand tons. They were photographed and evaluated as a Northern Sea Route convoy possibly en route from the port of Tiksi to the southeast or possibly to Pevek in the East Siberian Sea. All looked to be weather- and ice-beaten.

We returned to 180 feet several hours later and resumed our survey of the deeper depth contour first shifted to on 14 August. Meanwhile, we maintained sonar contact on the Soviet ships until late morning, at which time they gradually faded out to the east. The ice cover overhead averaged ten feet in thickness and remained an extremely compact mixture of first-year and deformed ice. Not a single polynya or lead was detected in which to make a vertical ascent. The depth contour we were recording, moreover, never steadied on a particular direction for any length of time. It just wandered back and forth as we did our best to follow and accurately record its path.

The ice pack overhead was still thick and extremely compact later in the morning on 16 August. We slowed and decreased depth sufficiently to stream the very low frequency (VLF) floating wire antenna so that Chief Radioman Mike Hein and his team could copy our radio broadcasts. The navigation team obtained several excellent Omega navigation fixes through the floating wire antenna as well. Although the ice pack overhead gradually thinned to between three and four feet during this time, it remained quite compacted, with very few leads or polynyas in evidence until almost midnight. The thickness and character of the ice remained well within *Queenfish's* capability to surface through it in an emergency, however.

Queenfish achieved her most southerly penetration into the Laptev Sea during the early evening of 16 August, at which time the bottom contour being traced steadied in an easterly direction for a short period of time and then began to curve gradually toward the northeast. The waters to the south of us must have been extremely shallow, because we were essentially in the center of the Laptev Sea and roughly 230 miles due north of the Lena River delta that projected from the Siberian coast.

We found a small polynya in which to ascend to periscope depth shortly before midnight but were unable to relocate it following completion of the William-son course reversal. The winds must have been quite strong, because the pack ice above us was moving at more than half a knot in a direction almost perpendicular to our course.

Ice conditions stayed much the same up to and through the early morning hours of 17 August. We decreased depth, slowed, and restreamed the VLF floating wire antenna to copy several early morning radio broadcasts and fix our position by Omega under the ice. Toby Warson and I looked forward to getting a satellite fix via the periscope antenna as soon as possible, however, because our most recent dead reckoning had plotted us three miles north of the SINS position and six miles south of the two Omega fixes just obtained. If others in the military and scientific community were to benefit from the hydrographic data we were collecting, our navigation would have to be more accurate than this! With increasing impatience we searched for suitable open water along our track. The ice pack remained steadfastly compact until early afternoon, when we eventually found several polynyas exceeding four hundred yards in length—more than sufficient in size for coming to periscope depth and accurately fixing our position.

The decision made on 14 August to back off and shift our survey to a deeper depth contour again proved wise when the ice pack overhead began to increase in thickness and draft during the afternoon. At mid-evening on 17 August, *Queenfish* passed over a broad ice scour, this time exceeding two hundred yards in width but only thirteen feet deeper than the surrounding bottom. Running down its axis along longitude 130°-20′ E was a sharp ridge that thrust some eighteen feet above the surrounding bottom. If we had encountered such a scour-and-ridge combination in either the Chukchi Sea or our present location while literally hugging the bottom as close as ten feet to avoid deep-draft ice massifs overhead, ours might have become one of those ill-fated expeditions so often written about in the history books.

Shortly before midnight on 17 August, we made a vertical ascent to periscope depth within a polynya that was considerably smaller than the one used in the afternoon in order to obtain a more accurate navigational position. I was pleased to note that all the chiefs of the watch—Torpedoman First Class Raymond Cheese-brough, Chief Sonar Technician Colorado Green, Chief Radioman Mike Hein, and Senior Chief Torpedoman Kenneth Ickes—who worked closely with the diving officers of the watch to deballast and reballast the submarine—had all become expert at routinely shifting the thirty-three thousand pounds of seawater out of, and then back into, the variable ballast tanks during the vertical ascents and stationary dives conducted thus far. They had also been able to stop our 292-foot, 4,640-

ton boat on a dime. *Queenfish* could not afford to lose depth control and risk collid-ing with the ice or touching bottom. One mishap or casualty could quickly lead to another in these waters. For example, a slight bump of an ice pinnacle or a massive ridge overhead could cause the boat to plow into a heavily silted or rocky seabed. A bounce off the bottom could then thrust her into the heavy ice overhead. Similarly, any inadvertent up or down bubble or aspect could cause one end of the submarine to collide with the ice overhead and the other end to plow into the bottom.

Visibility through the periscope was extremely poor, with fog everywhere. Drop-lets of water collected and condensed on the outer head window glass, requiring frequent dipping to clear them off. The sea ice surrounding us presented a quite for-midable and utterly chaotic sight. There was a tremendous amount of ice rubble, for lack of a better term, interlaced with randomly oriented, large pressure ridges of multiyear and deformed ice of at least fifteen feet or more in thickness. The general scene was breathtaking to behold—and spooky. As the fog slowly swirled around the huge ice ridges, we would not have been surprised to see the Frankenstein mon-ster or "The Thing" from the 1950s movie come out of the mist. The icescape and general environment were ideal for encountering such an apparition.

In short, it was absolutely the worst conceivable place for a serious casualty to occur. If we were required to abandon the submarine, we would find it extremely difficult to travel in any direction on foot. Added to this was the certainty of com-ing across a hungry polar bear no matter which direction one headed. We hovered at periscope depth just long enough to copy the next radio broadcast and fix our position.

Two days had passed since the navigator fixed our position by satellite. I was not unhappy to find that our hand dead-reckoning position was only eight miles off and that of SINS within five miles, with latitudes in both cases correct. I was con-cerned, however, that both hand dead reckoning and SINS were in error longitu-dinally in that the navigational positions in both cases were plotted too far to the east, an indication that we were being set to the west by a current of which we had not been previously aware.

Queenfish returned beneath the ice pack and resumed the survey shortly after midnight on 18 August. We spent the rest of the morning fully submerged as we proceeded in a direction from which to exit the northeastern Laptev Sea en route to a position well above the westernmost of the New Siberian Islands. From there we intended to send a check report to our bosses confirming that we were still alive and well. As we departed the more northerly reaches of the Laptev, we passed near waters visited briefly by *Seadragon* (Summitt) in 1962.[9]

With the exception of having to contend with dramatic changes in salinity and hence significantly reduced density within twenty feet of the surface, and a few grueling periods navigating through ice-covered shallow water, our survey of the first of the Siberian shelf seas had not been as difficult as we anticipated. The generous amount of open water and milder sea ice in the western and southern portions of the Laptev Sea had been an agreeable surprise, making that portion of the survey much easier.

On the other hand, the irregularly bottomed portion of the northeastern section that we were tasked with surveying proved to be extensively covered by compact deep-draft ice. I did not consider that the risks these conditions posed to both boat and personnel, were we to have rigorously adhered to the original survey plan, were worth taking and chose, instead, to survey a somewhat deeper depth contour of equal navigational value. This gave *Queenfish* a safer operational envelope within which to maneuver through the heavy, pack-ice–covered shallow waters of the Siberian continental shelf.

17
Northward around
the New Siberian Islands

We departed the Laptev Sea at best speed shortly after midnight on 18 August. We were en route to a position well out in the deep water of the Arctic Ocean from which to send a check report. Rear Admiral Small, Commander Submarine Forces Pacific, with whom we had not communicated since early August, had asked us to confirm that all was well before we resumed the survey.

On reaching latitude 80° N shortly before noon, we slowed, decreased depth, and began searching for a polynya in which to come to periscope depth. We located one almost immediately, and *Queenfish* made a vertical ascent through isothermal, 29.5° F, water into a small polynya with very little deballasting required. We ascended to the surface through exceptionally clear water. A quick look through the periscope revealed the polynya to be fringed with thick multiyear and deformed ice. "Great job!" I congratulated the diving officer of the watch, Steve Gray. "We're right in the center of the polynya."

"Hovering at six-eight feet, sir!" Gray reported back. I started to reply "very well" when a huge white shape rose from behind a large ridge, and I emitted an excited, "Polar bear, polar bear! It's on the edge of the polynya! Bearing, mark!"

"Bearing two-four-eight degrees true!" responded Quartermaster Clarence Williams, asking, "Estimated range?" "Close, Close!" I answered, followed by "Quick, hand me the camera!"

The command watch officer, Bob Baumhardt, placed a brand new Hasselblad 35-mm camera in my right hand while I continued to track the polar bear through the periscope. I removed the periscope eyepiece within a matter of seconds, rap-

Figure 17.1 Commander Alfred S. McLaren, USS *Queenfish,* on periscope during Siberian shelf survey. (Courtesy of the U.S. Navy)

idly snapped a series of pictures, and handed the camera back to Bob. I quickly re-mounted the eyepiece and stared at what was definitely a very large polar bear.

"Polar bear in the water!" I cried out. "He just reared up and dived into the wa-ter!" And then, "He's swimming right for us! He's closing fast!"

"Maybe he thinks we're a large seal," voiced an unidentified watch-section joker from within the control room.

Bob Baumhardt tried to place the camera back in my hand so I could take more photos. I attempted to remove the eyepiece and watch the rapidly approaching carnivore at the same time. I failed to get a firm grip on the camera, however, and

Figure 17.2 Female polar bear seen through periscope at edge of polynya in Arctic Ocean north of New Siberian Islands. (Courtesy of the U.S. Navy)

it slipped out of my hand, struck the edge of the periscope well, and fell in. Horrible metallic bangs and breaking-up noises were heard as the camera hit and then bounced off the bottom of the deep steel periscope well. I let out a few healthy curses, followed by "Stand by with the Minolta!"

I centered the periscope's crosshairs on the bear's large black nose and excitedly tracked it as it rapidly closed. Its great white head loomed larger and larger and soon filled the entire field of view. At that moment the idle thought entered my head, "How on earth are we going to explain teeth marks on our periscope when we return to port?"

"It's now getting a good whiff of us," I reported as the bear's glistening black nose closed to within inches of the periscope head window. "Polar bear turning away!" I then yelled out, adding, "It's a female! There are two bright-eyed cubs riding her stern! Quick, Bob, take a picture!"

I pulled the periscope eyepiece clear as Bob stepped up and snapped a fantastic series of photographs of the mother and her two fat cubs passing the periscope close aboard and rapidly swimming away. He took several more when they reached the edge of the polynya and scrambled onto the ice. A high state of excitement and

Figure 17.3 Three polar bears near *Queenfish* periscope above New Siberian Islands on 18 August 1970. (Courtesy of the U.S. Navy)

euphoria gripped the control room as many of the crew crowded in to find out what was going on. We continued hovering within the polynya, hoping that *Ursus maritimus* and her family would return, but they never did.

It soon began to snow. Visibility worsened, and the diving officer was directed to broach the boat up to fifty feet. The control room watch remained fully ready to submerge, however, in the event that heavy ice surrounding the polynya began to close or Chief Electronics Technician John Wilgus and his team picked up a strong or closing radar contact of any sort on the ECM equipment. The navigation team fixed our position, and we copied a series of radio broadcasts as we impatiently waited for confirmation that our check report had been received. In the meantime, photographs of the polar bears were developed and printed, and the best were posted throughout the boat for all to see.

We received confirmation about mid-evening on 18 August, after what seemed an eternity. Main vents were then opened, and as *Queenfish's* ballast tanks reflooded, all periscopes, masts, and antennas were lowered as a stationary dive took us beneath the surface of the polynya. The SPM was ordered housed and the main propulsion shaft reengaged as we passed one hundred feet. The engineering officer of the watch, Bill Blenkle, reported almost immediately, "Maneuvering ready to answer all bells!" At 140 feet, I ordered, "Ahead two-thirds, make turns for ten knots!" to regain depth control. Once the boat leveled off at 160 feet, I returned the conn to the officer of the deck, Bud Pezet. He was directed to proceed to a depth of 390 feet, increase speed to nineteen knots, and, as recommended by the navigator, head for a position northwest of the New Siberian Islands from which to resume the hydrographic survey.

All told, we had lost almost an entire day of survey time due to various communication problems and delays not of our making. It meant that we would not reach the survey resumption point until shortly after breakfast on 19 August, well behind *Queenfish's* PIM. It would be tough to make this time up, because a higher speed than the maximum we planned to use for safe navigation would be required.

The New Siberian Islands—Novosibirskiye Ostrova in Russian—make up an archipelago extending some 434 miles from west to east and covering a land area of some 14,670 square miles between the Laptev and East Siberian seas. There are three island groups in the archipelago: (1) the southern group (Bolshoy and Maly Lyakhov Stolbovoy islands); (2) the central group (Anzhu islands [or the New Siberian Islands proper] and Kotelny, Belkovsky, Novaya Sibir, and Faddeyevsky islands, with Faddeyevsky connected with Bunge Land by a sandy plain; and (3) the northern group, or DeLong Islands (Jeanette, Henrietta, Bennett, Vilkitsky, and Zhokhov). Altogether, there are now known to be some thirteen relatively large islands and more than thirty smaller islands in the group, representing remnants of a vast plain with isolated highlands and outcrops of igneous rocks.[1]

The shallow Sannikov Strait far to our south separated the southern group from the central group. The southern group lay in very shallow water, much closer to the Siberian coast and beyond our ability to approach, much less survey. Our intended track would take us well to the north of the major central group islands, which span approximately 250 miles between longitudes 136° and 151° E. Although we expected to encounter icebergs from one or more of these islands, it was not learned until years later that these islands were low-lying and, as a consequence, too dry and warm during the summer for ice caps or glaciers to build up. As will be discussed later, we had no idea just where the survey might take us in relation to the northern islands.[2]

The first Westerner to sight the New Siberian Islands was the Russian Maksim Mukhoplev, who discovered the southerly islands during an exploring expedition from Yakutsk in 1692. Merkuriy Vagin and the Cossack Yakov Permyakov, however,

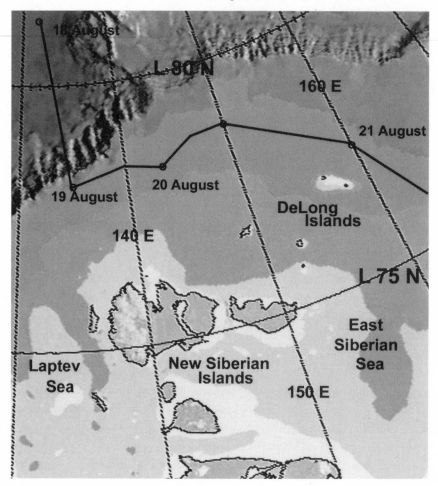

Chartlet 17.1 New Siberian Islands, 19 August to 21 August 1970.

were subsequently credited with discovering and landing on the largest of these islands, Bolshoy, in 1712.[3]

The islands were ultimately named after the Russian merchant Ivan Lyakhov, who landed on Bolshoy and the smaller island, Maly Lyakhov Stolbovoy, in search of prehistoric mammoth tusks during an expedition in 1770. His success led to a major industry in which ivory tusks from well over forty-six thousand mammoths were collected over the next 250 years. Lyakhov was later to find the first of the central New Siberian Islands—Kotelny (Kettle Island, because a copper kettle was found there)—during a 1773–74 expedition.[4]

Yakov Sannikov, chief foreman of a Russian hunting expedition, discovered two additional central islands, Faddeyevsky and Novaya Sibir, during 1805–6. Finally, a Russian foreman hunter, Belkov, completed the discovery of all the larger central New Siberian Islands with Belkovsky in 1808.[5]

The New Siberian Islands were later surveyed and mapped by a Russian exploring expedition led by Mattvey Gedenshtrom during the period 1808–11. P. Pshentsin continued the search for more islands during an extremely harrowing Russian expedition in 1811, which he and his companions barely survived.[6]

Queenfish reached the continental shelf north of the New Siberian Islands by mid-morning on 19 August. Following an unsuccessful attempt to come to periscope depth due to a phenomenal amount of thick, drifting brash ice, we resumed the hydrographic survey without an updated navigational fix. We were now operating 60 feet above the ocean floor at a keel depth of 180 feet and constantly maneuvering at approximately eight knots as we followed and recorded the deeper depth contour. Because the distance from the keel to the top of her sail was approximately 54 feet, *Queenfish*'s sail was 126 feet beneath the surface, enabling us to stay well clear of exceptionally thick and rugged sea ice overhead, which had an average thickness of 75 feet.

Most of the central and southern island groups of the New Siberian Islands archipelago were reported to be low-lying. The highest elevation of 1,227 feet was on Mt. Malakatyn-Tas, which was on Kotelny Island to our south. The central group was said to be nearly always covered by snow and ice. Although it would have been a real coup to sight several islands within this group, *Queenfish* was still too far north to do so.[7]

We made a second attempt to ascend to periscope depth in a polynya of almost five hundred yards in diameter shortly before noon. The surrounding water was heavily silted and of an extremely murky brownish-yellow color as we ascended from 140 to 80 feet. We were again defeated by thick drifting ice when *Queenfish*'s sail and port sail plane collided with and literally bounced off a sizable massif during the final stages of a slow ascent through water that was steadfastly isothermal at 29° F. The boat's screeching impact with the ice caused her to heel almost 15° and ricochet downward. The wind was driving such ice massifs across the polynya at speeds too great for us to detect in sufficient time to avoid them. The wind must have been of near gale force. After a harrowing few moments of uncontrolled descent, we regained control of *Queenfish* and returned to deeper depths and resumed the survey, grateful that no damage had occurred.

After passing under stretches of open water for the better part of an hour, *Queenfish* surfaced in a large polynya during the early evening of 19 August. The ascent had to be completed in stages due to the murkiness of the water above us and required frequent use of the SPM as hunks of deep-draft drifting ice were sighted and maneuvered around. We finally achieved periscope depth a half hour later under the same environmental conditions encountered earlier.

Grant Youngman used automatic depth control to hover *Queenfish* at periscope depth for the next eighty minutes to copy scheduled radio broadcasts. Our navigation team had to obtain satellite and Omega fixes in the midst of a heavy snowstorm. What Dick Boyle termed "typical marginal ice-zone conditions," characterized by strong winds, rapidly drifting ice, and low visibility, kept the officer of the deck, Tom Hoepfner, very busy. He had to use the SPM constantly to maneuver away from large ice chunks that were of even greater danger to periscope and communication masts than to the propeller or the rudder.

Toby Warson and Chief Quartermaster Jack Patterson obtained another series of satellite navigational fixes and proudly reported that their estimated position by hand DR had been within five miles, more accurate than the SINS, which held us some seven miles to the east of our actual position of 130 miles due north of Kotelny Island. Although Kotelny Island has the second highest peak in the archipelago, reaching an altitude of 1,230 feet, we were much too far away to see it even on a clear day.[8] Warson and Patterson further reported that latitudes by both hand DR and SINS were right on. I was pleased at this but cautioned that even greater navigational accuracy was required as *Queenfish* approached the northern group, the DeLong Islands, of the archipelago that still lay ahead.

We expected to pass by the volcanic DeLong Islands late on 20 August before entering into the East Siberian Sea the following day. The DeLong Islands consist of the quite small Jeannette, Henrietta, Bennett, Vilkitsky, and Zhokhov islands, which lie approximately seventy-five miles to the northeast of the most eastern of the large central group of islands, Novaya Sibir. Ice-capped Bennett, the largest of the DeLong Islands, lay more than 124 miles to our east at latitude 70°-67′ N, longitude 149°-08′ E. The volcano on Bennett is the northernmost active one on earth, and its peak at fourteen hundred feet is the highest in the entire New Siberian Archipelago, although we did not know this at the time. Lectures by Allan Beal and Dick Boyle on these remote and rarely seen islands had excited the curiosity of the officers and crew, and we hoped to pass sufficiently close to photograph them.[9]

We were uncertain just where the hydrographic survey might lead us with respect to this group of tiny scattered islands. Would water depths permit us to transit south of them or thread through, or would we be forced to skirt the entire group to the north?

If we were ever going to discover a new island or land during this survey mission, it would be within this island group. Nevertheless, the idea of threading through these islands in totally uncharted waters was not very appealing. Of immediate concern was the chance that the continental shelf seabed might suddenly shoal up, and we would stumble on a previously unknown very small island along our track, such as Figurina Island, which Petr Anzhu had discovered by accident due north of Faddeyevsky Island during his search for Sannikov's Land (Zemya Sannikova) in 1822. Our thoughts were similar with regard to the more northerly and larger so-called Sannikov's Land, supposedly sighted in 1810, 1811, and 1886 and still considered in existence as late as 1939.[10] Although *Queenfish* and her crew were avid to explore, discovery of a new landmass under the heavy pack ice and within already shallow water would have required some pretty adroit maneuvers and considerable rethinking of the expedition's overall survey plans.

A stationary dive during the middle of the evening actually drew cheers from the control room watch as we descended below the drifting brash ice and absolutely miserable atmospheric conditions that enveloped the polynya and surrounding area. We spent the remainder of the night and early morning of 20 August following the depth contour of interest as it wandered back and forth in a generally eastward direction north of the New Siberian Islands.

We returned to periscope depth and into a very open water area, via vertical ascent, shortly before breakfast on 20 August. Water beneath the polynya was heavily silted and populated with many small jellyfish when we began the ascent and then abruptly cleared about fifty feet from the surface. Seawater temperature remained a steady 29° F throughout, and salinity was essentially the same. Strange! At periscope depth we confronted the same miserable marginal ice-zone conditions as on the previous evening, although the heavy ice within and around the polynya appeared to be melting. *Queenfish* hovered beneath the surface with just No. 2 periscope and its protective fairing raised while we impatiently waited to copy priority radio messages that had somehow been preempted by almost half an hour of special "Family Grams" destined for another attack submarine somewhere in the Pacific.[11]

Navigation fixes placed us approximately 135 miles due north of Faddeyevsky Island. I was not altogether happy with either SINS or hand DR position estimates, however. Neither seemed to take into account a strong easterly "set" (direction of current) and drift of 0.5 knots from 90° that we had experienced since early on 17 August. The navigation team and I were later to be quite embarrassed when Allan Beal reminded us that the set and drift was, of course, the well-known Transpolar Drift Stream discovered and used by Fridtjof Nansen in the *Fram* between 1893 and 1896 in an attempt to reach the North Pole.[12]

We proceeded beneath the ice pack about mid-morning on 20 August and resumed the survey. *Queenfish's* last fix made it quite apparent that, unless we discovered a deep gulflike indentation in the continental shelf followed by deeper water toward the southeast, the area in the near vicinity of the DeLong Islands would be too shallow to negotiate, and *Queenfish* would have to pass well to the north, missing the archipelago altogether. This was disappointing news in that such a deep-water passage would have been a major geographic finding and of keen navigational and military interest.

We pursued the depth contour of interest throughout the rest of the morning and well into the afternoon without much difficulty. No ice keels were deep enough to require maneuvering around them, and the seabed was generally flat. The top sounder recorder revealed an increasing amount of deep-draft ice above us beginning about mid-afternoon on 20 August, although nothing with drafts that exceeded sixty-five feet beneath the surface.

Queenfish made a vertical ascent during the early evening into a very small polynya in order to fix her navigational position. Bill Enderlein did a superb job of getting us right up and into its center, but the slight forward way resulted in the bow passing beneath some thick first-year ice.[13] I immediately lowered No. 1 periscope and, as Bill increased depth slightly, ordered the SPM trained to 180°, using it to back sufficiently to bring us clear before the bow touched or scraped against the always-rugged underside of the ice.

No. 1 periscope was raised, and a quick look confirmed that our position within the polynya was good. I ordered Bill to bring us up several more feet. I then turned over the conn and responsibility for our well-being within the polynya to Ralph Beedle. In addition to being a superlative engineer officer, Ralph was one of *Queenfish's* best officers of the deck and command watch officers. Possessed of a keen situational awareness, forehandedness, and positive attitude the equal of Bob Baumhardt's, he was to share considerable credit with Bob for the high morale and successes of *Queenfish's* crew during my remaining years in command.

We hovered for about twenty minutes in what was clearly a shrinking polynya, threatening both rudder and screw. Because we had yet to receive our radio broadcast, I directed Ralph to broach *Queenfish* to a decks-awash condition and move the boat forward to position and hold our bow against the ice. This provided the stern area with sufficient clearance from the steadily closing ice. Chief Radioman Mike Hein had just enough time to finish copying the radio broadcast before it would be necessary to abandon this particular polynya. The broadcast was completed and copied a few minutes later. Tom Hoepfner opened the after main ballast tank vents, followed by the forward vents, and expeditiously took us below the surface with a modified stationary descent that ensured both rudder and screw were well below the ice before we began the descent. He then leveled the boat off smartly at 120 feet. *Queenfish* proceeded from there to 180 feet, increased speed to eight knots, and resumed what was beginning to seem a hydrographic survey that would never end.

The navigation fix obtained during the previous hour showed us to be more than 120 miles due north of Bennett Island. Thus, if the depth contour we had been tracing continued in the same slightly northeasterly direction that it had pursued all day, we would never have an opportunity to see this interesting island and would be certain to pass much farther north of the remaining DeLong Islands than we had originally anticipated. None of us, including Dr. Lyon before we departed, had expected the Siberian continental shelf to extend as far north of the New Siberian and DeLong island groups as we had found it. Our original thought was that the continental shelf might not extend much farther north than latitude 77° N, as it did across much of the northern Laptev Sea. Had this been the case, it would have resulted in our passing between thirty and forty miles north of the central group of New Siberian Islands and even closer to the more northerly DeLong Islands, with landfall being a real possibility on the most northerly of the group. But it was definitely not to be.

The ice overhead became increasingly compact as the evening progressed. Shortly before midnight on 20 August we began recording deep-draft ice whose keels extended as much as eighty feet below the estimated sea surface. Although they cleared the top of the sail by slightly less than fifty feet, none was detected by the top sounder for reasons not yet understood. Early on 21 August, the general direction of the depth contour being surveyed changed to due east, and we began to meander gradually toward the southeast as we passed to the north of Henrietta Island.

Mid-morning we encountered a very large polynya extending more than six hundred yards and reversed course, planning to ascend to periscope depth to obtain a navigational fix. When it appeared that *Queenfish* was clear of the numerous chunks of ice overhead, the diving officer of the watch, Steve Gray, brought us up with a well-controlled vertical ascent through exceptionally murky water to a keel depth of seventy feet.

As I raised No. 1 periscope, a slight shudder told us that *Queenfish* had touched ice. A combination of ice movement toward us and slight forward drifting on our part had placed us under the far edge of the polynya. I immediately lowered the scope and directed Steve to take us back down to one hundred feet so we could recheck our position within the polynya. The forward upward-beamed top sounder transducers indicated that *Queenfish's* bow was again under ice. We backed clear with the SPM and into the center of the open water above us. Steve brought us up smartly to a depth of forty-eight feet, which put the top of the sail awash. This enabled us to raise periscopes, radio, and ECM masts as the steel sail itself warded off the drifting blocks of ice. We had just developed a new method, providing there were no surface or air contacts, of accomplishing our daily chores at periscope depth in a complex environment of wind-driven drifting ice.

The latest navigational position confirmed our SINS and hand DR estimates that we were now more than seventy miles to the northeast of the nearest of the DeLong Islands of Henrietta and Jeannette.

The DeLong Islands have always evoked, for most Arctic explorers, the sad memories of the U.S. North Pole Expedition of 1879–81, commanded by U.S. Navy Lieutenant George Washington DeLong. In 1879, DeLong's ship *Jeannette* (named after his wife) followed the northeast coast of Chukotsky Peninsula from Laurenty Bay to Kolyuchinskaya Gulf and from there a course for the North Pole.[14] The tiny island that he named Jeannette was discovered as the expedition ship, frozen within and beset by the polar ice pack since 6 September 1879, drifted past it on 16 May 1881. Henrietta Island, to the northwest, was the next to be sighted on 24 May, and a sledge party was put off the ship onto the ice on 2 June to investigate. Catastrophically, *Jeannette* was crushed by the ice and had to be abandoned by its crew ten days later, 12 June 1881. It sank a day later, approximately nine miles to the west of Henrietta. From here DeLong and his men, despite their best efforts to sledge and drag their boats south, drifted north on the ice pack to latitude 77°-46' N. They subsequently discovered a third island, Bennett, in mid-July 1881, within what became known as the DeLong Islands, the northern group of the New Siberian Islands. From there, thirty-three crew members headed south on a journey in which twenty lives, including the captain's, were lost before they reached the vast Lena delta, eventual civilization, and rescue.[15]

Where might the remains of the *Jeannette* be now? In all probability they are scattered across the Arctic Ocean floor from where the ship first disappeared beneath the sea above the New Siberian Islands, to as far away as southwest Greenland several thousand miles away, where pieces were discovered in 1884, having drifted there in just three years.[16] *Queenfish* was neither equipped for nor tasked with locating and investigating marine wrecks on the seafloors of the Siberian continental shelf. It would have been interesting, however, to have had a remote operating vehicle, or side-scan sonar, back in 1970 with which to search for major parts of *Jeannette* that might still lie on the seabed in the near vicinity of where she sank.

As it was, water depths were far too shallow and the pack ice too thick to permit us to get anywhere near.

The depth contour curve that we had delineated and recorded on a southeasterly heading throughout the night had now taken us into the northwest corner of the East Siberian Sea. We all knew we were approaching what might soon prove to be the most arduous and dangerous weeks of the entire expedition.

The Even Shallower East Siberian Sea

We passed well to the northeast of the New Siberian and DeLong islands and entered the northwestern corner of the East Siberian Sea late on 21 August. We had at last reached this vast and mysterious sea, the least known of the seven fringing the Arctic Ocean. Although we had become quite expert and experienced in piloting our boat through the shallow, ice-covered waters of the Chukchi and Laptev, we were anything but overconfident about the East Siberian. *Queenfish's* crew approached the formidable challenges posed by this perennial ice-covered sea with respect and some trepidation.

The average bathymetry of the East Siberian Sea is now known to be shallower than either the Laptev's or the Chukchi's, as we were to discover during late August of 1970. Its largely pack-ice–covered waters are fresh and cold from the discharge of approximately 5,332,414 cubic feet of fresh water per year from the north-flowing Kolyma, Indigirka, and Alazeya rivers. Ninety percent of this water enters the southern East Siberian Sea between June and September of each year; the remainder of the year the northernmost reaches of these rivers are frozen almost solid. Surface temperatures vary between 32° F and 35.6° F throughout, and bottom temperatures are always near the freezing point of 29.5° F, according to recent reports that confirm *Queenfish's* own 1970 observations.[1]

The coastal waters of the East Siberian Sea were first explored early in the seventeenth century, during the harshest years of the Little Ice Age. Ivan Rebrov of the Russian exploring expedition from the Yana River in the Laptev Sea was the

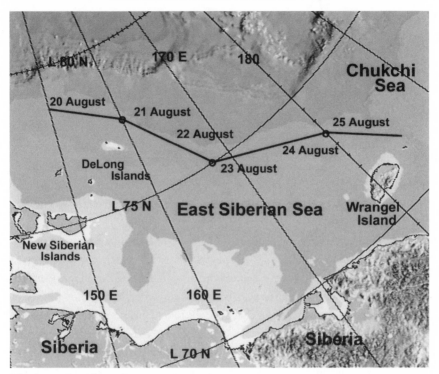

Chartlet 18.1 East Siberian Sea, 21 August to 25 August 1970.

first known discoverer of the East Siberian Sea. In 1638 he passed through Dmitri Laptev Strait, between Bolshoy Island and the Siberian coast, eastward into the East Siberian Sea, and subsequently discovered the mouth of the Indigirka River. He was soon followed by Dmitri Zyryan, who headed an expedition in 1642 that sailed from the mouth of the Indigirka eastward into unexplored waters of the East Siberian Sea. He discovered the Alazeya River.[2]

Close behind Zyryan was Mikhail Stadukhin, of a Russian exploring expedition from Yakutsk, who joined Zyryan at the Alazeya River in July of 1643 and continued the voyage of exploration farther east, where he discovered the Kolyma River. Finally, Stadukhin completed the first sea voyage from the Kolyma River, which flows into the East Siberian Sea, westward to the Lena River flowing into the Laptev Sea, during the autumn of 1645. Their discoveries soon led to large-scale shipments of valuable cargos of sable skins from the Kolyma to the Lena.[3]

Exploration farther east of this offshore route across the East Siberian Sea was undertaken in 1648 by a seven-ship Russian exploring and hunting expedition led by

Semen Dezhnev. The expedition proceeded from the Kolyma River northward into the East Siberian Sea and eastward along the Arctic coast of Siberia for conquest and trade and to find the fur-rich Anadyr River country.[4] Dezhnev's discovery of the easternmost extremity and of the strait dividing the Asian and American continents preceded Vitus Bering's by eighty years. Six of Dezhnev's seven ships and their crews were lost, however, and the expedition was considered a failure. Dezhnev's report was "misplaced," and the strait was eventually named for Bering.

Dezhnev's great achievement was not to be fully recognized until 1898, when Russia adopted Nordenskiöld's recommendation that East Cape, the easternmost promontory of Asia, be named Cape Dezhnev. So Vitus Bering, erroneously believed to be the discoverer of the strait in 1729, was in fact the second to pass northward through it.[5]

As large-scale exploitation of these Siberian coastal fur trade routes developed, many of the hunters and traders who sailed them began to form convoys to lessen the dangers. The first such convoy, consisting of up to ten vessels and four hundred men, was led in 1649 by a party of Cossacks commanded by Timofey Buldakov. Over the next thirty years, convoys between the main Siberian rivers and a number of small islands, such as the Medvezhyi Islands, discovered offshore, became almost routine, although severe weather, contrary winds, and impassable ice took a heavy toll of ships, cargo, and men.[6]

East Siberian Arctic seafaring began to die out at the end of the 1680s as the sable trade declined and hunters and traders migrated to more promising regions farther south.[7]

Voyages along the Siberian coast resumed following the Russo-Japanese War of 1904–5, more than two hundred years later. Fear of increased foreign penetration in the Far East and the need to protect Russian territories there prompted the Russian government to encourage the extension of private Russian shipping to the mouth of the Kolyma River in the East Siberian Sea. The first vessel to achieve this successfully was the *Kolyma* in July 1911. A small number of ships have continued such voyages each summer season to the present day.[8]

Particularly noteworthy in the early days of the century were the east-west and return voyages of the icebreakers and *Taymyr* (Vilkitsky) and *Vaygach* (Novopashennyy) each summer from 1910 to 1915 via the coastal waters of the East Siberian Sea.[9]

Our intensive study of all information available from these early Russian reports, together with Nordenskiöld's historic transit in *Vega* of the Northeast Passage from August 1878 through July 1879 (see also chapter 13), strongly suggested to us that the East Siberian Sea's shallow depths and heavily compacted sea ice might well prove the most treacherous of all to survey on the Siberian continental shelf.[10]

As *Queenfish* transited to the east of Henrietta and Jeannette islands during the early morning hours of 22 August, she encountered an increasing number of deep-draft ice keels of anywhere from eighty to almost one hundred feet. The seabed grew rocky and irregular. As the morning progressed, we discovered and passed over three more deep ice scours like those encountered in the Laptev Sea. These passages were the scene of two of the most dangerous moments of our entire voyage.

The first incident occurred as we crossed over the scours. The seabed was just sixty feet beneath our keel. A sudden decrease of twenty to thirty feet in overall water depth was followed, within minutes, by an abrupt and quite dramatic shoaling upward of the seafloor. Only through the exceptionally alert and adroit response on the part of both the ship's control team and the command watch officer, Toby Warson, did *Queenfish* avoid plowing into the rugged seabed. Almost simultaneously Toby changed course to the east with considerable rudder, decreasing the ship's depth as much as the ice overhead would allow and reducing speed.[11]

The second incident occurred shortly after we had gingerly returned to the original southeasterly course, speed, and depth and resumed the survey. We were just beginning to calm down and congratulate ourselves on avoiding a collision with the bottom when the quartermaster of the watch, Clarence Williams, reported excitedly from the depth sounder that a pingo had suddenly shot up some forty feet. It peaked and passed with less than twenty feet of clearance under our keel before we could even react. Within seconds water depth had returned to approximately sixty feet beneath our keel. I was not the only one who paled at what had just occurred. There were anxious expressions all around.

For reasons that could not be explained to anyone's satisfaction, our under-ice piloting sonar, or iceberg detector, had failed to give us advance warning of either close call. It should have provided warning of the possible pingo at ranges in excess of one thousand yards, but did not. These two near misses underscored once again the wisdom of shifting to a deeper depth contour in the interest of ship and crew safety. If we had doggedly continued to survey the original depth contour of interest in the East Siberian Sea, it would have required us to transit within twenty to thirty feet of the bottom, and *Queenfish* would have collided with the bottom twice this day.

The eight-knot survey speed that we had been using to catch up to our PIM, whenever conditions permitted, was immediately reduced to not more than five knots in order to gain more reaction time with which to deal with the next un-

Figure 18.1 Artist's concept of USS *Queenfish* passing over an ice scour in the East Siberian Sea. (Courtesy of the U.S. Navy)

derwater obstacle. It was definitely time to slow down, calm down, collect our thoughts, and review once again the operational procedures and watch-standing requirements for completing our mission in the safest manner possible.

The first order of business was to find a polynya in which to ascend and fix our navigational position. That completed, we took time to reflect on the dangers of pingos, ice scours, and ice gouges. Although they had hitherto provided an interesting diversion from an otherwise grueling and sometimes boring hydrographic survey, our unpleasant experience with them was fair warning for the unwary in the East Siberian Sea.

Allan Beal, Dick Boyle, and I once again turned to speculation on what might have created these deep trenches. Were they caused by the northward movement of glaciers or icebergs toward the sea in ancient times, as we thought might be the case in the Laptev Sea? The ones here were oriented in a roughly north-to-south direction perpendicular to the Siberian coast. Although we were too far from the coast to tell whether any of the trenches or scours originated from the discharge of a northward-flowing river, we did note the presence of a considerable amount of deep-draft ice nearby.

In subsequent discussions in the control room and throughout the boat, it occurred to more than one crew member that these scours, gouges, or trenches might be of future military value, some of the deeper ones as patrol or prelaunch safe havens for ballistic missile submarines. A suitably equipped Arctic nuclear attack submarine could conceivably use them as routes for penetrating southward from the Arctic Ocean to an excellent interdiction position for employing mines and torpedoes against submerged adversaries as well as for shipping along a northern convoy route.

We could not find any open water along our survey track to the southeast during the remainder of the morning. The pack ice above us remained steadfastly thick and heavily compacted. Shortly before noon, therefore, we decreased depth, slowed to minimum turns, and streamed our floating wire VLF radio antenna beneath the very thick, jagged ice overhead. We hoped for the best as we copied our radio broadcast at minimum turns. For the second time in a row, messages of importance to us, such as ice forecasts, were preempted by some twenty minutes of nonoperational Family Grams to another nuclear attack boat deployed to the western Pacific (which had apparently made special arrangements).

This was a new and unforeseen problem—one that could affect both mission and safety if vital radio traffic continued to be preempted. The risk of colliding with moving sea ice, not to mention the chance of counterdetection, mounted with each passing minute we spent at communications depth. Such a situation would be totally unacceptable if we were on a higher-priority cold war mission. Chief Radioman Mike Hein, Communications Officer Lars Hanson, and I would have some firm and well-thought-out recommendations to make in this regard to the submarine force commander on *Queenfish's* return to Pearl Harbor.

Toby Warson and Chief Quartermaster Jack Patterson managed to get several Omega fixes that checked well with SINS and our hand DR, but both men expressed a strong desire to get a more accurate satellite fix at the first opportunity. We returned to 180 feet and resumed the hydrographic survey over what was developing into very different bottom topography from that observed around the New Siberian Islands or throughout the Laptev Sea.

In reviewing the current operational environment and what might lie ahead, Allan Beal, Dick Boyle, my officers, and I agreed that the probability of running into sudden shoaling, more ice scours, and even larger pingos was high. In addition, the meanderings of the depth contour we were following posed a serious challenge for both ship control and navigational teams. Rarely would the contour remain steady on any particular southeasterly direction. Like a mountain road or winding riverbed, it would suddenly turn south, then head briefly toward the southwest, and finally return to the southeast or some other unanticipated combination of the three.

There was no question in anyone's mind now that an inadvertent up- or down-angle of just one-half degree could cause the boat's rudder to dig into the seabed or collide or become entangled with the very thick ice overhead. A moment's inattention or distraction, any misinterpretation of navigation, under-ice sonar information, or maneuvering order, or fatigue could bring the expedition to an abrupt and possibly calamitous end.

I strongly reinforced with each command watch officer that, as in the Chukchi and Laptev seas, all piloting of the boat in ice-covered shallow water was to be conducted from the iceberg detector watch station in the control room. Safe navigation of *Queenfish* through the much harsher East Siberian Sea called for even closer coordination and communication between the officer doing the piloting and the control room watch standers and ship control team. Each member of the watch team was to provide "forceful backup" whenever the operational situation demanded it. In reporting ice thickness overhead and depth below, the quartermaster of the watch was not to hesitate to recommend the safest course, depth, and speed. The ship control party, which consisted of the diving officer of the watch, planesmen and helmsman, and the engineers aft, was to respond promptly and correctly to all orders subsequently given, even to shutting down one side of the engineering power plant if bottoming was imminent. Kenneth Ickes was to make sure that each watch team had recourse to additional qualified planesmen and helmsman to allay the fatigue that would most certainly set in from the stress of continually maneuvering in close quarters.

Finally, the current operational situation dictated that Toby Warson and I should be either in the control room or close at hand at all times for extra direction, backup, and support and that either Allan Beal or Dick Boyle should be in the control room from this day forward until we were clear of the Arctic ice pack.

Complete confidence in our collective ability to handle whatever came our way in the East Siberian Sea and beyond was never in doubt. It was well known throughout the boat that at least three of *Queenfish's* officers, Ralph Beedle, Toby Warson, and Bob Baumhardt, had each proved more than equal to the task of piloting *Queenfish* beneath or around deep-draft ice keels in our path and avoiding going aground in rapidly shoaling water. Moreover, *Queenfish* had a superb ships diving officer in Tom Hoepfner and three top-notch diving officers of the watch, Grant Youngman, Steve Gray, and Bill Enderlein, backed up by three solid ship control teams. All had shown they could keep the boat on depth and bubble and in trim in even the tightest of maneuvering situations. Adding to our overall comfort level and confidence were our superb engineering department watch standers headed by the engineering officers of the watch, Frederick Moore, William Blenkle, and Lars Hanson, and our machinery watch supervisors, Senior Chief Electronics

Technician Richard Dietz, Master Chief Electricians Mate Mike Kotek, and Chief Machinist Mate Harry Tample.

The rest of 22 August was as difficult as expected for each successive watch section as we followed and recorded the depth contour of interest across an irregular and sometimes rocky bottom. The ice cover overhead remained relentlessly thick and heavily compacted. A break in the ice pack during the evening at last presented a brash-ice–filled polynya of sufficient size for us to make a vertical ascent to periscope depth and confirm our navigational position by satellite. Jeannette Island, the most easterly island of the DeLong Archipelago, was now almost 140 miles to the west of us. The navigator estimated that, with luck, *Queenfish* could be more than halfway through the East Siberian Sea in another twenty-four hours.

The ice surrounding the polynya largely consisted of multiyear and deformed ice conglomerates and ridges of thicknesses approaching seventy-five feet. As I rotated the periscope to conduct a lengthy series of air and surface sweeps on a thoroughly dark, overcast, and generally dismal evening, it struck me as quite remarkable that the surface of the ice pack did not give a hint of its actual thickness in any direction. If anything, considerable weathering of the many pressure ridges and the floe surfaces in between made the ice seem far thinner and milder than it actually was when viewed from underneath.

The mid-watch, morning, and early afternoon watches of Sunday, 23 August, were just as exhausting as on the previous days. We seemed to have the situation well in hand, though, and had no further encounters with ice scours or pingos. It should have been a warning that we would not have long to wait before experiencing the most serious threat yet to the safety of *Queenfish* and her crew.

Until late afternoon, the day had not posed any great difficulties in under-ice navigation. Many crew members were watching one of their favorite westerns, *Shane,* in the crew's mess. A number of officers and I joined them to see Alan Ladd once more finish off the dark and villainous gunfighter, Jack Palance. I was thoroughly engrossed when a messenger suddenly touched my shoulder and informed me that *Queenfish* was at all-stop and hovering and that Toby Warson needed me to come to the control room at once. Heart in my mouth, I ran up to the afterport side of the control room, where Bob Baumhardt was positioned behind the AN/BQS-8 under-ice sonar. He did not need to say a word. Saturating the iceberg detector scope was bright sea-ice-return in all directions.[12]

Baumhardt quickly briefed me on the situation. *Queenfish* had somehow entered a cul-de-sac while in the process of closely following and recording the bottom contour as it curved through due south, or 180°, and then steadied on a backtracking, southwesterly direction. All forward way on the boat had been killed, and we were now hovering at approximately ten feet above the bottom with the starboard main condenser sea suctions just ordered shut in order to keep at least that side from silting up. To make matters worse, deep-draft keels extending from the pack ice were no more than fifteen to twenty feet above us. Our under-ice piloting sonar indicated that we were also blocked to port and starboard by deep-draft ice at or very close to our depth. Still shallower water lay dead ahead of us. We were stuck in the equivalent of an ice garage.

Because there was insufficient water beneath the keel to permit lowering the SPM, I immediately ordered that present depth and state of neutral buoyancy be maintained as closely as possible. Nothing should be done inadvertently to change our fore and aft trim, or bubble, which was holding steady at 0°. All water for flushing to all heads was secured and red tagged. Further movement by all personnel throughout the boat was prohibited except in an emergency and only then by the express permission of the command watch officer. The next step was to extract ourselves, as calmly and carefully as possible, from this tightest of operational envelopes without grounding *Queenfish* or colliding with the ice in the process.

Heavily dependent on the finest of communication and coordination possible between the ship control party and the maneuvering room watch, I gave a series of orders to spin the propeller astern, several revolutions at a time, in order to develop slight sternway, or movement of the boat aft. The rudder had to be positioned slightly to starboard to prevent backing to port, and the diving officer of the watch, now Tom Hoepfner, had to order very slight adjustments of the stern planes as necessary to counter any tendency of the boat to squat.

Steady calm and patience were the watchwords for us all as we worked to achieve and preserve each small gain in an astern direction so as to extract ourselves from the undersea cocoon in which we had found ourselves. We gradually accomplished this without touching either the bottom or the ice over the space of what seemed an eternity but in actuality took no more than an hour. Back in deeper water, with more comfortable clearance from the ice overhead and on either side, all throughout the boat gave out a huge collective sigh of relief.

The fact that we had fallen into this hazardous situation so suddenly with one of my best command watch officers and watch teams on duty was stunning. It would haunt my mind and my dreams for the rest of the voyage and for years to come.[13] Dick Boyle recalled that *Sargo* (Nicholson) had been in tight situations within the Chukchi and Bering seas during the winter of 1960, but they were nothing like this. *Sargo* was, of course, shorter and had almost half the displacement of *Queenfish*; she also had the benefit of two small screws versus one large one. All I could say to the watch section, after our successful extraction, was, "Well done, men! Good old *Queenfish* has demonstrated her fantastic stability and maneuverability, not to mention luck, once again!" The occasion definitely called for a liberal "splicing of the main brace" as soon as we were finally clear of the Arctic ice pack.

I had been the diving officer on three previous submarines, *Greenfish, Seadragon,* and *Skipjack,* and was an experienced officer of the deck with many underways and landings under my belt on all three; I had now served on *Queenfish* for more than three years, two as her new construction and commissioning executive officer and one as her commanding officer. Of the four submarines, *Queenfish* was proving, without a doubt, to be the most responsive, easiest to maneuver, and most dependable under adverse circumstances. Unlike the other boats I had served on, *Queenfish* never gave me any unpleasant surprises with regard to her capabilities. During the course of my four-year command, she almost "talked to me." I could sense or feel in my feet her degree of stability and response to any maneuvering situation or order.

By early evening we were heading in a southeasterly direction once again and safely within what had become a standard safe-operations envelope in the East Siberian Sea: sixty feet above the bottom and clearing the ice overhead by at least fifty feet. Getting out of our earlier tight squeeze had just consumed most of the afternoon and almost all our emotional energy. It could never be allowed to occur again.

Queenfish's watch-to-watch survey instructions were, therefore, immediately changed: The command watch officers were instructed to follow the depth contour being traced to a compass heading of not more than 180° or due south. If the bottom contour continued past 180° toward the southwest, *Queenfish* was to remain on course 180°, ice conditions permitting, until the bottom contour returned to 180°, at which time we would resume following and recording it once again.

Once we were back on course, speed, and depth, we looked for and soon found a large polynya during the early evening. It was covered with a three- to four-inch-thick "skylight" of ice, which did not keep us from making a vertical ascent to periscope depth and a quite cheeringly bright, sunny day. The radio schedule was copied once the usual collection of Family Grams had cleared, and our navigational position was fixed. We were delighted to discover that *Queenfish* was now more than halfway through the East Siberian Sea and slightly above latitude 75° N, with the nearest land being Jeannette Island almost 230 miles away. We returned beneath the surface about mid-evening and resumed the survey.

Monday, 24 August, produced no surprises that came close to the main events of the past two days. We did encounter one or more unusually deep ice keels thrusting some 110 feet downward toward us in the early afternoon. At the time, we were in the process of surveying a quite irregular seabed that required us to increase depth beneath us from sixty to eighty feet. Two deep ice keels showed up as bright spots on the iceberg detector. As the spots got larger and brighter, *Queenfish* maneuvered to avoid them at a range of four hundred yards. They then completely disappeared from the iceberg detector scope at a range of two hundred yards. Just when we thought we were well clear, the top sounder recorded that the deeper of the two keels had cleared the top of our sail by less than fifteen feet. The East Siberian Sea was definitely living up to its reputation for severity, to which one would add the word "treachery." It was not finished with *Queenfish* yet.

We located a large polynya shortly after evening meal on 24 August and made a brisk vertical ascent into our first brash-ice–free polynya in some time. The relatively quick vertical ascents followed by stationary dives in the East Siberian Sea were helped by the fact that water temperature remained more or less constant around the freezing mark throughout the water column between transit and periscope depth. This was expected to change after we rounded Wrangel Island and proceeded southward in the western Chukchi Sea.

We had now surfaced or ascended to periscope depth a total of twenty-two times out of thirty tries in the Arctic ice-pack–covered waters. As might be expected, except for several long stretches in the northeastern Laptev Sea and the northwestern East Siberian Sea, surfaceable areas along our track were scarce. Yet we always managed to find a polynya or lead when we needed to. One factor of the dynamic Arctic Ocean environment with its high winds, even in winter, was that there would be patches of open water throughout most of the Arctic Basin year-round.

A stationary dive was conducted as soon as the radiomen reported that the radio broadcast copied and the navigation team was satisfied with its satellite and Omega fixes. As we returned to survey depth, course, and speed, the navigator reported that *Queenfish* would be approximately 150 miles due north of Wrangel Island by midnight, 24 August. We departed the East Siberian Sea, to no one's regret, shortly after midnight, crossed the 180° meridian, or international date line, and entered the Chukchi Sea. *Queenfish's* survey of the bottom topography of the East Siberian Sea stood to add more than one thousand miles of continuous depth soundings to what had been a very limited bank of hydrographic and oceanographic data beyond its Siberian coast offshore waters.

19
Return to Survey
the Northwestern Chukchi Sea

Queenfish crossed the international date line at longitude 180° early on 25 August, passing from the Eastern into the Western Hemisphere. We were now approximately 150 miles north of Wrangel Island and heading in a generally easterly direction. The pack ice above us remained steadfastly thick and heavily compacted through the night, with few areas of open water in evidence. The depth contour of interest began to lead us gradually toward the southeast, and by mid-morning we found ourselves in the northwestern Chukchi Sea. With the exception of a relatively narrow offshore route along the northern Siberian coast, around the Chukotsky Peninsula, and south to the Bering Strait, these waters were for the most part unexplored and uncharted in 1970.

Reentering the third and last of the three seas that covered the Siberian continental shelf, our feeling was one of suppressed excitement, akin to being only a few days from homeport following a long deployment and looking forward to embracing the familiar and friendly atmosphere of our own world. It was hard to believe. With luck we could be completely clear of the Arctic pack ice and back in ice-free open water within a day or two.

The day-by-day, mile-by-mile routine of having to thread our way through hundreds of miles of uncharted, ice-covered, shallow waters had been exhausting for us all. As we proceeded across the Laptev Sea, over the New Siberian Islands, and through the East Siberian Sea, we had been faced with the ever-present risk of colliding with the jagged keel of an ice massif or a seamount/pingo or of running aground on a rapidly shoaling bottom. There was no respite from such a re-

Figure 19.1 National Oceanic and Atmospheric Administration satellite view of Wrangel Island, eastern East Siberian Sea, and northwestern Chukchi Sea. (Courtesy of the National Oceanic and Atmospheric Administration)

lentlessly hostile environment or the concerns it engendered, even in our sleep.[1] We were tired and in some ways approaching burnout. The forthcoming stop in Nome for much-needed rest and recreation was looked forward to with the keenest anticipation, though the visit would be short.

Dick Boyle and Allan Beal, as part of their series of informative lectures, had already acquainted the officers and crew with many of the Arctic pioneers who had braved the ice-covered regions of the Chukchi Sea before us. It was a surprise to most of them to learn that the first Western explorer to discover and navigate the Siberian offshore waters of the Chukchi Sea, all the way to and through the Bering Strait, was not Bering but Semen Dezhnev. After Dezhnev, more than eighty years would pass before Russian naval explorers resumed exploration of the Chukchi Sea. Mikhail Vasilyev and Gleb Shishmarev, in *Otkrytiye* and *Blagonamerennyy*, respectively, sailed northward from Kotzebue Sound, Alaska, into the Chukchi to latitude 71°-06′ N, longitude 166°-08′ W on 29 July 1820.[2]

Shishmarev returned the following year, penetrating up to latitude 70°-13′ N and then exploring the Chukotsk coast northwestward to Cape Serdste-Kamen.

Ferdinand Wrangel followed in April 1823, surveying the Chukchi coast from Cape Shmidt to Kolyuchinskaya Gulf. He heard numerous reports during the voyage of "a mountainous land to the north," which came to be called Wrangel Island. Of considerable commercial significance, but of catastrophic ecological impact, was the entry into the Chukchi Sea in 1848 by the American whaling ship *Superior* (Thomas Roys), the first of twenty-seven hundred whaling ships of varying nationalities that would exploit its rich bowhead whaling grounds to the point of near extinction by 1921.[3]

The USS *Vincennes* (John Rodgers) explored the Chukchi Sea from Arakamchechen Island near the eastern extremity of the Chukotsky Peninsula, traveled northwest to Herald Island, and concluded with a brief survey in the northwest Chukchi Sea during August of 1855. Wrangel Island was sighted by two significant voyages eleven years later: the first in 1866 by the trading ship *W. C. Talbot* (Eduard Dallmann) and the second in 1867 by the whaler *Nile* (Thomas W. Long).[4]

By the end of the nineteenth century, Russian hydrographic expeditions, such as those led by Tyrtov in *Gaydamak* in 1875, Novosilsky in *Vsadnik* in 1876, Strelok in 1882, Ostolopov in *Kreyser* in 1886, and Vulf in *Razboynik* in 1889, had thoroughly surveyed an offshore route along the northeast and northern coasts of the Chukotsky Peninsula and Siberia. Calvin Hooper in *Thomas Corwin* of the U.S. Revenue Marine Service also cruised and explored this area during 1880 and 1881 and was, in all probability, the first to land on Wrangel Island. He was followed two weeks later by Robert Berry in USS *Rodgers,* who conducted the first geographical and scientific survey of the island.[5]

The century's concluding years of exploration of the Arctic were to see both great success and tragic failure. Adolph Nordenskiöld became the first to navigate the entire length of a Chukchi Sea offshore route, from due south of the eastern end of Wrangel Island, around the Chukotsky Peninsula coast and on to the Bering Strait, during the summers of 1878 and 1879, as part of his successful voyage through the Northeast Passage (see chapter 13).[6] As noted earlier, in 1879 George Washington DeLong's ship *Jeannette,* of the U.S. North Pole Expedition, became entrapped in the Chukchi Sea pack ice north of Herald Island in early September the same year.

During 1909 and 1910, the Russian government sent a hydrographic surveying expedition, under the command of Innokentiy Tolmachev, to determine whether there was a navigable sea route between the Lena River and the Bering Strait. This effort led a year later to the steamer *Kolyma's* (P. A. Troyan) single-season commercial trip from Vladivostok to the Kolyma River and the advent of increased marine traffic along the coastal waters of the Chukchi in the decades that followed.[7]

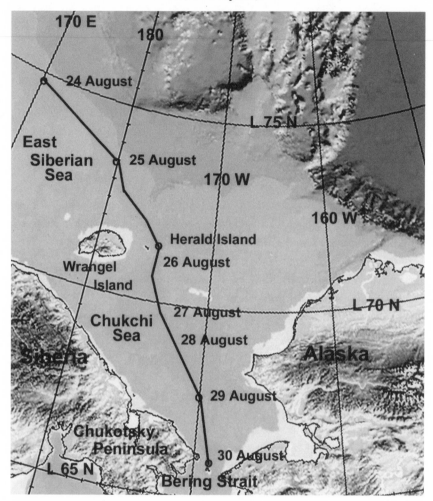

Chartlet 19.1 Northwestern Chukchi Sea to Bering Strait, 25 August to 30 August 1970.

Marine traffic through the higher latitudes of the Chukchi Sea has, however, remained the sole province of nuclear-powered submarines and icebreakers to the
present time.

Queenfish reached the Chukchi Sea on the morning of 25 August. The plan
was to continue the bottom-contour survey in a generally southeasterly direction
through a significant uncharted section of the northwestern Chukchi Sea that lay
to the west of *Sargo's* (Nicholson) inbound track to the Arctic Ocean during the
winter of 1960.[8] Our survey would then be terminated in already charted waters

well to the southeast of Wrangel and Herald islands. Although *Sargo* did not see either of these two extremely interesting islands that had taken so many years to discover, we had high hopes that the depth contour we were tracing would take us sufficiently close to view and photograph them both.

Herald Island was associated with Arctic explorer Vilhjalmur Stefansson's 1913 Canadian Arctic Expedition to search for a possible new continent between Alaska and the North Pole in his expedition ship *Karluk*. Stefansson had hoped as well to colonize and claim the much larger and completely uninhabited Wrangel Island for the United States during the 1920s.[9]

Our hydrographic survey took us increasingly to the southeast during the remainder of 25 August. We hoped to reach the edge of the Arctic ice pack and open water by 71° N, the midlatitude of Wrangel Island, and then continue southward toward the Bering Strait.

We located a very large polynya during the early evening hours and conducted a vertical ascent from 120 feet to periscope depth through a dense population of large jellyfish and a virtual snowstorm of organic material. Hovering beneath the surface just long enough to copy our radio broadcast and obtain a satellite fix, we then returned beneath the ice to resume the survey. Our position showed that *Queenfish* was some seventy-seven miles to the northeast of Wrangel Island. If the next day, 26 August, was clear, there would be an excellent chance to spot this glacier-free island's highest point of 3,598 feet as we passed it to our west.[10] Hopes of finally emerging from the pack ice were raised when *Queenfish* began to encounter numerous stretches of open water shortly before midnight.

The areas of open water were soon to disappear, though, and by early morning we were once again looking for a polynya in which to make a vertical ascent to periscope depth. We felt an added sense of urgency to fix our position as quickly and accurately as possible, for the bottom contour we were tracing was unexpectedly headed directly for Herald Island and Soviet territorial waters almost due south of us.

A suitable polynya was found within a half hour, and we made a vertical ascent through extremely murky water, dense with diatoms and jellyfish. Grant Youngman was on the dive and had little difficulty with deballasting, seawater temperature remaining essentially isothermal at 33° F. The view through the periscope was of an exceedingly bleak icescape engulfed in thoroughly miserable weather. To our great disappointment, the day held little promise for viewing either Herald Island or Wrangel Island. The polynya was filled with numerous chunks of heavy ice capriciously blown across the open water areas by the strong winds. Tom Hoepfner, the officer of the deck, was kept busy maneuvering *Queenfish* with the SPM to keep the ice away from periscope No. 2, then in use. Toby Warson and Chief Quartermaster Jack Patterson soon obtained an excellent series of satellite and Omega fixes that placed us fifty-nine miles north of Herald Island. We resubmerged shortly thereafter and resumed the survey.

It became clear during the next hour that the depth contour of interest, were we to continue following it, would take us closer to Herald Island than we were authorized to go. We had no choice but to suspend this part of *Queenfish*'s survey of the Siberian continental shelf before we came any closer. We then shifted maximum attention and concentration toward passing Herald Island by a comfortable margin to the east and getting sufficiently south to locate the edge of the ice pack and clear it. Course was therefore changed to the southeast to achieve this, and the navigator proceeded to work out a course for the Bering Strait that would keep us in deep water.

By dawn of 26 August, the sea surface seemed clear of ice. It looked as if it would be possible to make a final vertical ascent to periscope depth and remain there as we maneuvered around the last vestiges of the pack en route to the Bering Strait.

Execution of the foregoing plans turned out to be easier said than done. Coming to periscope depth, we observed the horizon to be ice-free to the south. What appeared to be the edge of the ice pack was now well astern of us. By mid-morning, however, *Queenfish* was confronted by heavy concentrations of sea ice off her port side—our "escape direction" toward deeper water to the east. The sea was becoming increasingly choppy, with enough white caps to make it very difficult to pick out those smaller pieces of ice in our path that would pose a hazard to the periscope.

Shortly before noon, we were surrounded by a quite compact ice pack extending all across the horizon to the south and solidly connected to the heavy ice that was much closer to the east. Seeking a way out of the ice and into deeper water, *Queenfish* descended and leveled off at 150 feet, slowing to three knots as we altered course to a southeasterly direction and then gradually a more southerly one. Just as it seemed we were finally approaching the end of this history-making voyage, *Queenfish* was once again caught between treacherous ice and shallow water. The Siberian continental shelf was not done with us yet.

Allan Beal, Dick Boyle, Toby Warson, and I held an urgent conference over the best of our western Chukchi Sea charts and pertinent information from Beal's Ph.D. dissertation to try to determine the best course of action for safely clearing the ice pack en route to the Bering Strait.[11] It appeared we might have to reverse course and backtrack a considerable distance north in order to find more favorable ice conditions and deeper water from which to exit the Chukchi Sea. A reversal would not only lengthen an already-long undersea voyage but also be professionally embarrassing for the entire *Queenfish* team.

As we quickly pored over and examined every scrap of information on board concerning the Chukchi Sea, Beal brought to our attention the recently discovered Herald Sea valley. Using the Chukchi Sea charts and his dissertation, he showed us where there was a southern entrance to a seemingly northerly oriented valley. Beal estimated that we could expect depths within the valley to be as much as thirty feet below the surrounding seabed, although the undersea valley's overall length and width and northern egress into the ice-covered northwestern Chukchi Sea were not known. He suggested that if we could find a northern entrance into the valley, we might find a more direct route through deeper water from which to exit the Chukchi Sea. He concluded with a strong warning, however, to avoid the definitely known shallow Herald Reef area just to the east of the postulated upper reaches of the valley.[12]

Weighing our present situation, we concluded that it would be well worth the time to locate that northern entrance to the Herald Sea valley—if there was one—rather than prematurely commit to the much less attractive backtracking option. The so-named northern entrance was estimated to be "somewhere near" Herald Island and Soviet territorial limits.[13] *Queenfish* was at present about twenty-five miles north of Herald Island. With the navigator's concurrence, I chose a southeasterly heading that would take us well to the east of the island. With luck we could expect to find an entrance into the valley within the next several hours.

The Chukchi Sea did us no favors as we slowly proceeded southeast. The pack ice above remained quite compact, with very little indication of open water. I instructed the command watch officer, Bob Baumhardt, to make a short excursion to the east every half hour, if ice conditions permitted, similar to a lengthy baffle clearing, in the hope of locating deeper water, which would indicate we had reached what might be the northern mouth of the Herald Sea valley.

I became increasingly anxious with each passing hour to locate the northern entrance, for we knew that once we were past Herald Island and headed toward the Bering Strait, depths within the Chukchi Sea would become even shallower. The ability to gain a few extra feet of depth as we cleared the last remnants of a compact Arctic ice pack was becoming imperative.

As *Queenfish* was clearing baffles to the east during the late afternoon of 26 August, the quartermaster of the watch raised our spirits by reporting that the secure depth sounder was showing the seafloor to be deeper to the east. Toby Warson, Chief Quartermaster Jack Patterson, Allan Beal, Dick Boyle, and I quickly verified a definite trend toward the deeper depths.

I immediately took the conn from Bob Baumhardt and ordered, "Steady as you go!"

"Steady on course one-zero-zero, sir!" responded the helmsman.

We remained on course for another fifteen minutes to ensure that we had reached the deepest water possible and then changed our heading to the previous one to the southeast. I returned the conn to Bob Baumhardt. Toby Warson soon recommended a revised course that best paralleled the estimated northwest-southeast axis of the Herald Sea valley and that would, with luck, take us clear of the ice pack and Herald Island.

I therefore ordered Baumhardt to resume the hydrographic survey immediately and, working closely with the navigator, to adjust course as necessary to remain along the deepest axis of the sea valley as it headed in a southeasterly direction. With a sigh of relief I noted that our hand DR showed we were still well to the northeast of Herald Island and within international waters.

Within minutes we were transiting at five knots within a sea valley whose water depths remained as much as 20 to 30 feet deeper than the 180 feet that we had been experiencing a half hour earlier. It appeared that it might be the previously undiscovered northern extension of the Herald Sea valley. If so, *Queenfish* would have sufficient room to navigate safely clear of the Arctic ice pack before we reached the 150-foot depth curve. Of course, we were still in largely uncharted waters, and if our first hours in the East Siberian Sea were any example, anything could happen.

The secure depth sounder continued to reassure us that we were in deep water throughout the night, and the acoustic top sounder recorder revealed a steadily decreasing amount of ice and increasing areas of open water. We reached the 180-foot depth contour shortly before breakfast on 27 August. This required us to plane up to a new transit depth of 110 feet. Within a half hour we crossed the 150-foot depth curve, with only occasional bands of very mild ice appearing overhead. We continued past and to the southeast of Herald Island. Now certain that we were finally clear of the pack ice and had only open water above us, I took the conn, reversed course to port, slowed to minimum turns, and raised No. 2 periscope to search for residual fragments of pack ice and other obstacles such as timber and other flotsam within the flat-calm surface above us.

It occurred to me at the time that *Queenfish's* discovery of the northern entrance to the Herald Sea valley, and the subsequent charting of its deepest axis from where

Figure 19.2 A last look at the southern edge of the Arctic ice pack before heading for the Bering Strait on 29 August 1970. (Courtesy of the U.S. Navy)

we first entered until we finally emerged from the valley at its southernmost point in the southern Chukchi Sea, could well prove of great value to future Arctic submarine navigators.

Satisfied that all was clear, I ordered, "All stop!" followed by "Vertical ascent to six-eight-feet!" The diving officer, Steve Gray, responded, "Vertical ascent to six-eight-feet, aye sir!" and brought *Queenfish* up smartly. I raised No. 1 periscope and commenced a rapid series of air and surface searches just before the boat broke the surface. We were now approaching an area more closely monitored by both the Soviet Union and the United States. No contacts of any sort were in sight and, best of all, no ice. The navigator soon fixed our position by satellite and recommended a more direct course for the Bering Strait. Remaining at periscope depth, we secured from the special under-ice watch bill several hours later, during the early morning hours of 28 August, and set the regular watch for submerged operations.

Like prisoners on their release from a lengthy confinement, we were jubilant. *Queenfish* had made it. We had completed a most successful and historic first hydrographic survey of the Laptev, East Siberian, and northwest Chukchi seas. Cheers could be heard throughout the boat as we congratulated ourselves for having successfully completed a most difficult mission and emerging from it unscathed.

I asked our chief cook, Michael Knaub, to prepare a very special celebratory meal and our chief hospital corpsman, Andrew Gunn, to make immediate preparations for "treating" more than 117 cases of "exposure."

We now had only to pass through the southern Chukchi Sea and Bering Strait safely and undetected, enter the Bering Sea, and head for Nome, Alaska, where we were looking forward to stretching our legs and relaxing for a day or so. Because the results of our Arctic expedition would not be made public until after our arrival in Nome, *Queenfish* remained at periscope depth, maintained radio silence, and took continuous satellite and Omega fixes throughout the early morning hours of 28 August. Shortly after breakfast I asked Warson to lay down our track such that everyone would have an opportunity to see both Big Diomede (Soviet) and Little Diomede (U.S.) islands through the periscope as we proceeded through the famous Bering Strait on 29 August.

Nome and the Long Journey Home

Queenfish was well south of the Bering Strait and heading for Nome, Alaska, on the morning of 30 August. It would be our first visit ashore in almost two months. To say that our forthcoming rest-and-relaxation stop was eagerly looked forward to would be a gross understatement. The crew was particularly excited at the prospect of going ashore in an exotic Bering Sea port, if only for two days. I was looking forward to Nome as well, having thoroughly enjoyed my brief visit there just ten years before, following my transpolar voyage from the Atlantic to the Pacific as a young officer on board USS *Seadragon*. As we proceeded at almost twenty knots on the surface, we entertained ourselves with enthusiastic speculations on the welcome we would receive.

I noted with some curiosity that certain members of the crew seemed to have special advance intelligence, unknown to the rest of us, about the amenities of this remote northern frontier town. When Chief of the Boat Kenneth Ickes informed me that members of the engineering department, in particular, were submitting overnight-liberty requests, I was incredulous. My memories of Nome were of a very small gold-mining community with board sidewalks and unpaved roads, inhabited largely by miners and Eskimos in native dress. Other than the old Bering Sea Hotel, there was no place to stay overnight that I could remember.

At the time I visited Nome in 1960, it seemed as if every other building contained an old-time western saloon with long walk-up bars with mirrors behind them and sawdust-covered floors that definitely catered to a rough clientele. It was easy to conclude that a significant portion of the population spent most of their time in the local saloons and made their living by selling hard liquor to one another.

The day promised to remain clear and beautiful as we rounded the Seward Peninsula en route to Nome. We had been on the surface since passing between Big and Little Diomedes islands midway in the Bering Strait the previous afternoon. The seas were exceptionally calm and almost mirrorlike. Crew members came to the bridge from time to time to enjoy the scenery and breathe in the wonderful clean, crisp air. Their obvious pleasure made me chuckle when I recalled their loud complaints about "the air smelling too fishy" following our shift from full submerged atmospheric control, which we had been on since the North Pole more than three weeks ago, to ventilating *Queenfish* from the outside atmosphere.

Ten years before, the town of Nome had turned out in force to greet USS *Seadragon* on her arrival. She had just completed a historic first submerged survey of the Northwest Passage through the Canadian Arctic Islands and surfaced at the North Pole and was soon to be the first submarine in history to travel from the Atlantic to a new homeport in the Pacific via the Arctic Ocean. A Coast Guard cutter had conveniently anchored just a half-mile offshore, and *Seadragon* was able to moor alongside the cutter and to avail herself of the cutter's liberty boats. Coming into Nome today, I wondered, as I continued to daydream on the bridge, if there might be another huge banquet awaiting us at the old Bering Sea Hotel, with a typical native feast and the blanket-tossing of the commanding officer at the local Eskimo village, such as the crew had enjoyed in 1960.[1] Our excitement and anticipation grew as the morning passed.

Queenfish rounded Cape Rodney, passed Sledge Island to port, and was soon less than twenty miles from Nome. All seemed quiet as we continued our approach during the early afternoon. As Nome gradually came into view, we were surprised to see no ships of any sort anchored offshore. The town had no pier or offshore moorings that could be used by deep-draft ships, which meant that *Queenfish* would have to anchor several miles offshore. The Nome area is noted for sudden high winds and an offshore seabed that is quite flat. Our single and relatively lightweight "mushroom" anchor could not be depended on to hold, and it would certainly drag if the weather deteriorated. With her relatively large sail area, *Queenfish* would run the risk of suddenly being blown into very shallow water and aground if we were not supremely alert and careful. Anchoring offshore also meant we would have to keep a sufficient number of men on board and on watch throughout our visit in order to be able to raise the anchor quickly and get underway in the event of an emergency.

As we closed to within a few miles, the town was still quiet—unusually so for a late afternoon in the middle of the week. Nome had a small fishing fleet, and many of its residents had small runabouts, but there were no people in sight, either on the beach or the landing area. Nor were there any curious onlookers gathered on the shore. I was thoroughly mystified.

On reaching a suitable anchorage several thousand yards to seaward of Nome, the chief radioman, Mike Hein, was instructed to send off the required arrival messages to Admiral Walter Small, Commander Submarine Forces Pacific in Pearl Harbor, and to the nearest local-area commander. After repeatedly trying on both high- and very high-frequency circuits for the better part of the next half hour, Chief Hein reported that atmospheric electromagnetic disturbances appeared to be preventing communication with anyone on any of the primary or secondary frequencies assigned.

Chief Hein was instructed to keep trying to make contact with Pearl. We were expected to have surfaced safely and anchored off Nome today. If *Queenfish* did not establish communication with someone soon, a fleetwide "Submarine Overdue" message, followed by "Sub Miss, Sub Sunk," would be initiated by those in the submarine force expecting to receive a safe-arrival report from us. It was now urgent that Chief Hein and I go ashore and attempt to contact COMSUBPAC by whatever means possible.

A rubber life raft was quickly prepared and lowered into the water alongside. Chief Hein and I, both in uniform, slid down the rounded hull of the submarine and into the raft. Once securely seated in our life jackets, we proceeded to paddle toward shore, grumbling the whole way about the unaccustomed physical exertion. The long stretch was covered in a little less than an hour. As we approached Nome's small dock, we noticed a small group of men beginning to assemble. They looked quite somber; there was definitely no response to our friendly waves.

What could possibly be the matter? Had the navy or coast guard been here earlier with their crews behaving so badly that all military visitors were now unwelcome? Was there some kind of serious health crisis in Nome? We even thought about the advisability of turning around and rowing back to the boat. As we closed to less than one hundred yards, I shouted to the group on the pier that we were from the U.S. submarine *Queenfish* and needed to use a radio or telephone. Impassive and unfriendly stares were their only response. As we rowed closer, I went on to explain that we had just come from the Arctic Ocean and had planned to visit Nome for the next several days. As I kept on talking, I noted that three of the people in the forefront of the somber reception party were policemen. From their midst suddenly came the question, "Are you American?"

"Of course we are!" I replied indignantly. "We're from the U.S. nuclear attack submarine *Queenfish*," I repeated, "manned by your fellow citizens!"

Uncertain smiles began to appear. Someone of obvious importance finally stepped forward and said, "We thought you were a Soviet submarine."

"Why would you think that?" I asked. We came alongside the dock and threw a light mooring line to one of the men standing there. As we secured the life raft and stepped out, the policemen, followed by the mayor of Nome, sheepishly introduced themselves. We shook hands and showed them our military identification cards.

The mayor then uncomfortably explained that no one had been informed of our impending arrival. Not only that, but when they saw a large black submarine suddenly appear offshore without any of the normal identification numbers appearing on its sail or hull, they thought it had to be Russian.

Looking out to sea toward our submarine, I could easily understand their reaction. *Queenfish* looked quite sinister as she rode at anchor: large, almost jet black, and, for security reasons customary outside local waters, not displaying a clue as to her national identity except for a small American flag flying just abaft the sail.

As it turned out, all radio frequencies normally used locally for long-distance communication were affected by the same adverse atmospheric disturbances that we had encountered. This left us no option but to find the nearest telephone booth and make a collect call to our bosses in Pearl Harbor informing them that *Queenfish* had reached Nome safely and to please notify all concerned.

The Commander Submarine Forces Pacific duty officer who received my call was initially suspicious, but I managed to convince him that, yes, I really was the commanding officer of *Queenfish* and was submitting our formal arrival report.

The entire episode was a very low-tech and somewhat embarrassing denouement to a multimillion dollar, two-month voyage of exploration by one of the United States Navy's most technically advanced and capable warships.

Chief Hein and I joined the mayor and several leading citizens for a much-needed hot drink and quickly made the necessary arrangements to ferry crew members to and from the boat and town. We also made arrangements to deliver our outgoing mail and Admiral Rickover's letters to the local post office.

When the first of *Queenfish*'s crew stepped ashore, the citizens of Nome wasted no time in more than making up for their initial unfriendliness, and we were all to enjoy their gracious and warm Alaskan hospitality during our two-day visit.

Nome was almost unrecognizable from the remote frontier outpost that I remembered from 1960. It was visibly more modernized, most certainly in response to both increased tourism and economic development of this area of Alaska's Seward Peninsula. The formerly deeply rutted dirt roads were now paved, as were the treacherous board sidewalks, and there were interesting gift shops and small restaurants and signs of all the other businesses that characterize most towns.

One thing had definitely not changed: there were as many, if not more, saloons. All were packed with plenty of local color, in the main just as friendly as in 1960, although some of the customers were still of the rough-and-ready type and definitely not to be messed with, as a few of our younger and less-experienced members soon found out. In 1960, other than a well-escorted Wein Alaska Airlines flight attendant or two, there were few available women whom one would want to be seen with in broad daylight. Nome in 1970 was different. The number of attractive and fashionable young Eskimo ladies who came forth to show our crew members a good time was astonishing.

One thing that had not changed was the long, cold walk back to the boat landing where a local craft ferried us to and from our submarine at anchor. There were the same added hazards of having to avoid discarded whale bones strewn along the unlighted path, not to mention other unpleasant deposits, which added spice to the overall adventure of navigating one's way safely back to the boat following a night on the town.

Queenfish's crew departed two days later, on 1 September 1970, happy and without incident, vowing to their newfound lady friends to return again soon, as sailors have done from time immemorial. The remainder of the journey back to Pearl Harbor seemed overly long, probably because we had not received any mail in Nome as a result of our unexpected arrival. Hence, the only communication with family or friends before we departed Nome was a few brief and very expensive minutes on the telephone, with no time to find out what had transpired at home during our absence. A few of the crew members had the exceedingly frustrating experience of not being able to reach a wife, girlfriend, or family member whom they had not seen or talked to since *Queenfish* left Seattle on 21 July.

We had arrived in Nome in a high state of excitement, filled with pride in having completed without mishap our lengthy and arduous undersea expedition in unknown waters. The chief of the boat, executive officer, officers, chief petty officers, and I now had to work to overcome any feeling of letdown among the crew and to make sure that both morale and performance were sustained during what would be our final and probably longest ten days at sea.

The best solution for any submarine captain in this circumstance is to keep his crew busy on routine and preventive maintenance, submarine and watch station qualification, and advanced training with attendant boatwide drills and to involve as many as possible in the preparation of our final patrol report.

Dick Boyle and Allan Beal conducted briefings on the main achievements of the

Figure 20.1 USS *Queenfish* returns to Pearl Harbor, Hawaii, on 11 September 1970, on completion of the Arctic-Siberian Shelf Expedition. (Courtesy of the U.S. Navy)

voyage, during which crew members had an opportunity to volunteer their own ideas and thoughts about what *Queenfish* had accomplished. Groundwork was also laid for the production of a post–Arctic expedition "cruise book" for all hands.

The chief of the boat organized contests and tournaments with prizes that included "basket leave" (leave that does not count against a sailor's normal thirty days' leave per year) on arrival in Pearl Harbor. The games included cribbage; acey-deucy; a board game called "horse races" in which each division made up its own unique entry piece, few of which resembled any horse known to mankind; and a chocolate pie-eating race without benefit of eating utensils. Another contest was to determine the most creative tailors among the more imaginative crew members who fashioned hats, jackets, and even costumes out of the fascinating pieces of colored fabric found in each bale of wiping rags loaded on board.

The days did pass, one by one, and we finally surfaced off southwest Oahu just before dawn on 11 September and set course for the entrance to Pearl Harbor Channel. Breakfast was *Queenfish*'s traditional end-of-deployment: all the steak and fresh-baked apple pie one could eat washed down with a lot of fresh coffee. The weather could not have been more perfect. We slowed to take on board *Queenfish*'s division commander and former commanding officer, Commander Jack Richard, shortly after entering the channel, and he soon joined me on the bridge.

There is really nothing quite like the joy of returning home after a lengthy deployment. As we headed into Pearl Harbor Channel and rounded Hospital Point, we saw our excited families waiting on the pier in front of Commander Submarine Forces Pacific headquarters. Some of our loved ones were dressed as polar bears and other Arctic animals, and many were carrying signs and posters warmly welcoming us home. A navy band was playing away, and hula dancers were there to present leis and to give us a welcoming aloha. Admiral Small and many of his staff were among the group to greet *Queenfish*'s crew and their families.

We made a perfect approach to our berth, literally handing over our lines, and moored *Queenfish* securely alongside. As soon as the gangway from boat to pier was laid down, all rushed ashore to embrace loved ones and greet submarine force staff and friends. I had special reason to rejoice at the reunion with my family, because my wife and I were soon to be joined, on 22 September 1970, by a fourth child and second son, John Bandini McLaren.

Epilogue

This Inquiry I must confesse is a gropeing in the Dark: but although I havee
not brought it into a cleer light; yet I can affirm, that I havee brought it from
utter darkness to a thin mist.

—John Aubrey, 1693

Queenfish and her crew received due recognition from both their military superiors
and the press following the successful completion of our Arctic operation. The
Commander Submarine Forces Pacific and staff and the Commander in Chief
Pacific Fleet and his staff received detailed briefings on the expedition during the
week following *Queenfish's* return to Pearl Harbor. I was flown back to Washington,
D.C., to brief Admiral Rickover and his principal assistants at the Pentagon as well
as the oceanographer of the navy. The admiral was particularly attentive, asking
detailed questions, and seemed pleased with the overall success of the voyage. It was
certainly the most pleasant time I was ever to spend with him.

On our return, Toby Warson was immediately detached with orders to become
the second commander of the U.S. Navy's only deep-diving nuclear submarine, the
NR-1. Tom Hoepfner was to follow a few months later with orders to the Georgia
Institute of Technology to pursue a graduate degree in mechanical engineering.
Tom was later to command the USS *Woodrow Wilson (SSBN-626)*.

The state flags flown at the North Pole were presented to the U.S. state gover-
nors during 1970 and 1971 on behalf of the U.S. Navy and the submarine force.

In 1971 *Queenfish* received a Navy Unit Citation for the Arctic-Siberian Continental Shelf Exploration and the cold war mission that preceded it in 1970. I subsequently received a Legion of Merit for each of the two missions, and individual
officers, senior petty officers, and crew were suitably recognized with medals or letters of commendation for their outstanding performance.

Queenfish and her crew were also recommended for a Presidential Unit Cita-

Figure E.1 Commander Alfred S. McLaren, USS *Queenfish,* receiving second Legion of Merit for the successful completion of the Arctic-Siberian Shelf Expedition. (Courtesy of the U.S. Navy)

tion by the Commander in Chief of the Pacific Fleet, Admiral Bernard A. "Chick" Clarey, for three other missions conducted in 1971. This unique recognition was overruled at the Washington level, however, and a second Navy Unit Citation was awarded instead. I received the Distinguished Service Medal (the nation's top peacetime award), and *Queenfish*'s key officers and petty officers were suitably recognized with medals or letters of commendation in early 1972. The Navy Unit Commendation was not received by *Queenfish*'s crew until my change of command in early May of 1973, however. It will always be difficult for me to understand how this happened. How much better it would have been if a deserving ship-crew team had been recognized as a whole as soon as possible. The effect on morale, unit pride, reenlistment, and future performance would have been immense. In my view, individual officer and petty officer awards should always follow rather than precede unit-crew team awards.

Queenfish in addition received the Battle Efficiency "E" twice and was the second submarine in the Pacific Fleet to be certified to carry the new multicapable MK-48 torpedo. In late 1972 she was awarded the first Golden Anchor Award in the Pacific submarine force for her exceptional reenlistment rate.

Our submarine's successes during the period 1969–73 were due to the consistently superb teamwork, individual performance, and steadfast loyalty to ship and service of all her officers, chief petty officers, and crew. Particular individuals stand out: *Queenfish's* chief of the boat for most of this period, the late Senior Chief Electronics Technician (Nuclear) Richard Leroy Dietz; Senior Chief Sonar Technician James Carl Petersen; Chief Radioman Michael Hein; and Chief Quartermaster Jack Patterson. These men received Meritorious Service and/or Navy Commendation medals while serving on board *Queenfish*.

Worthy of special recognition as well were the superlative performances and efforts of Lieutenants Steve Gray, Lars Hanson, and Fred Moore; *Queenfish's* engineer officer, Lieutenant Commander Ralph Beedle, who earned several Meritorious Service and Navy Commendation medals on board *Queenfish* and was later to command the USS *Los Angeles (SSN-688)*; and sonar officer and later operations officer and navigator, the late Lieutenant Commander Robert James Baumhardt, recipient of both Meritorious Service and Navy Commendation medals and, for his superb performance during *Queenfish's* 1971 cold war operations, the Legion of Merit. Bob later became executive officer of the USS *Barb (SSN-596)*. He would have made a superb nuclear attack submarine captain but chose to leave the navy, quite understandably, to spend more time with his family.

Finally, and absolutely essential for *Queenfish's* success during these demanding and difficult years, both at sea and in port, was the loyalty and understanding support of our spouses and families, particularly the chief of the boat's wife, the late Shirley Dietz, the chief radioman's wife, Terry Hein, and my wife of twenty-five years, Mary Eisenhower McLaren.

Queenfish was to remain almost continually at sea until my change of command in early May of 1973. In addition to the Siberian shelf expedition, during this time the boat completed two six-month western Pacific deployments, two short Vietnam "excursions," and six successful cold war missions during the spring of 1970, summer and fall of 1971, and winter of 1972–73. Most of the Arctic odyssey crew remained together until the boat entered Bremerton Naval Shipyard in Washington State for overhaul later in 1973.

Queenfish upheld her very full and illustrious career as a frontline nuclear attack submarine during the remainder of the cold war under a continuous succession of outstanding crews and commanding officers. She undertook many special missions outside of and during the course of eight more six-month deployments in the western Pacific. She returned to the Arctic Ocean and the North Pole in 1985 and 1988. During the latter expedition, she surfaced with two other submarines at the North Pole on the thirtieth anniversary of *Nautilus's* historic transpolar voyage. She was ultimately to be awarded the Navy Unit Commendation six times and the Meritorious Unit Commendation three times. Members of her crew at the time of my command have remained exceptionally close and have consistently made up the majority of attendees at every reunion since she was decommissioned.

Queenfish was also, unfortunately, to become one of the early casualties of victory in the cold war, a victory in which she had played a key role, when she was deactivated on 21 September 1990, just ten weeks short of the twenty-fourth anniversary of her commissioning.[1]

I left *Queenfish* to become operations officer and later chief staff officer at the submarine force's tactical development and analysis squadron, Submarine Development Group Two in Groton, Connecticut. From there I went on to become chief of staff for operations and plans on the staff of Commander Submarine Forces Pacific. Following selection for major shore command, I received orders to become commander of the Naval Underwater Systems Center, a part of the Naval Material Command and the principal scientific laboratory for the submarine force. This center comprised thirty-two hundred scientists, engineers, and military personnel stationed at facilities in Newport, Rhode Island; New London, Connecticut; Seneca Lake, New York; Bermuda; West Palm Beach, Florida; and a sizable portion of Andros Island in the Bahamas.

My retirement from the United States Navy came on 31 July 1981, and I immediately entered graduate school at Cambridge University (Peterhouse) in England, thanks to the G.I. Bill and generous grants from ARCO International and the Office of Naval Research's Arctic programs. Working at the Scott Polar Research Institute in the Department of Geography and Geology, I had an outstanding opportunity to draw on the knowledge and experience gained on *Queenfish*'s 1970 Arctic expedition as I pursued a master's of philosophy degree in polar studies. My lengthy thesis, titled "The Arctic Submarine: An Alternative to Ice Breaker Tankers and Pipelines," argued that a conventionally (nonnuclear) powered submarine, towing hydrodynamically shaped oil-filled bladders, would be the safest and most efficient way to transport petroleum from Canada's Arctic islands to Atlantic coast refineries year-round. In late 1982, I was awarded an M.Phil. by the University of Cambridge. This degree and two key articles relating to my research led to a number of extremely interesting consultancies in conjunction with the transport of petroleum from the Canadian Arctic islands to U.S. and European refineries via submarine.[2]

The wonderful years of "reading for my degree" at Cambridge were followed by a semester of intensive geography and computer courses at Keene State College in New Hampshire. In January of 1983 I embarked on a full-time Ph.D. program at the University of Colorado, Boulder, where I pursued a doctor of philosophy degree in the physical geography of the polar regions in association with the Cooperative Institute of Environmental Sciences and the Department of Geography.

Research support and also considerable data were provided by Dr. Lyon and Dick Boyle at the Arctic Submarine Laboratory, San Diego, and by Dr. Peter Wadhams at Scott Polar Research Institute, University of Cambridge. Financial support also came from the G.I. Bill, a graduate teaching assistant's position in the University of Colorado's Geography Department, ARCO International, and the Office of Naval Research.

While I was at the University of Colorado, Dr. Leonard Johnson, the Office of Naval Research's director of Arctic programs, encouraged me to establish an off-campus research company, called Arctic Analysts, with Ron Weaver of the National Snow and Ice Data Center, at the university. His suggestion, which I followed, greatly facilitated my obtaining the necessary research grants to digitize and analyze the raw analog under-ice thickness and topography data from the *Nautilus* and *Queenfish* voyages and to compare and report the results in my dissertation. The analysis showed that *Queenfish* encountered uniformly milder ice conditions throughout the Arctic Basin or Arctic Ocean than *Nautilus* did twelve years earlier, with the mean ice draft across the basin determined to be 0.7 meters thinner in 1970 than in 1958. These broad conclusions were reported in my dissertation, titled "Analysis of the Under-Ice Topography in the Arctic Basin as Recorded by USS *Nautilus* in 1958 and USS *Queenfish* in 1970."[3]

All requirements for a Ph.D. were met on 21 April 1986, and the doctor of philosophy degree was conferred on me by the regents of the University of Colorado during graduation ceremonies in late May of 1986.

I remained at the Cooperative Institute of Environmental Sciences as a senior research associate and as an associate professor in the Department of Geography at the University of Colorado, Boulder, thanks to a multimillion-dollar congressionally mandated University Research Initiative grant for five years to the University of Colorado, which I helped obtain, with my Ph.D. supervisor, Dr. Roger Barry, and Dr. Russ Schnell. Its purpose was to examine Arctic ocean-ice-atmosphere interactions and their implications for global climate change. In the course of this research, graduate student Mark Serreze and I made the major discovery that the huge Beaufort Gyre in the Canada Basin reversed from clockwise to counterclockwise each summer, with tremendous effects on ice movement and concentration and with implications for global warming.[4]

In early 1990, following an announcement in the *Navy Times* that the U.S. Navy intended to decommission seven *Sturgeon*-class nuclear attack submarines during the coming year, I submitted an article to the *U.S. Naval Institute Proceedings* urging that these submarines be saved to study global change. I have since been informed that this article played a significant role in stimulating the thinking and planning that led to the creation of the very successful Science Ice Exercise program developed by the U.S. Navy and the U.S. National Science Foundation that have used *Sturgeon*-class submarines to investigate the geology, biology, oceanography, and sea-ice thickness distribution of the Arctic Ocean with reference to global climate change.[5]

Thirty-four years were to pass, however, before the water depth/bottom contour data recorded by *Queenfish* throughout the Chukchi, Laptev, and East Siberian seas in 1970 were analyzed and entered on appropriate navigation charts. The data finally appeared on the International Bathymetric Chart of the Arctic Ocean (ICBAO), RP-2, in 2004. To the best of my knowledge, however, the analog recordings of ice-draft measurements throughout the Laptev, East Siberian, and western Chukchi seas remain to be digitized and analyzed.

Shortly after being promoted to full research professor in 1991, I was exceedingly fortunate in being selected to become president of the nonprofit corporation Science Service, headquartered in Washington, D.C. As its president, I was responsible for running the Westinghouse Science Talent Search program and the International Science and Engineering Fair and was publisher of the weekly magazine, *Science News*. I remained in this most interesting position, with its myriad opportunities to encourage and work with young scientists throughout the world, until March of 1996.

From March 1996 to March 2000 I served as the thirty-seventh president of the Explorers Club, a membership organization founded in 1904, whose presidents have included such Arctic exploration luminaries as General Adolphus Greely, General David Brainerd, Admiral Robert Peary, Dr. Frederick Cook, and Vilhjalmur Stefansson and whose distinguished membership also included polar explorers Captain Robert Scott, Roald Amundsen, Ernest Shackleton, Admiral Richard Byrd, Sir Hubert Wilkins, Captain William Anderson, Admiral James Calvert, Admiral John Nicholson, Admiral George Steele, Will Steger, and Sir Wally Herbert. It was during this presidency that I returned to the Arctic in July of 1996 during a voyage to the North Pole on the Russian nuclear icebreaker *Yamal*.

Through the Explorers Club I made five more trips to the North Pole, the last being in 2003. I have also participated as a lecturer and group leader in seven North American, Greenlandic, European, and Siberian Arctic expedition cruises on board Russian icebreakers, including a transit from north to south of the Kara Sea; numerous visits to Franz Josef Land, Svalbard, and Novaya Zemlya; a voyage following Amundsen's route through the Canadian Northwest Passage; a first-ever circumnavigation of Baffin Island; and, in August 1999, a monthlong, east-to-west passage on the Russian icebreaker *Drenytzn* along the Northern Sea Route or

Northeast Passage from Providenya to Svalbard. It was during this passage that I had an opportunity to return to the Chukchi, East Siberian, and Laptev seas and actually set foot on Kolyuchin Island, Wrangel Island, Vilkitsky Island, Bennett Island, the New Siberian Islands, Shmidt Island, Cape Chelyuskin, Galomuanyy Island, and the four major islands of the Severnaya Zemlya Archipelago.

I am now in my fifth career, this time in deep-sea exploration and science, but that is another story. Each year becomes more interesting, yet passes even more rapidly than the last, and there never seem to be enough hours in the day for all that I would like to do in the way of Arctic and deep-sea research, exploration, and field science. Oh, to have another twenty to thirty years . . .

Appendix
USS Queenfish (SSN-651)
List of Ship's Company

Personnel aboard *Queenfish* during SUBICEX 1-70

Officers

Alfred Scott McLaren
Lincoln Henry Mueller
Toby Gene Warson
Walter Angell Pezet
Ralph Eugene Beedle
Karl Thomas Hoepfner

Robert James Baumhardt
Stephen Vern Gray
Grant Hughes Youngman
Frederick Cranford Moore
William George Blenkle
Lars Parker Hanson

Crew

Gerald Ray Acock
Harold Lee Albertson
Kenneth William Allen
Martin Douglas Angell, Jr.
Lawrence Skidmore Angus
Steven George Apple
Harold Odell Berg
Joseph Rolin Boston
Gordon William Branin
Michael Wayne Brown
Michael Francis Budner

Dennis Theodor Kawakami
Michael James Keck
James Stuart Kennedy
David Arthur King
Steven Wayne Kirchner
Michael Laddie Knaub
Mike Kotek
Donald William Krieg
Perry Rees Kuhn
Michael Don Lanque
Jesse Ernest Long III

Wayne Lee Burnaine

Michael Alan Calhoun

Raymond Henry Cheesebrough

Charles Wesley Clifton

Robert Thomas Coia

James Elva Cook

Charles Dean Cranmer

James Franklin Craver, Jr.

Howard Warner Curry

Owen Shannon Denman

Robert John Diehl

Richard Leroy Dietz

Padraic Anthony Doyle

William Bailey Dunford

Grant Richardson Elam

Michael Edward Falconer

Dennis Charles Foster

Thomas Michael Fursman

Artemio Velasco Gapasin

Gary Forrest Gillette

Arthur Rudolph Gnepper

Roger Edward Gouldberg

Richard Wayne Grafton

Colorado Printis Green III

Andrew Jackson Gunn

Gary Stephen Hanlin

James Robert Harrick

Daniel Ray Harrison

Charles Richard Hazeltine

Allen Heisler

Michael Steven Hein

Richard Charles Hery II

John Frederick Hildenbrand

Kenneth Earl Ickes

Lawrence Claude Invie

Patrick Harold Jeremy

Larry Stephen Johnson

Steven Edward Kasprzak

James Joseph Lyons

Peter Colin Magoon

Christopher Anthony Marino

James William Mehaffey

Frederick Miller III

Patrick Charles Mills

Jerry Charles Moseley

John Wayne Nice

William Aubrey Ogden, Jr.

Dale Howard Olson

Jack Bowman Patterson

Allan Victor Peña

Ronald Eric Peters

James Carl Petersen

Lance Peterson

Hugh Frank Pringle

Keith John Randolph

David George Rowe

Charles Michael Ruth, Jr.

Frederick William Schueneman

Donald Thomas Shipley

Thomas Charles Sizer

Louis William Soukey

Paul Scott Speaker

James Anthony Stachelski

David Val Stewart

Leonard Egerton Sully

Harry Tample, Jr.

Nicholas Conrad Theis

Craig Gilmour Thorne

Vernon Nelson Tolar

Kenneth Michael Tucker

Gerald Edwin Uffelman

Michael Dale White

John Adams Wilgus

Clarence Frank Williams

Edward Jack Wise

Eric Frank Zavadil

Military Riders

William P. Enderlein   Charles Lee Wright, Sr.
Raymond A. Chamlis

Civilians

M. Allan Beal,   Richard J. Boyle,
Senior Scientist   Assistant to Dr. Waldo Lyon
Arctic Submarine Laboratory   Arctic Submarine Laboratory
San Diego, California   San Diego, California

Notes

Chapter 2

1. The name in parentheses given after the name of a particular ship indicates the last name of the commanding officer at the time.

Chapter 3

1. Herbert C. Fyfe, *Submarine Warfare Past, Present, and Future* (New York: E. P. Dutton and Co., 1902), 157–65; John Wilkins, *Mathematical Magick, Or, The Wonders That May Be Performed by Mechanical Geometry,* chap. 5, pt. 2 (London: Brasen Serpent in Paul's Church Yard, 1648).

2. U.S. Navy Submarine Force Museum, "History of USS *Nautilus (SSN-571),*" www.ussnautilus.org/history.html.

3. William M. Leary, *Under Ice: Waldo Lyon and the Development of the Arctic Submarine* (College Station: Texas A&M University Press, 1999); U.S. Navy Electronics Laboratory, USS *Redfish (SS-395), Report of Beaufort Sea Expeditions* (San Diego: U.S. Naval Electronics Laboratory, 7 October 1952 and 3 December 1953).

4. William R. Anderson, *Nautilus 90 North* (Cleveland: World Publishing Company, 1959), 33–37.

5. "Welcome Aboard USS *Nautilus (SSN-571),* The World's First Nuclear Powered Ship," www.subguru.com/nautilus571.htm.

6. Leary, *Under Ice,* 95, 98.

7. Ibid., 94, 95, 97, 98–99.

8. Ibid., 99–100; Anderson, *Nautilus 90 North,* 64.

9. "Welcome Aboard USS *Nautilus*"; Leary, *Under Ice,* 102–6; Anderson, *Nautilus 90 North,* 94–97.

10. Wilkins, *Mathematical Magick;* "A New Plan for Reaching the North Pole," *Geographical Journal* 17, no. 4 (1901): 435; George H. Wilkins, *Under The North Pole* (New York: Brewer, Warren, and Putnam, 1931); Leary, *Under Ice,* 107.

11. Anderson, *Nautilus 90 North,* 106–8, 113–14. This navigation system was designed to be used by the intercontinental Navaho missile.

12. A dead-reckoning system is a manual plotting method of determining position by course, speed, and distance traveled; it has been used by mariners for hundreds of years. Relative motion is calculated through the use of at least three gyroscopes and accelerometers to measure the change in angular direction and acceleration in three axes and a computer to calculate the resultant changes in position relative to an initial start-up or subsequent reset position.

13. Errors creep in, however, due to less-than-optimum crew course, speed, and depth control plus the effect of external forces such as current and wind. These forces must be periodically corrected for by updating or resetting the "initial starting position" as new navigational positions or "fixes" are obtained.

14. Leary, *Under Ice,* 107, 112, 117.

15. Anderson, *Nautilus 90 North,* 166–68; Leary, *Under Ice,* 117–18, 122–23.

16. Leary, *Under Ice,* 127; Anderson, *Nautilus 90 North,* 197, 201, 203–8.

17. Anderson, *Nautilus 90 North,* 208–9, 223, 233.

18. James Calvert, *Surface at the Pole: The Extraordinary Voyages of the USS Skate* (New York: McGraw Hill Book Co., 1960); Leary, *Under Ice,* 135–36.

19. Leary, *Under Ice,* 141, 143, 144, 145–53; Calvert, *Surface at the Pole,* 183–87.

20. Leary, *Under Ice,* 156–59, 180. The iceberg detector used a transducer similar to that of the QLA mine detection sonar. Roshon's iceberg detector projected a frequency-modulated scanning sonar signal (FM) from 24 to 32 kHz. It had a vertical beam pattern of 4° and a horizontal pattern of 90°. Vice Admiral John H. Nicholson, USN (Ret.), personal communication, 13 March 2005.

21. Leary, *Under Ice,* 173.

22. George P. Steele, *Seadragon: Northwest under the Ice* (New York: E. P. Dutton and Co., 1962), 52–53, 62.

23. Ibid., 98, 127; Leary, *Under Ice,* 190, 145–53.

24. Steele, *Seadragon: Northwest under the Ice,* 69, 90.

25. Ibid., 67, 71, 97, 113, 116–18, 138–39, 146, 148, 187, 200.

26. Ibid., 225–34.

27. Leary, *Under Ice.*

28. Waldo K. Lyon, "The Submarine and the Arctic Ocean," *Polar Record* 11 (1963): 699–705; Alfred S. McLaren, "Exploration under the Arctic Ice," *Explorers Journal* (March 1982): 34–39.

29. Leary, *Under Ice,* 241–47.

Chapter 4

1. Technology support areas included such positions as sonar technicians, torpedomen, radiomen, electricians, interior communications operators, machinists, enginemen, electronic technicians, fire-control technicians, and nuclear radiologists.

2. The Submarine Safety Program or SUBSAFE was initiated by the U.S. Navy Bureau of Ships Letter serial no. 525-0462 of 20 December 1963, following the loss of USS *Thresher (SSN-593)* with all hands earlier that year. The program's design, construction, and certification requirements covered the structure, systems, and components critical for submarine watertight in-

tegrity and recovery capability and required, among many other changes, welded joints for all seawater piping and an emergency main ballast tank blow system.

Chapter 6

1. Alfred S. McLaren, "Military Control of the Marginal Sea Ice Zone: Its Importance to Our National Security" (master's thesis [classified], U.S. Naval War College, 1968), 120. The same thesis for the War College also satisfied the requirement for an M.S. degree in international affairs from George Washington University, which I was also awarded in 1968.

Chapter 7

1. Jack Knudsen and "Tiger Al" Davis, USS *Greenfish (SS-351)*, 1958–59; George Steele, USS *Seadragon (SSN-584)*, 1960–61; Les Kelly, Shep Jenks, and Paul Tomb, USS *Skipjack (SSN-585)*, 1962–65; Jack Richard, USS *Queenfish (SSN-651)*, 1965–67; Guy Schaffer, USS *Greenling (SSN-614)*, 1968.

Chapter 8

1. Because the modern digital computer had not yet been invented when we returned to port, the data from both voyages did not lend itself to digital analysis until the early 1980s, when I undertook the research as part of my Ph.D. dissertation at the University of Colorado, Boulder.

2. In this regard, Admiral Rickover was to explain, when nuclear submarines were later named after important political figures instead of fish, that "fish don't vote!"

3. The letters would actually be mailed from Nome, Alaska.

Chapter 9

1. U.S. Central Intelligence Agency, *Polar Regions Atlas* (Washington, DC: U.S. Central Intelligence Agency, 1978; repr., 1981), and *The CIA World Fact Book,* rev. ed. (Washington, DC: U.S. Central Intelligence Agency, 1999), 10.

2. Ye. R. Akbalyan, comp., *Practical Dictionary of Siberia and the North* (Moscow: European Publications and Severnye Prostory, 2005), 57.

3. U.S. Central Intelligence Agency, *Polar Regions Atlas,* 10.

4. Josh Newell, *The Russian Far East: A Reference Guide for Conservation and Development,* 2nd ed. (McKinleyville, CA: Daniel and Daniel, 2004), 417; Willy Østreng, ed. *The Natural and Societal Challenges of the Northern Sea Route: A Reference Work* (Dordrecht, Netherlands: Kluwer Academic Publishers, 1999), 6.

5. Newell, *Russian Far East,* 417; Østreng, *Natural and Societal Challenges,* 5–6.

6. Ibid.

7. Akbalyan, *Practical Dictionary of Siberia and the North,* 57, 501.

8. A. H. Markham, *The Great Frozen Sea* (London: Daldy, Isbister and Co., 1878); B. D.

Zetler, "Arctic Tides by Rollin A. Harria (1911) Revisited," *EOS Transactions,* American Geophysical Union, 67, no. 7 (February 18, 1986): 73–76.

9. K. O. Emery, "Topography and Sediments of the Arctic Basin," *Journal of Geology* 57 (1949): 512–21; Miah A. Beal, "Bathymetry and Structure of the Arctic Ocean" (Ph.D. diss., Oregon State University, June 1968), 9.

10. Ya. Hakkel', "Structural and Tectonic Features of the Arctic Basin," *Problems of the Arctic and Antarctic,* no. 11 (1962); reprinted in special issue commemorating the twenty-fifth anniversary of drift station North Pole-1, translated in *Arctic Institute of North America* (May 1966): pc-1–c-13, 1–13.

11. Beal, "Bathymetry and Structure," 16–17, 21, 201 (fig. 30, track of *Skate* 1962 expedition), 203 (fig. 32, track of *Seadragon* 1962 expedition).

Chapter 10

1. Anderson, *Nautilus 90 North,* 68; John H. Nicholson, "Sargo," in Dugan and Vahan, eds., *Men Under Water* (Phila.: Chilton Books, 1965), 53–67; track information for 1962 provided by Dr. Waldo Lyon, Arctic Submarine Laboratory, San Diego, July 1970; Steele, *Seadragon,* 244–47.

2. The "sector" method of determining jurisdiction over the Arctic, wherein lines of longitude drawn from the stern edges of each Arctic state's coastline to the North Pole, defined or encompassed each state's area of sovereignty. This method was first proposed by V. L. Lakhtin 'of the USSR during the 1920s (John McCannon, *Red Arctic: Polar Exploration and the Myth of the North in the Soviet Union, 1932–1939* [New York: Oxford University Press, 1998], 194). It has never been accepted by the international community. Up to 1970 the USSR had never made any attempt to enforce it within "their sector." With regard to the First United Nations Convention on Law of the Sea, this agreement was entered into force on 10 June 1961 (International Law Commission, *Conventions and Other Texts* [New York: United Nations, Office of Legal Affairs, 1998–2001]) (last modified 30 November 2001). It would not be until 1994 that a ratified United Nation's Third Law of the Sea would address Arctic regions and be applicable to all signatories.

3. International Law Commission, *Conventions and Other Texts.*

4. Camil Simard, "Soviet Sovereignty in the Arctic Seas: Northern Perspectives," *Canadian Arctic Resources Committee* 16, no. 4 (July–August 1988). This edict was based on the fact that Soviet jurists had traditionally considered the Laptev and East Siberian seas as waters historically belonging to the Soviet Union. Final international agreement on a two-hundred-mile EEZ was also not achieved until 14 November 1994, when the Third United Nations Convention on Law of the Sea was finally ratified. International Law Commission, *Conventions and Other Texts.*

5. In order to update or reset the initial or "departure navigation position" set into the SINS several days earlier.

6. "Keel depth" is the distance from the submarine's lowest point or keel to the bottom.

7. Peter Wadhams, *Ice in the Ocean* (Amsterdam: Gordon and Breach Science Publishers, 2000), 195.

8. "Three-section" here refers to four hours on watch, eight hours off watch.

9. In order to use its better optical qualities for underwater search and viewing.

10. Wadhams, *Ice in the Ocean,* 247.

11. The velocity of sound in water varies in direct proportion to changes to water temperature, that is, if water temperature increases, the speed of sound in water or sound velocity increases; if it decreases, sound velocity decreases.

12. This was from a NAVSAT (TRANSIT) satellite navigation system of only four satellites, which was what was available in 1970. This was replaced by the twenty-four satellite GPS system in 1996 (John Rousmaniere, "Navigation," Microsoft Encarta Online Encyclopedia, 2005, http://encarta.msn.com).

13. I served as antisubmarine warfare and gunnery officer on USS *Gregory (DD-802)* from 1955 to 1957. "Bell-like" tones or echoes from targets that we were searching for with our active sonar were often the first indication that we had detected the target acoustically. Evidence of detection on the active sonar indicator or "screen" might not show up for another five hundred to one thousand yards.

14. "Zero bubble" refers to the longitudinal aspect or up- or down-angle. We focused maximum attention on keeping *Queenfish* at a completely level or "zero bubble."

15. To clear baffles meant to change course 60°, in this case to port or the west, and conduct a careful passive sonar search for any surfaced or submerged contacts down our previous track.

16. "Ice blink" refers to glare in the sky over an ice field.

17. Most of us had heard stories for years about the early experiences of the crew members on the first German Type XXI class submarine, with similar long trunks to the bridge, during World War II. Apparently a lack of recognition of the importance of fully equalizing a higher interior pressure with that of the atmosphere resulted in literally "shooting" into the air the crew member opening the upper hatch, with resultant serious injury.

18. Anderson, *Nautilus 90 North,* 203.

19. Steele, *Seadragon,* 110.

20. National Snow and Ice Data Center (NSIDC), *The Cryosphere, 2002* (Boulder, CO: University of Colorado, 2002).

21. Alfred S. McLaren, "The Under-Ice Thickness Distribution of the Arctic Basin as Recorded in 1958 and 1970," *Journal of Geophysical Research* 94 (15 April 1989): 4971, 4974, 4976. First-year ice can be further divided into "young" (0–29.99 cm), "thin" (30–69.99 cm), "medium" (70–119.99 cm), and "thick" (120–199.99 cm) for analysis. Multiyear ice can be further divided into second-year (200–299.99 cm) and multiyear (300–399.99 cm) for analysis. Deep-draft independent keels can be further divided into number, mean drafts, and percentages of those greater than 5.0 and 9.0 meters for operational use and analysis. "Surfaceable areas" can be further divided into percentages and numbers greater than 400 m long of surfaceable areas (<200 cm thick), skylights (<100 cm thick), and open water (<30 cm thick) for both operational use and analysis.

22. McLaren, "Under-Ice Thickness Distribution," 4971.

23. Ibid., 4971, 4974, 4975.

24. Ibid., 4974, 4975.

25. *Queenfish's* "Moving Haven" occupied a rectangle defined by leading and after boundaries, one hundred miles ahead and one hundred miles astern, and lateral boundaries fifty miles either side of our plan of intended movement. It is established and promulgated (in our case to classified recipients) in order to prevent misidentification by air or surface forces and mutual interference and possible collision with other submarines.

26. Anderson, *Nautilus 90 North,* 166–68.

27. I learned much from the gentlemanly and most genial Walt Wittmann when we were shipmates on USS *Seadragon's* 1960 Arctic voyage. I consulted him frequently not only in connection with my Naval War College thesis on the marginal sea ice zone but also on this voyage as well. I also spent a day with him at his office in Washington prior to departing on this expedition.

Chapter 11

1. "Under-ice topography" refers to under-ice thickness or sea-ice draft morphology below sea level.

2. In the Williamson Turn, right or left full rudder is usually used until a course 60° from the previous or base course has been reached. It is followed by rudder in the opposite direction of equal magnitude, left or right. The latter is then reduced or adjusted as necessary to permit steadying on the reciprocal or reverse of the submarine's original course. This type of turn or maneuver should enable a ship or submarine to right a position on and retrace its previous course exactly. A submerged submarine would ordinarily use only that amount of rudder that can be used without causing cavitation. Cavitation noise of any sort will make any ship or submarine and its weapons vulnerable to detection and destruction by potential adversaries.

3. A secondary propulsion motor is essentially a large outboard motor that can be trained through 360 degrees and operated as a slow speed "thruster"; it is housed and faired into the outer hull at keel level, approximately two-thirds of a ship's length from the bow.

4. Regarding first-year ice, see McLaren, "Under-Ice Thickness Distribution," 4974.

5. Anderson, *Nautilus 90 North,* 208–9; McLaren, "Under-Ice Thickness Distribution," 4971.

6. National Geophysical Data Center, *The International Bathymetric Chart of the Arctic Ocean (IBCAO),* research publication RP-2 (Boulder, CO: National Geophysical Data Center, 2004).

7. Leary, *Under Ice,* 241–47.

8. "Zero bubble" here refers to a completely level longitudinal or fore and aft aspect.

9. McLaren, "Under-Ice Thickness Distribution," 4978.

10. Steele, *Seadragon,* 95.

11. Waldo Lyon and Walt Wittmann, personal communication, Arctic Submarine Laboratory, Naval Oceanographic Laboratory, May 1970.

12. I later had an opportunity to examine closely the top sounder record from this near miss as I was digitizing the analog records of the under-ice draft or thickness recorded by *Queenfish* along *Nautilus*'s 1958 track for my Ph.D. It was a very close call indeed!

13. Steele, *Seadragon,* 134–46.

14. Because Arctic Ocean sea ice is constantly in motion, any pole planted in the ice at the exact geographical location of the North Pole could be several miles away from it by the next day.

15. G. W. DeLong, *The Voyage of the Jeannette: The Ship and Ice Journals of George W. DeLong, 1879–1881* (Boston: Houghton Mifflin, 1884).

16. Wally Herbert does an excellent job of explaining why this would have been nearly impossible in his *Noose of Laurels: The Discovery of the North Pole* (London: Hodder and Stoughton, 1989).

17. McLaren, "Under-Ice Thickness Distribution," 4975.

18. Ibid.; Alfred S. McLaren et al., "Variability in Sea-Ice Thickness over the North Pole from 1958 to 1992," *Nature* 358 (16 July 1992): 224–26.

Chapter 12

1. "Seismic activity" here means acoustically monitoring the area for "seismic frequencies" below fifty kilohertz; Akbalyan, *Practical Dictionary of Siberia and the North,* 302; W. Jacquelyne

Kious and Robert I. Tilling, *This Dynamic Earth: The Story of Plate Tectonics,* U.S. Geological Survey, http://pubs.usgs.gov (September 1996).

2. Beal, "Bathymetry and Structure of the Arctic Basin," 68.

3. Akbalyan, *Practical Dictionary of Siberia and the North,* 352, 837–38.

4. McLaren, "Analysis of the Under-Ice Topography," 21.

5. Each site could be populated by exotic ecosystems, such as I saw during an extended dive in a Russian MIR deep-diving submersible to the Mid-Atlantic Ridge in 1999, wholly dependent on chemosynthesis for energy from oxidation of the hydrogen sulfide within the high-temperature water (i.e., 600–800° F) being emitted from the vents. See also National Science Foundation, Office of Legislative and Public Affairs (OLPA), "Behavior of Arctic Ocean Ridge Confounds Predictions," http://www.nsf.gov/od/lpa/news/03/pr0367.htm (25 June 2003); Kious and Tilling, *This Dynamic Earth.*

6. A pingo is "a large frost mound, especially a relatively conical mound of soil-covered ice (commonly 30 to 50 meters high and up to 400 meters in diameter) raised in part by hydrostatic pressure within and below the permafrost of Arctic Regions, and of more than one year's duration" (U.S. Department of Agriculture, Natural Resources Conservation Service, "Glossary of Landform and Geologic Terms," *National Soil Survey Handbook,* pt. 629 [Washington, D.C.: U.S. Government Printing Office, 2002], 46).

Chapter 13

1. Clive Holland, *Arctic Exploration and Development: C. 500 B.C. to 1915* (New York: Garland Publishing, 1994), 16.

2. Østreng, *Natural and Societal Challenges,* xxxv.

3. Ibid., xxxv, 3.

4. Ibid., xxxv.

5. Ibid., 5, 9, 15. With as many as six nuclear and more than thirty diesel-powered icebreakers in operation plus almost two hundred ice-strengthened freighters, the Russians can now make transits between the Atlantic and Pacific as early as May and as late as October.

6. Holland, *Arctic Exploration and Development,* 3, 16.

7. Ibid., 20, 21, 24, 30–32; Østreng, *Natural and Societal Challenges,* 20.

8. Holland, *Arctic Exploration and Development,* 44–45.

9. Ibid., 66, 70–71.

10. Ibid., 90, 129.

11. Ibid., 99–107.

12. A. E. Nordenskiöld, *The Voyage of the Vega round Asia and Europe* (London: Macmillan and Co., 1883), 276; Fridtjof Nansen, *Farthest North,* vols. 1 and 2 (London: George Newnes, Ltd., 1898).

13. Holland, *Arctic Exploration and Development,* 522–23; Østreng, *Natural and Societal Challenges,* 22.

14. Roald Amundsen, *My Life as an Explorer* (Garden City, NY: Doubleday, Page, and Co., 1927).

15. McCannon, *Red Arctic,* 12, 23–25, 31, 33, 60–61.

16. Ibid., 34–35.

17. Ibid., 61–68.

18. Ibid., 63.

19. Ibid., 63–67.

20. Ibid., 56, 148.

21. Ibid., 68, 166, 172.

22. Ibid., 174; S. D. Waters, *German Raiders in the Pacific* (Bennington, VT: Merriam Press, 2000), 19–20; McCannon, *Red Arctic*, 174.

23. Waters, *German Raiders in the Pacific*, 175.

24. Østreng, *Natural and Societal Challenges*, 38.

25. Terence Armstrong, George Rogers, and Graham Rowley, *The Circumpolar North: A Political and Economic Geography of the Arctic and Sub-Arctic* (London: Methuen and Co., 1978), 63.

Chapter 14

1. McLaren, "Analysis of the Under-Ice Topography," 150–51.

2. Susan Barr, ed., "Franz Josef Land," in *Polarhandbok No. 8* (Oslo: Norsk Polarinstitutt, University of Salzburg, Oslo, 1995), 8, 107–22. Little did I know that I would have an opportunity to visit a great deal of this fascinating archipelago, pass through the beautiful British Channel and Markham and Austrian straits, helicopter to and walk on top of several huge tabular icebergs calved from its glaciers, and explore a number of the islands and former Soviet Union polar stations during each summer from 1997 to 2000. These special opportunities were afforded me when I lectured on the North Pole voyages of the Russian nuclear icebreakers *Yamal* and *Sovetsky Soyuz* and the Northeast Passage voyage of the diesel-powered Russian icebreaker *Kapitan Dranitsyn*.

3. Wadhams, *Ice in the Ocean*, 10.

4. "Red tagged" refers to the red tags placed on valves, switches, and equipments indicating that it is forbidden to move or operate the item or items because of severe/life-threatening safety hazards.

5. On 26 August 1999, during a Northeast Passage voyage on board the Russian icebreaker *Kapitan Dranitsyn*, I had an opportunity to fly by helicopter to the eighty-nine-meter-high glacier-covered summit of Mys Arkticheskiy. A crashed Soviet *Li2* cargo/transport aircraft now marks it.

6. Akbalyan, *Practical Dictionary of Siberia and the North*, 455, 968.

7. Holland, *Arctic Exploration and Development*, 108, 511; Nordenskiöld, *Voyage of the Vega*, 105–7.

Chapter 15

1. Akbalyan, *Practical Dictionary of Siberia and the North*, 500–501; Holland, *Arctic Exploration and Development*, 52, 55.

2. Steven K. Baum, *Glossary of Physical Oceanography and Related Disciplines* (College Station: Texas A&M University, Department of Oceanography, May 26, 2004), 236.

3. Ibid., 237.

4. Information from www.yuktia.com. This site is currently shut down and inaccessible; interested readers might want to look at the following: (1) *Encyclopedia of the Arctic* (three-volume set), http://www.routledge-ny.com/ref/arctic/lena.html; (2) "Discharges of Major Rivers into the Laptev Sea during 1976–1979," http://psc.apl.washington.edu/ANWAP/LaptevRivers.html; (3) Janiel Rivera, "Preliminary Evidence for Lena River Discharge Events in the Laptev Sea, Russian Arctic," abstract, http://gsa.confex.com/gsa/2004am/final program/abstract; and (4) Jsrq.

Bareiss et al., "Impact of River Climatology on the Decay of Sea Ice in the Laptev Sea during Spring and Early Summer," *Arctic, Antarctic, and Alpine Research: An Interdisciplinary Journal* 31, no. 3 (August 1999).

5. See Wadhams, *Ice in the Ocean*, 195.

6. On 24 August 1999, while embarked on the Russian icebreaker *Kapitan Dranitsyn* in Marata Fjord and during a transit of the Shokalsk Strait between Bolshevik Island and October Revolution Island, I finally had an opportunity to view and photograph the huge and quite spectacular glacier that covers the entire southwest portion of October Revolution Island. I also saw a surprising number of very large polar bears at close range.

7. I visited the former Soviet Union polar station Prima at Cape Baronov on the northern tip of Bolshevik Island on 24 August 1999. Following the end of the cold war and until 1997, it remained open as a base from which to fly wealthy people to the North Pole, via long-range helicopter. We sighted hundreds of beluga whales in Shokalsk Strait en route to the Laptev Sea.

8. Visual, acoustic, and electromagnetic.

9. An ice island or tabular iceberg calves off from the deep-water extension of an ice shelf, which is the seaward extension of glacial-formed ice. See Terence E. Armstrong, B. Roberts, and C. Swinthinbank, *Illustrated Glossary of Snow and Ice*, Scott Polar Research Institute, special publication no. 4, 2nd ed. (Menston Yorkshire, UK: Scholar Press, 1973) and American Meteorological Society, *Glossary of Meterology*, 2nd ed. (Boston: American Meteorological Society, 2000).

10. Robert Headland, Scott Polar Research Institute, Cambridge University, personal communication, August 1999, and personal observation.

11. Holland, *Arctic Exploration and Development*, 311.

12. Office of Naval Intelligence Review, *German U-Boats in the Arctic,* vol. 6, pts. 1–5 (Washington, DC: U.S. Office of Naval Intelligence, 1951). It is interesting that Soviet Rear Admiral I. Kolyshkin's *Submarines in Arctic Waters* (Moscow: Progress Publishers, 1966) makes no mention of any Soviet submarines going farther east than the Kara Sea during World War II.

13. Office of Naval Intelligence Review, *German U-Boats in the Arctic,* 279, 328; Kenneth Wynn, *U-Boat Operations of the Second World War, Vol. 1: Career Histories, U1–U510* (Annapolis, MD: Naval Institute Press, 1997), 133, 143, 233.

14. Office of Naval Intelligence Review, *German U-Boats in the Arctic,* 278, 414.

15. Ibid., 329–30.

16. Paul Kemp, *U-Boats Destroyed: German Submarine Losses in the World Wars* (Annapolis: Naval Institute Press, 1997), 172, 181, 199, 214, 258; Manfred Dörr, *Die Ritterkreuzträger der Deutschen Wehrmacht, 1939–1945, Teil IV: Die U-Boot-Waffe,* Band 2: Knights' Crosses of the Germany Navy (Osnabruck, Germany: Biblio Verlag, 1989), 62, 217; Wynn, *U-Boat Operations,* 143, 191–92.

Chapter 16

1. I visited Cape Chelyushkin, the northernmost point of the Eurasian continent on the Taymyr Peninsula, on 23 August 1999, while embarked in the *Kapitan Dranitsyn.* There I had an opportunity to see the "Amundsen Cache" or stone monument that replaced an earlier wooden memorial to Chelyushkin, Nordenskiöld, and Amundsen. Although the meteorological and radar station was in operation, the surrounding area was an environmental disaster, surrounded as it was by thousands of rusting oil drums and machinery fragments of every description.

2. Possibly a pingo.

3. Akbalyan, *Practical Dictionary of Siberia and the North,* 507.

4. This team comprised diving planes operators, helmsmen, chief of the watch, and diving officer of the watch.

5. First-year ice, between 3.28 and 6.6 feet thick; multiyear ice, between 6.6 and 13.1 feet thick; deformed ice, thickness greater than 13.1 feet created by rafting of thinner sea-ice floes, one on top of another, by strong Arctic winds. See McLaren, "Under-Ice Thickness Distribution."

6. This depth sounder used a much higher acoustic frequency, considerable narrower band width, and lower power output that made it virtually undetectable. It was also more accurate.

7. The Little Ice Age was a period of cold climate worldwide from the fourteenth through nineteenth centuries.

8. "Spoking" refers to a bright band of light that radiates outward on a fixed bearing from the center of the scope.

9. Beal, "Bathymetry and Structure of the Arctic Ocean," 203, fig. 32.

Chapter 17

1. Akbalyan, *Practical Dictionary of Siberia and the North,* 655.

2. Holland, *Arctic Exploration and Development,* 647; J. Dowdeswell and M. Hambrey, *Islands of the Arctic* (Cambridge: Cambridge University Press, 2002), 87, 92.

3. Holland, *Arctic Exploration and Development,* 78, 86.

4. Ibid., 134, 137; Akbalyan, *Practical Dictionary of Siberia and the North,* 540.

5. Holland, *Arctic Exploration and Development,* 170, 174.

6. Ibid., 174–75, 176–77.

7. Dowdeswell and Hambrey, *Islands of the Arctic,* 87. I had an opportunity to see the four northern islands, Belkovsky, Kotelny, Faddeyevsky, and Novaya Sibir, on 20 and 21 August 1999 while embarked on the *Kapitan Dranitsyn* during a Northeast Passage expedition. We transited the very shallow Blagovyeshchenski Passage between Faddeyev and Novaya Sibir islands and went ashore on Belkovsky Island. We saw hundreds of the Laptev Sea walrus population that are smaller in size and considered almost a separate species from the Pacific population on Wrangel Island. We were disappointed not to have seen either the polar bears or polar wolves of this area. The latter are reported to be the largest in the Arctic.

8. Akbalyan, *Practical Dictionary of Siberia and the North,* 655.

9. The DeLong Islands were named after the ill-fated DeLong North Pole Expedition. George Washington DeLong's ship, the *Jeannette,* was crushed by the ice close to Bennett Island in 1881. See Holland, *Arctic Exploration and Development,* 317. I went ashore on Vilkitsky Island, a small, unglacierized volcanic island with spectacular pinnacles that resembled Arnold Böcklin's classic 1886 painting, *Isle of the Dead,* on 19 August 1999. The chart used by the *Kapitan Dranitsyn* for its approach from the northwest had no sounding information. This island is one of the most remote and inaccessible in the Arctic, and we were only the second passenger ship to visit. We found a shipwreck on the island, along with an almost intact lifeboat. I visited Bennett Island on 20 August 1999 and spent most of the morning climbing to the top of the highest (1,400 feet) of its two domed glaciers. The Bennett Island volcano erupted in the late 1990s. See also Newell, *Russian Far East,* 228; Akbalyan, *Practical Dictionary of Siberia and the North,* 655.

10. Holland, *Arctic Exploration and Development,* 175, 177, 189, 353; McCannon, *Red Arctic,* 40.

11. "Family Grams" are short messages from family members to deployed boats; they had been standard for the ballistic missile boats for some time. This was the first time in our experience, however, that they had ever appeared on attack submarine broadcasts, much less caused "unhandy" delays in the retrieval of higher-priority radio traffic. My crew was not in favor of receiving family grams, and possible bad news, during deployments until late in 1972.

12. Nansen, *Farthest North.*

13. Four to five feet thick. See McLaren, "Under-Ice Thickness Distribution of the Arctic Basin," 4976.

14. I had the opportunity to visit the Gulf of Kolyuchin and Kolyuchin Island and its polar station and lighthouse (closed down in 1993) on 14 August 1999. This particular gulf had been the scene of destruction for many Arctic expeditions in the past. The tundra-covered Kolyuchin Island had been used by Chukchi natives as a walrus hunting ground for hundreds of years. The island was covered with more than a thousand walrus skulls of varying degrees of antiquity.

15. Holland, *Arctic Exploration and Development,* 316–17.

16. Ibid., 382.

Chapter 18

1. Newell, *Russian Far East,* 417; Sveta Berezovskaya, "Changes in River Runoff over the East-Siberian Sea Basin," (abstract, University of Alaska Fairbanks, Water and Environmental Research Center, October 27, 2003); Baum, *Glossary of Physical Oceanography,* 125.

2. M. M. Naurzbaev and E. A. Vagarov, "Variation of Early Summer and Annual Temperature in East Taymir and Putoran (Siberia) over the Last Two Millennia Inferred from Tree Rings," *Journal of Geophysical Research* 105 (2000): 7317–26; Holland, *Arctic Exploration and Development,* 52, 55.

3. Holland, *Arctic Exploration and Development,* 56, 57.

4. Ibid., 58–59.

5. Ibid., 94.

6. Ibid., 59, 63, 64, 67.

7. Ibid., 74.

8. Østreng, *Natural and Societal Challenges,* 22.

9. Ibid.

10. Nordenskiöld, *Voyage of the Vega.*

11. We missed by less than six feet!

12. "Bright sea-ice-return" refers to "bright spots" all over the sonar scope, indicating the proximity of ice.

13. I still frequently dream about this close call or something very similar some thirty-eight years later. It was, in retrospect, one of the two or three most challenging situations I had ever experienced in my entire submarine career.

Chapter 19

1. Some thirty-eight years later, I still dream, almost monthly, about conducting similar surveys in a submarine or submersible.

2. Holland, *Arctic Exploration and Development,* 59, 187.

3. Ibid., 187, 189, 225, 226.

4. Ibid., 249, 269, 272.

5. Ibid., 296, 299, 328, 333, 355, 364.

6. Ibid., 311.

7. Ibid., 486, 495.

8. Leary, *Under Ice,* 186.

9. Holland, *Arctic Exploration and Development,* 517–18; Jennifer Niven, *The Ice Master:*

The Doomed 1913 Voyage of the Karluk (New York: Hyperion, 2000); Vilhjalmur Stefansson, *Discovery: The Autobiography of Vilhjalmur Stefansson* (New York: McGraw-Hill Book Co., 1964), 256–63.

10. Dowdeswell and Hambrey, *Islands of the Arctic*, 27. I visited Wrangel Island, known for the recent discovery that the last mammoths on earth—a dwarf species—lived there until 3,500 years ago, on 15 and 16 August 1999. According to the UNESCO World Heritage Center (http://whc.unesco.org/), this mountainous island of some 2,937 square miles was not glaciated during the last ice age, resulting in an exceptionally high level of biodiversity. It has the world's largest population of Pacific walrus and the highest density of ancestral polar bear dens.

11. Beal, *Bathymetry and Structure of the Arctic Ocean*.

12. Ibid., 147.

13. Waldo Lyon, personal communication, June 1970.

Chapter 20

1. "Blanket tossing" refers to placing the commanding officer in a blanket and tossing him into the air. The custom derives from an old Eskimo method of "seeing over the horizon" for game or polar bears.

Epilogue

1. J. Christey, *United States Naval Submarine Force Information Book, 2004* (Groton, CT: Submarine Force Library and Museum, 2004); John Donlon, *The Klaxon* (Groton, CT: Submarine Force Library and Museum, 1991).

2. Alfred S. McLaren, "The Arctic Submarine: An Alternative to Ice Breaker Tankers and Pipelines" (Master's thesis, University of Cambridge, 1982); Alfred S. McLaren, "The Development of Cargo Submarines for Polar Use," *Polar Record* 21, no. 133 (1983): 369–81; Alfred S. McLaren, "Transporting Arctic Petroleum: A Role for Commercial Submarines," *Polar Record* 22, no. 136 (1984): 7–23.

3. Alfred S. McLaren, "Analysis of the Under-Ice Topography in the Arctic Basin as Recorded by USS *Nautilus* in 1958 and USS *Queenfish* in 1970" (Ph.D. diss., University of Colorado, Boulder, 1986).

4. A. S. McLaren, M. C. Serreze, and R. Barry, "Seasonal Variations of Sea Ice Motion in the Canada Basin and Their Implications," *Geophysical Research Letters* 14, no.11 (1987): 1123–26; A. S. McLaren, M. C. Serreze, and R. G. Barry, "Summertime Reversals of the Beaufort Gyre and Its Effects on Ice Concentration in the Canada Basin," *Journal of Geophysical Research* 94 (15 August 1989): 10955–70.

5. D. S. Steigman, "Fleet Could Shrink to 488 Ships," *Navy Times,* 4 June 1990, 26; Alfred S. McLaren, "Save the *Sturgeons* to Study Global Change," *U.S. Naval Institute Proceedings* 116 (October 1990):108–9; Margo Edwards, "Arctic Ocean SCICEX Explorations," in *National Geographic Atlas of the Ocean: The Deep Frontier,* ed. Sylvia A. Earle (Washington, DC: National Geographic, 2002).

Glossary of Naval, Submarine, and Arctic Terms and Acronyms

AN/BQN-4 five-unit upward-beamed fathometer
: Deck- and sail-mounted active sonar equipment used to measure distance from hull to sea ice directly above each of the five units or transducers installed between the bow and the stern of the submarine.

AN/BQN-4 topside upward-beamed echo sounder
: Sail-mounted narrow-band active sonar equipment used to measure distance from top of submarine sail to sea ice directly overhead. Also used to estimate sea ice thickness above submarine.

AN/BQQ-5 passive sonar
: Medium-range passive or "listening" sonar used to detect and analyze noise from submarines and ships.

AN/BQR-7 long-range sonar
: Long-range passive or "listening" sonar used to detect and analyze low-frequency noise from submarines and ships.

AN/BQS-7 polynya delineator
: Active frequency-modulated sonar used to delineate the shape and size of a polynya ahead of and above the submarine.

AN/BQS-8 Arctic under-ice sonar suite	Active sonar equipments installed that permit a submarine to operate safely under ice and transit to and from the ice-covered surface year-round.
AN/BQS-4	Active search sonar that provides short to medium range and bearing to a submerged or surface contact.
Arctic suite	Special hull, mast, and control surface modifications and equipments (sonar and navigational) that enable a submarine to operate safely under ice for sustained periods and to break through to the surface or submerge through the ice-covered sea at will.
Baffle	Acoustically blind area that covers an arc approximately from 30° to port to 30° to starboard from directly astern of the submarine.
Bathymetric	Relating to the measurement of depths of water in oceans, seas, and lakes.
Battle Efficiency "E"	Award given annually to the submarine that demonstrates the highest degree of readiness for combat/wartime for that particular year within a particular submarine division or squadron.
Bells	Speed and direction orders sent from the submarine ship's control panel to the maneuvering room in the engineering plant.
Bergy bits	Small house-size icebergs or pieces of iceberg of up to 5,400 tons.
Bettis training manuals	Nuclear power plant engineering systems and

	equipments training manuals published by the Bettis Corporation.
Brash ice	Fragments of broken-up or disintegrating ice floes.
Bubble	Indication of horizontal level measured in degrees.
Bummocks	Downward-projecting ice masses.
Chatter	Periscope vibration; a special fairing that encompasses the periscope can be raised to prevent or reduce.
Check report	Required radio communication at a specified time or within a specified time range.
CNO	Chief of Naval Operations, normally headquartered in Washington, D.C.
COMSUBPAC	Commander Submarine Force Pacific, normally headquartered in Pearl Harbor, Hawaii.
Conn	Maneuvering, i.e., course, speed, and depth control of submarine.
Deep-draft ice	Sea ice whose draft extends more than nine meters beneath the sea surface.
Deformed ice	Wind-driven floe-over-floe sea ice whose draft beneath the sea exceeds four meters.
DR	Dead reckoning.
DRT	Dead-reckoning tracer.
ECM	Electronics countermeasures mast.

EEZ	Economic Exclusion Zone.
Envelope	Three-dimensional operational volume under water.
Fairing	Protective housing for a periscope.
Fathometer	Active acoustic depth sounder.
FM	Frequency modulated.
Four-transducer topside echo-sounder array	Same as AN/BQN-4 five-unit upward-beamed fathometer less one transducer.
Gyrocompass	Compass used to determine true north and true direction/course relative to true north by means of gyroscopes.
Height of eye	Height of eye above earth or water surface.
High look	Act of raising one's height of eye using any method available, such as decreasing a submarine's depth, while at periscope depth to see further over the horizon.
HY-80 steel	High-yield-strength, low-carbon, low-alloy steel with nickel, molybdenum, and chromium used to construct deep-diving submarine hulls.
IBD	Iceberg detector.
Ice blink	Glare in sky over an ice field.
Ice scour	Irregular depression or gouged out-area of seabed created by passage of massive ice, such as an iceberg or glacier, whose draft exceeds the overall water depth.

Keel depth	Distance from submarine's lowest point or keel from sea surface.
Lead	Narrow opening of water within an ice field or pack.
Loran C navigation system	Very accurate worldwide electronic navigation system.
Military rider	Member of special team assigned to submarine to augment crew or provide special skills.
MIZ	Marginal sea-ice zone; area encompassed by the extension of year-round or perennial ice pack during late fall, winter, and early spring.
MK-19 gyrocompass	Primary submarine gyrocompass used to indicate true north and determine true direction/course in relation to true north by means of gyroscopes.
MK-23 gyrocompass	Secondary submarine gyrocompass.
MK-48 antisubmarine warfare torpedo	Primary submarine weapon against enemy submarines and ships.
Multiyear ice	Sea ice that has grown thicker than the normal maximum of two meters per year.
NK variable-frequency topside echo sounder	Same as upward-beamed fathometer or top sounder, except that frequency can be varied as operationally desired.
North American N6A inertial navigation system	Aircraft inertial navigation system modified for use on first nuclear submarines to operate under Arctic sea ice.

Omega navigation system	A worldwide electronics navigation system.
PCO	Prospective commanding officer.
PDR	Precision depth recorder; used to present depth sounding results graphically.
PIM	Plan of intended movement.
Pingo	Underwater low hill or seamount forced up from seabed by hydrostatic pressure in area underlain by permafrost.
Polynya	A generally oval or circular open water area within a sea ice field or pack.
RDF	Radio direction finder.
Red tagged	Method of removing switches, levers, and equipments from operational use for safety reasons.
SINS	Shipboard inertial navigation system.
Skate class	The first class of nuclear attack submarines to be built; altogether there were four submarines in this class.
Skeds	Dedicated radio broadcasts.
SPM	Secondary propulsion motor; backup and special-use system of propulsion.
SSMG	Ship's service motor generator; provides DC power to a distribution bus or panel.
Sturgeon class	Fourth class of nuclear attack submarine to be built. A total of thirty-seven were built, all

designed to operate in sea-ice–covered polar regions year-round.

Tonals	Acoustic frequencies displayed as finite lines on electronic scope or graphic plotter.
Top sounder	Term generally applied to narrow-beam, high-frequency active sonar used to measure distance to, and estimate draft of, sea ice directly above top of submarine's sail.
UQN fathometer	Early standard U.S. Navy depth-determining sonar.
UQS-1B	Short-range active mine-detection sonar.
VLF	Very low frequency.
Warfish	Torpedo fully configured for combat use.
Watch bill	Posted/promulgated individual crew in port and at sea-watch station assignments.
Williamson Turn	Use of right or left full rudder to reach a course 60° from the previous or base course. It is followed by rudder in the opposite direction of equal magnitude, left or right. Latter is then reduced or adjusted as necessary to permit steadying on the reciprocal or reverse of the submarine's original course. This type of turn or maneuver should enable a ship or submarine to achieve a position on and retrace its previous course exactly.
Zero bubble	Completely level longitudinal aspect or up/down angle.

Bibliography

Akbalyan, Ye. R., comp. *Practical Dictionary of Siberia and the North.* Moscow: European Publications and Severnye Prostory, 2005.

American Meteorological Society. *Glossary of Meterology.* 2nd ed. Boston: American Meteorological Society, 2000.

Amundsen, Roald. *My Life as an Explorer.* Garden City, NY: Doubleday, 1927.

Anderson, William R. *Nautilus 90 North.* Cleveland: World Publishing Co., 1959.

Armstrong, Terence, B. Roberts, and C. Swinthinbank. *Illustrated Glossary of Snow and Ice.* Scott Polar Research Institute, special publication no. 4. 2nd ed. Menston Yorkshire, UK: Scholar Press, 1973.

Armstrong, Terence, George Rogers, and Graham Rowley. *The Circumpolar North: A Political and Economic Geography of the Arctic and Sub-Arctic.* London: Methuen and Co., 1978.

Barr, Susan, ed. "Franz Josef Land." In *Polarhandbok No. 8.* Oslo: Norsk Polarinstitutt, University of Salzburg, Oslo, 1995.

Baum, Steven K. *Glossary of Physical Oceanography and Related Disciplines.* College Station: Texas A&M University, Department of Oceanography, May 26, 2004.

Beal, Miah A. "Bathymetry and Structure of the Arctic Ocean." Ph.D. diss., Oregon State University, 1968.

Berezovskaya, Sveta. "Changes in River Runoff over the East-Siberian Sea Basin." Abstract, University of Alaska, Fairbanks, Water and Environmental Research Center, October 27, 2003.

Calvert, James. *Surface at the Pole: The Extraordinary Voyages of the USS Skate.* New York: McGraw-Hill Co., 1960.

Christey, J. *United States Naval Submarine Force Information Book, 2004.* Groton, CT: Submarine Force Library and Museum, 2004.

DeLong, G. E. *The Voyage of the Jeannette: The Ship and Ice Journals of George W. DeLong, 1879–1881.* Boston: Houghton Mifflin, 1884.

Donlon, John. *The Klaxon.* Groton, CT: Submarine Force Library and Museum, 1991.

Dörr, Manfred. *Die Ritterkreuzträger der Deutschen Wehrmacht 1939–1945, Teil IV: Die U-Boot-Waffe.* Band 2: K-Z. Osnabruck, Germany: Biblio Verlag, 1989.

Dowdeswell, J., and M. Hambrey. *Islands of the Arctic.* Cambridge: Cambridge University Press, 2002.

Edwards, Margo. "Arctic Ocean SCICEX Explorations." In *National Geographic Atlas of the Ocean: The Deep Frontier,* ed. Sylvia A. Earle. Washington, DC: National Geographic Society, 2002.

Emory, K. O. "Topography and Sediments of the Arctic Basin." *Journal of Geology* 57 (1949): 512–21.

Fyfe, Herbert C. *Submarine Warfare Past, Present, and Future.* New York: E. P. Dutton and Co., 1902.

Hakkel', Ya. "Structural and Tectonic Features of the Arctic Basin." *Problems of the Arctic and Antarctic,* no. 11 (1962). Reprinted in special issue commemorating the twenty-fifth anniversary of drift station North Pole-1, translated in *Arctic Institute of North America* (May 1966): pc-1–c-13, 1–13.

Herbert, Wally. *The Noose of Laurels: The Discovery of the North Pole.* London: Hodder and Stoughton, 1989.

Holland, Clive. *Arctic Exploration and Development: C. 500 B.C. to 1915.* New York: Garland Publishing, 1994.

International Law Commission. *Conventions and Other Texts.* New York: United Nations, Office of Legal Affairs, 1998–2001.

Kemp, Paul. *U-Boats Destroyed: German Submarine Losses in the World Wars.* Annapolis, MD: Naval Institute Press, 1997.

Kious, W. Jacquelyne, and Robert I. Tilling. *This Dynamic Earth: The Story of Plate Tectonics.* U.S. Geological Survey, http://pubs.usgs.gov. September 1996.

Kolyshkin, I. *Submarines in Arctic Waters.* Moscow: Progress Publishers, 1966.

Leary, William M. *Under Ice: Waldo Lyon and the Development of the Arctic Submarine.* College Station: Texas A&M University Press, 1999.

Lyon, Waldo K. "The Submarine and the Arctic Ocean." *Polar Record* 11, no. 75 (1963): 699–705.

Markham, A. H. *The Great Frozen Sea.* London: Daldy, Isbister and Co., 1878.

McCannon, John. *Red Arctic: Polar Exploration and the Myth of the North in the Soviet Union, 1932–1939.* New York: Oxford University Press, 1998.

McLaren, Alfred S. "Analysis of the Under-Ice Topography of the Arctic Basin as Recorded by USS *Nautilus* in 1958 and USS *Queenfish* in 1970." Ph.D. diss., University of Colorado, 1986.

———. "The Arctic Submarine: An Alternative to Ice Breaker Tankers and Pipelines." Master's thesis, University of Cambridge, 1982.

———. "Assessment of 16-Year (1975–91) Record of Inter-seasonal and Inter-annual Trends in Arctic Basin Ice Draft and Estimated Thickness as Measured by U.S. Nuclear Submarines: Final Report." National Oceanic and Atmospheric Administration, Washington, DC, 1994.

———. "The Development of Cargo Submarines for Polar Use." *Polar Record* 21, no. 133 (1983): 369–81.

———. "Exploration under the Arctic Ice." *Explorers Journal* (March 1982): 34–39.

———. "Military Control of the Marginal Sea Ice Zone: Its Importance to Our National Security." Master's thesis (classified), U.S. Naval War College, 1968.

———. "Save the *Sturgeons* to Study Global Change." *U.S. Naval Institute Proceedings* (October 1990): 108–9.

———. "Transporting Arctic Petroleum: A Role for Commercial Submarines." *Polar Record* 22, no. 136 (1984): 7–23.

———. "The Under-Ice Thickness Distribution of the Arctic Basin as Recorded in 1958 and 1970." *Journal of Geophysical Research* 94, no. C4 (15 April 1989): 4971–83.

McLaren, Alfred S., R. G. Barry, and R. H. Bourke. "Could Arctic Ice Be Thinning?" *Nature,* 28 June 1990, 762.

McLaren, Alfred S., and R. H. Bourke. "Contour Mapping of Arctic Basin Ice Thickness and Roughness Parameters." *Journal of Geophysical Research* 97 (1992): 17, 715–17, 728.

McLaren, Alfred S., R. H. Bourke, R. L. Weaver, and R. L. Woodfin. "Arctic Sea-ice Statistics from Recent Submarine Topsounder Measurements." Technical Report SAND 86-7094, Sandia National Laboratories, Livermore, California, 1989.

———. "Digitization and Statistical Analysis of Submarine Under-ice Profiles." Technical Report SAND 86-7090, Sandia National Laboratories, Livermore, California, 1988.

McLaren, Alfred S., M. C. Serreze, and R. Barry. "Seasonal Variations of Sea Ice Motion in the Canada Basin and Their Implications." *Geophysical Research Letters,* no. 11 (1987): 1123–26.

———. "Summertime Reversals of the Beaufort Gyre and Its Effects on Ice Concentration in the Canada Basin." *Journal of Geophysical Research* 94 (15 August 1989): 10955–70.

McLaren, Alfred S., J. E. Walsh, R. H. Bourke, R. L. Weaver, and W. Wittmann. "Variability in Sea-ice Thickness over the North Pole from 1977 to 1990." *Nature,* 16 July 1992, 224–26.

Nansen, Fridtjof. *Farthest North.* Vols. 1 and 2. London: George Newnes, Ltd., 1898.

National Geophysical Data Center. *The International Bathymetric Chart of the Arctic Ocean (IBCAO).* Research publication RP-2. Boulder, CO: National Geophysical Data Center, 2004.

National Science Foundation, Office of Legislative and Public Affairs (OLPA). "Behavior of Arctic Ocean Ridge Confounds Predictions." http://www.nsf.gov/od/lpa/news/03/pr0367. htm (25 June 2003).

National Snow and Ice Data Center (NSIDC). *The Cryosphere, 2002.* Boulder: University of Colorado, 2002.

Naurzbaev, M. M. and E. A. Vagarov. "Variation of Early Summer and Annual Temperature in East Taymir and Putoran (Siberia) over the Last Two Millennia Inferred from Tree Rings." *Journal of Geophysical Research* 105 (2000): 7317–26.

Newell, Josh. *The Russian Far East: A Reference Guide for Conservation and Development.* 2nd ed. McKinleyville, CA: Daniel and Daniel, 2004.

"A New Plan for Reaching the North Pole." *Geographical Journal* 17, no. 4 (1901): 435.

Nicholson, John H. "Through Bering Strait in Mid-Winter." www.ssn583.com/nicholsonReview. htm.

Niven, Jennifer. *The Ice Master: The Doomed 1913 Voyage of the Karluk.* New York: Hyperion, 2000.

Nordenskiöld, A. E. *The Voyage of the* Vega *Round Asia and Europe.* London: Macmillan and Co., 1883.

Office of Naval Intelligence Review. *German U-Boats in the Arctic.* Vol. 6, pts. 1–5. Washington, DC: U.S. Office of Naval Intelligence, 1951.

Østreng, Willy, ed. *The Natural and Societal Challenges of the Northern Sea Route: A Reference Work.* Dordrecht, Netherlands: Kluwer Academic Publishers, 1999.

Rousmaniere, John. "Navigation." Microsoft Encarta Online Encyclopedia, 2005. http://encarta. msn.com.

Simard, Camil. "Soviet Sovereignty in the Arctic Seas: Northern Perspectives." *Canadian Arctic Resources Committee* 16, no. 4 (July–August 1988).

Steele, George P. *Seadragon: Northwest under the Ice.* New York: E. P. Dutton and Co., 1962.

Stefansson, Vilhjalmur. *Discovery: The Autobiography of Vilhjalmur Stefansson.* New York: McGraw-Hill Book Co., 1964.

Steigman, D. S. "Fleet Could Shrink to 488 Ships." *Navy Times,* 4 June 1990, 26.

U.S. Central Intelligence Agency. *The CIA World Fact Book.* Rev. ed. Washington, DC: U.S. Central Intelligence Agency, 1999.

———. *Polar Regions Atlas.* Reprint, Washington, DC: U.S. Central Intelligence Agency, 1981.

U.S. Department of Agriculture, Natural Resources Conservation Service. "Glossary of Landform and Geologic Terms." *National Soil Survey Handbook,* pt. 629. Washington, DC: U.S. Government Printing Office, 2002.

U.S. Navy Submarine Force Museum. "History of USS *Nautilus* (SSN-571)." www.USSNautilus.org/history.html.

USS *Redfish (SS-395). Report of Beaufort Sea Expeditions.* San Diego: U.S. Naval Electronics Laboratory, 7 October 1952 and 3 December 1953.

Wadhams, Peter. *Ice in the Ocean.* Amsterdam: Gordon and Breach Science Publishers, 2000.

Waters, S. D. *German Raiders in the Pacific.* Bennington, VT: Merriam Press, 2000.

"Welcome Aboard USS *Nautilus* (SSN-571), The World's First Nuclear Powered Ship." www.subguru.com/nautilus571.htm.

Wilkins, H. *Under the North Pole.* New York: Brewer, Warren, and Putnam, 1931.

Wilkins, John. *Mathematical Magick, Or, The Wonders That May Be Performed by Mechanical Geometry.* Chap. 5, pt 2. London: Brasen Serpent in Paul's Church Yard, 1648.

Wynn, Kenneth. *U-Boat Operations of the Second World War, Vol. 1: Career Histories, U1-U510.* Annapolis, MD: Naval Institute Press, 1997.

Zetler, B. D. "Arctic Tides by Rollin A. Harria (1911) Revisited." *EOS Transactions,* American Geophysical Union, 67, no. 7 (18 February 1986): 73–75.

Index